Drag

The Cassell Lesbian and Gay Studies list offers a broad-based platform to lesbian, gay and bisexual writers for the discussion of contemporary issues and for the promotion of new ideas and research.

COMMISSIONING:
Steve Cook
Roz Hopkins

CONSULTANTS:
Liz Gibbs
Christina Ruse
Peter Tatchell

I had written about *Drag* when it was first published – thinking the book entertaining, informative and, quite honestly, unique. For although men in frocks have been a part of British theatrical tradition since the Middle Ages, the subject had not previously come under so close and comprehensive a scrutiny. Although others followed Roger down the path he had so stoutly beaten (notably Peter Ackroyd with his *Dressing Up: Transvestism and Drag, The History of an Obsession (1979)* and Kris Kirk and Ed Heath with their *Men in Frocks (1984)*, *Drag* remained the most useful and pithily written history of the subject.

It seemed a pity that *Drag* had gone out-of-print and with what must have become monotonous regularity, I prodded Roger about getting the book back into print – probably in a revised and updated edition. The launching of the Cassell Sexual Politics list propelled him into contacting his agent and setting up this new edition.

By the time we reached the 1990s, Roger and I had both abandoned London – he for South West Scotland (with his lover, Ian Buckley) and me to Brighton. But we talked regularly on the 'phone and I was aware of the progress of the new edition of *Drag*. When I pondered the fate of the book in the days after Roger's death, I felt it criminal for it to languish unfinished and unpublished. Both Richard Smith and I mooted to Steve Cook, publisher for the list, that we could finish the book.

So, as it now stands, *Drag: A History of Female Impersonation in the Performing Arts* is two thirds by Roger Baker, with my chapters, 'Glamour Girls and Terrifying Termagants' and 'Hollywood and Bust', bringing the story up to date and looking at drag on film, and Richard Smith's 'Frock Tactics' dealing with drag on the gay scene, in gay politics and in popular music.

The first edition of *Drag* contains no notes and a fairly small bibliography. Where Roger indicated a need for a note in his revised text, I have included the relevant information – but otherwise the reader is directed to the rather fuller Bibliography in which I have included, for example, Braybrooke's edition of the *Diary and Correspondence of Samuel Pepys* as the edition most likely to have been used by Roger in 1967, not least because the definitive Lathan and Matthews edition didn't commence publishing until 1969.

Preface

WHEN he died in November 1993, aged fifty-nine, from complications arising from an attack of Beijing 'flu and the emphysema which had plagued him for years, Roger Baker was 'still hacking away at the workface' of *Drag: A History of Female Impersonation on the Stage*, the book he had published in 1968 and which, partly at my prompting, he was revising, rewriting and bringing up-to-date for this new and re-titled edition.

At the time of his death, Roger had almost finished work on the original text: substantially sharpening it and noticeably pointing up the homosexual context of much he was writing about, but which he had been rather more discreet about when writing the original edition in 1968. He had made a tentative start on a chapter entitled 'Swinging London' – now called 'Glamour Girls and Terrifying Termagants' – and was looking forward to tackling the material which now makes up the final third of the book, including the explosion into popular culture of drag (Dame Edna Everage, barely mentioned in the first edition, is a prime example of this) as well as its use within the gay community.

I had known Roger since the late 1960s. He and I were probably the first journalists to contribute under our own names to the then fledgeling gay press – fumblingly trying to identify our constituents and work out what it was they expected from us – in the pages of such publications as *Timm*, *Spartacus* and *Jeremy*. By the time *Gay News* appeared in 1972, we were old hands. And adaptable. Roger and I knew each other as fellow contributors to a wide variety of publications, straight and gay. We also met as editor and commissioned writer. We had great respect for each other regardless of the position either of us occupied at any given professional moment.

viii: Contents

Contents

From the AIDS Awareness series:

How can you write a poem when you're dying of AIDS?
(ed.) John Harold

'This is a moving anthology. So many pieces mention people going away, leaving a room, parting, missing one another, but there's also much about renewal and reunion, in dreams or reality, and about hope and love; it's very inspiring.' Antony Sher

Positive Lives: Responses to HIV – A Photodocumentary
(eds) Stephen Mayes and Lyndall Stein (Terrence Higgins Trust)

'An exciting demonstration of how powerfully photography can communicate one of the most critical global challenges of our age.' Richard Branson

From the Women on Women series:

Daring to Dissent: Lesbian Culture from Margin to Mainstream
(ed.) Liz Gibbs

'Radical, readable and feisty, this new collection of essays from very different dykes gives us all the courage to insist on our difference and the energy to dissent.' Patricia Duncker, University of Wales, Aberystwyth

Challenging Conceptions: Planning a Family by Self-Insemination
Lisa Saffron

'This pioneering book will be invaluable for lesbians contemplating motherhood.' Angela Mason, Executive Director, Stonewall

Portraits to the Wall: Historic Lesbian Lives Unveiled
Rose Collis

'In this all-too-slender volume, Collis has captured the danger and exuberance of some dozen historic lesbian lives. The book is well researched and accessible, journalistic and witty.' Fiona Cooper, novelist

Also available from the Cassell Sexual Politics List:

*Coming Out of the Blue: British Police Officers Talk about their Lives
in 'The Job' as Lesbians, Gays and Bisexuals*
Marc E. Burke

'Marc Burke's path-breaking study helps give a voice to the previously hidden
pains and dilemmas of lesbian, gay and bisexual police. It will become
required reading for all those who wish to understand this controversial issue
of the 1990s.' Ken Plummer, University of Essex

Safety in Numbers: Safer Sex and Gay Men
Edward King

'In the proliferation of writing about AIDS, *Safety in Numbers* stands out for
its careful analysis of one of the most important areas of all – the need to
develop and support effective prevention programmes for those most at risk.
This book will play an important part in helping to save lives and combat
homophobia.' Dennis Altman, La Trobe University, Australia

Speaking of Sex: The Limits of Language
Antony Grey

'. . . beautifully written in his usual easy and felicitous style. The plea for sex
respect should convince anyone; but it was his chapter on love I found
especially moving.'
Francis Bennion, author of *The Sex Code: Morals for Moderns*

*Broadcasting It: An Encyclopedia of Homosexuality on Film,
Radio and TV 1923–1993*
Keith Howes

'Its range, rigour and thoroughness are breathtaking. More impressive still,
it's a great read – fun, insightful and surprising.'
Richard Dyer, University of Warwick

Male Impersonators: Men Performing Masculinity
Mark Simpson

'Discussions of masculinity have hitherto been characterized by a timid tone
of pious apology – here at last is the antidote to that all-too-sombre debate.
Sharp, astute and decidedly spunky, Simpson's essays are guaranteed to
amuse, provoke and illuminate.' Andy Medhurst, University of Sussex

In Memoriam Roger Baker

Cassell
Villiers House
41/47 Strand
London WC2N 5JE

First published 1994

British Library Cataloguing-in-Publication Data
A catalogue record for this book is available from the British Library.

ISBN 0-304-32836-7 (hardback)
    0-304-32855-3 (paperback)

Typeset by Fakenham Photosetting Limited, Fakenham, Norfolk
Printed and bound in Great Britain by Mackays of Chatham

Drag

A History of Female Impersonation in the Performing Arts

Roger Baker

With contributions by Peter Burton and Richard Smith

CASSELL

Divine: 'The most beautiful woman in the world.'

Lily Savage: A gutsy, gritty and witty woman who is neither grotesque nor glamorous. Photograph from the Gay Times picture library.

vague and speculative, pieced together from contemporary documents, gossip and internal evidence from the plays. Even more speculative must be any conclusions we may draw about how the boys acted and what they looked like while they were doing it.

Chapter three

Acting Style and the Sound of Juliet

CURIOUSLY, it has only been in recent years that any kind of focus has been placed on this particular aspect of the Elizabethan and Jacobean theatre – and these discussions have emerged largely as a by-product of textual analysis rather than from any thoughts about the purely practical business of acting and staging. It always puzzled me slightly as to why theatre historians should have placed so much emphasis on attempting to reconstruct the shape and architectural detail of the actual playhouses and either ignored questions of acting style or dealt with them in the most casual way. Certainly the position of Juliet's balcony is important, but so surely is the quality and style of the person who played Juliet.

Today we may be able to make informed guesses about what kind of stage pictures were created but much else remains a mystery. We have, for example, no idea how the actors sounded – by which I mean what kind of vocal delivery was used and also what accents the actors possessed. Did each player retain his own regional cadence, or did the imperative of the verse coupled with regular performances gradually synthesise into a particular sort of voice recognisable as that of the actor? Were the boys and young men playing female parts at first using their natural, unbroken, voices and later encouraged or trained to distort their gruffer, more identifiably masculine tones by using a higher register, even a falsetto perhaps? The plays do offer us some internal clues, and I shall return to them.

47: Acting Style and the Sound of Juliet

A major turning point in the study and analysis of Shakespeare's texts (and by extension those of his fellow dramatists) came with the publication in 1964 of *Shakespeare Our Contemporary* by the Polish theorist Jan Kott, who insisted on the dramatist's urgent relevance to the upheavals of the mid-20th century – a bracing and controversial voice especially to those commentators who were, in Peter Brook's phrase 'far from life ... sheltered figures behind ivy-covered walls'. In his work Kott addressed, among other things, the treatment and imagery of sexuality in a group of Shakespeare's comedies and in doing so explored for the first time what significance there might have been (and still lies) in the fact that the ambiguous heroines Viola, Rosalind and the others were originally written for boys in drag.

Previous commentators, those behind their ivy-covered walls, if they mentioned the boy players at all, have tended to make a series of automatic and highly questionable assumptions: that no teenage boy could possibly play the female roles with any conviction; that having to use boys as girls was a grave disadvantage to Shakespeare; that many heroines were asked to disguise themselves as young men simply to make it somehow 'easier' all round. Even Jan Kott, usually both sensitive and sensible, offers a couple of limitations of his own suggesting that the (hypothetically) short attention span of boys explain why Shakespeare's female roles (and those of his contemporaries) are so much shorter than the male; and that their (again hypothetical) range was limited to playing either young girls or old women was why Shakespeare created so few portraits of women in the full bloom of sexual maturity.

Essentially I interpret this dismissive attitude to the question as a cultural rather than a practical response. Cultural because, behind these various assumptions, lies the belief that audiences and theatres were exactly the same in the sixteenth century as in the nineteenth and twentieth centuries; that the expectations of the one and the goods delivered by the other have remained constant over three hundred years. A practical response would begin by trying to dismantle received ideas about the theatre, by asking different questions – such as how they might imagine an Elizabethan dramatist, actor or playgoer would have reacted to a partnership of real woman and real man acting together on the public stage.

One problem every modern commentator shares, of course, is that there is virtually no opportunity these days to see boys or young men actually playing female parts. Once upon a time school plays represented one kind of experience, that of seeing boys acting with seriousness and dedication. The tradition of all-male casts performing at single-sex schools continued well into the 1960s. Some reached a remarkably high standard. However, with the sexes first less severely segregated and then not at all (or rarely) school Portias and Violas are now most likely to be teenage girls – that is if Shakespeare hasn't given way to Tennessee Williams or Joe Orton as a school play choice.

The cultivated Englishman of the Renaissance placed a high priority on education and dozens of schools were founded all over the country at this time; we see them still, named after Queen Mary or Queen Elizabeth. Drama was a regular part of the curriculum in the schools, not just (as today) a relaxing end-of-term entertainment, but as an integral part of a young man's education. Doing plays, it was asserted, taught the boys 'good behaviour and audacity', which meant an appropriate social manner and self-confidence. Rhetoric of voice and gesture were acquired skills, had their own quite stylized vocabularies, and were used in legal and political debate as well as tools of diplomacy. Boys being educated at Eton and Westminster were hardly destined to become actors, but they shared the actors' skills and demonstrated them in school productions.

It was a schoolmaster, Nicholas Udall (or Uvedale), who wrote *Ralph Roister Doister*, now referred to as the first formal English comic play. Udall was headmaster of Eton and later Westminster and his play was performed at one of these schools (historians are undecided), possibly in 1540, perhaps a few years earlier. The plays of the Roman comic stylist Terence, whose work was studied in all Tudor schools and translated by Udall, was the model for this and other plays. The tradition of an annual performance of Terence at Westminster School continued through the twentieth century. In 1846 Terence was, for some reason, dropped and an outcry was the result. He was reinstated the following year, however, with a prologue specially written to apologise for the omission. The choice in 1847 was *Adelphi* and the critic of the

recently founded *Illustrated London News* was impressed: 'Of the acting of Mr Clapcott, as Dostrata the widowed mother, we cannot speak too highly. Her grief at the supposed desertion of her daughter ... was very touchingly given. It drew forth, as it deserved, prolonged applause.' No suggestion of limitations, or unease at a boy playing the part is suggested here. In 1966 Westminster chose Terence's comedy *Eunuch* and gave it in modern dress – with high-heeled shoes, nylon-clad legs and mini-skirts.

In 1933 the theatre critic and historian W A Darlington wrote an article on school plays and noted that, as far as he could see, only Westminster and Bradfield (with its triennial Greek play) had maintained a solid acting tradition. As a result other schools were quick to get in on the act and claim long traditions for themselves as well, which initiated a revival of classical drama first among the public schools and later in the less prestigious grammar schools. Many of these reached a standard of excellence and confidence which made them worth the attention of those who were neither parent or prefect.

One headmaster had more than common insights. This was Guy Boas, who recorded his years of producing plays at Sloane School in Chelsea and argued persuasively that the Elizabethan dramatists are by no means beyond the range of schoolboys. Sean O'Casey and Walter de la Mare were among the people who advised Boas on his productions and his theories derive directly from practical experience which gives them authority. The implications of this work, however, did not seem to filter through to the academic commentators. It might have influenced their appraisal of what the boy actors were capable of.

As I suggest, a seriously acted and produced school play is the nearest a modern audience may come to seeing boys act. It gives a flavour, but no matter how good and convincing such productions may be I don't think they can be equated with what an Elizabethan audience saw either at St Paul's and Blackfriars or on the public stage of the Globe.

There must, I think, have been a considerable difference in style and production values between the shows put on by the children's companies and those of the adult troupes, especially when the children were still firmly attached to the chapels of great houses.

From the evidence of the plays themselves, whether early pieces by Lyly or the later works created by Ben Jonson, it would appear that there was an air of formal artificiality about the plays and masques. Since the performances would take place in the great halls of the houses and palaces (enclosed spaces) and before an attentive audience, there would be no need for the young actors to strain their voices to gain a hearing. And since the boys were in any case trained choristers one can assume that they knew something about projection and that their clear, pure vibrato-free voices possessed a musical, asexual quality which suited the delicate language of their material.

Perhaps on summer evenings they performed with the light of the setting sun streaming through the huge windows beloved of Elizabethan architects, and at other times in the flattering glow of dozens of candles. With their richly brocaded clothes, they probably had the effect of particularly brilliant puppets. These qualities must have been at least part of the attraction of the children's companies when they were taken away from the shelter of the great houses and placed on the semi-private stages in the City of London – a great contrast to the vigorous, heroic sweep of the dramas presented by the adult companies.

Those elements of ribaldry and apparently graphic representations of love interest which eventually upset the authorities came later and it is possible that those satirical, lampooning plays acquired a heightened pleasure from the spectacle of seeing a child mouthing a rude word he doesn't quite know the meaning of, an effect which encouraged those writers with axes to grind and scores to settle to go even further, with the results we have already noted. Certainly the performances that took place behind the walls of Blackfriars must have had an extraordinary quality unknown to us today.

How the boy apprentices attached to the adult companies played presents a different problem. The most obvious difference lies in the nature of the plays themselves. Although the children played female parts, these roles seem to have demanded little more than a kind of stylised representation of a woman. The plays of Shakespeare, Marlowe, Tourneur and their contemporaries ask for much more realistic and emotional portrayals, which in turn would

demand a different kind of acting. Few commentators can bring themselves to believe that the appearances of the boys in such roles could have been anything but odd and ruinous to the full effect of the play.

In *Shakespeare and the Modern Stage* (1906) Sir Sydney Lee comments: 'How characters like Lady Macbeth and Desdemona were adequately rendered by youths, beggars description.' And even Ivor Brown, who was one of the more sympathetic and down to earth of Shakespeare commentators, finds himself unable to imagine a boy playing Cleopatra. 'Were there some full grown but sexually neutral types specially sought out and retained for parts of this kind?' he speculates. What he means exactly by 'sexually neutral' is unclear, but there is no evidence whatsoever that castration was ever practiced in England to retain a particularly outstanding pre-adolescent voice as in Italy. If he was thinking of an adult homosexual, then he was clearly harbouring limited, stereotyped notions. But Brown's reaction was not unique. In 1958 A M Nagler published a useful little book called *Shakespeare's Stage* and he is similarly baffled: 'A lad of sixteen could not possibly have played Lady Macbeth realistically,' he states, defying any opposition. 'To get away with it,' he argues, 'the boy must have acted stylistically and so, therefore, to retain a common denominator of style, the adult actors must also have acted stylistically.'

It is a seductive argument. By referring to the classical theatres of China and Japan – both highly stylised and both using male actors in female roles – Nagler reminds us that 'stylisation does not exclude emotional reaction'. He also makes the rather obvious point that the Jacobeans knew that their theatre was theatre and not reality. Of the boys' companies he says: 'It would be hard to imagine that these children played realistically' and supposes that Nathaniel Field made such a successful transition from the Chapel Royal to the King's Men because he had learned this art of stylisation.

As far as the children's companies are concerned he has a point and, as already indicated, I'm inclined to agree that their work probably was stylised rather than realistic. But when thinking about the adult companies the analogy with oriental theatre does not really stand up. The long, elaborate dramas of China and Japan

were expressed in an accepted and universally understood code which governed their language, music, movement, costume and makeup. The finished productions approached something like a religious ritual, and they were always identical whoever acted them and wherever they were played. The human personality of the performers was submerged by the demands of the code, and technique became paramount.

This kind of stylisation seems alien to the realistic, free-flowing public dramas of Elizabethan and Jacobean times. There was probably a use of rhetoric in gesture and vocal delivery that touched on a kind of stylisation (rather like those employed by barristers in a modern courtroom), but the sheer variety of dramatic levels within the plays indicates a similar variety of dramatic styles. Nor would such an elaborate and refined technique seem to be a logical evolution from the streets where drama began. The public had its favourite stars and its response – just like today – was to the personality that shines through performance. Nor is there any evidence, either from the plays themselves or from contemporary notes, that the theatre of this time was anything other than realistic and firmly related to contemporary life. My contention is that the female impersonators were quite able to present realistic accounts of their roles – with acting, appearance and sound united into a seamless whole.

As already noted, how Shakespeare's actors sounded is something we shall probably never know with any certainty. But there are a few clues scattered through the plays which may lead us to some idea of how at least the boy actresses sounded. The starting point must be harmony, revered by the Elizabethans as a kind of perfection representing heaven. Shakespeare's plays are threaded through with music, songs and references to those divine harmonies which mean order and sanity. When reason seems to totter it is like sweet bells jangled 'out of tune and harsh'. We may be confident that Shakespeare – and his contemporaries – were sensitive to the sound of voices.

In *Twelfth Night*, the Duke Orsino says to Viola who is disguised as the boy Cesario:

Diana's lip
Is not more smooth and rubious; thy small pipe
Is as the maiden's organ, shrill of sound
And all is semblative a woman's part.

Today we tend to use the word 'shrill' to suggest an unpleasant sound, but its use in this context is almost certainly straight-for-wardly descriptive, meaning high-pitched and piercing. Like a choir boy, in fact. Which seems to indicate quite clearly that the boy actresses had clear, unbroken voices.

But did they? The possibility of a voice breaking seems to have been a constant hazard. Hamlet greets one of the boys in the troupe of strolling players that visits Elsinore with the remark: 'Pray God your voice, like a piece of uncurrent gold, be not cracked within the ring.' In *Cymbeline* Arviragus observes that the voices of himself and his brother Guiderius 'have got the mannish crack'. And there is a clear suggestion that the song 'Fear no more the heat o' the sun' could have been spoken rather than actually sung. 'I cannot sing, I'll weep and word it with you,' says Guiderius.

Orsino specifically requests Viola/Cesario to sing 'that old and antique song, Come away death' – but he doesn't: Feste the jester is quickly produced to perform it. Perhaps the boy who originally played Viola had that mannish crack in his singing voice but enough control over his speaking voice to emulate the 'maiden's organ'. To support this supposition is the incidental thought that the boy who played Viola's twin brother Sebastian must have appeared grown up and masculine enough to satisfy Olivia as a Cesario-substitute. This is the climactic moment when all sexual options are open and the youth (Cesario) turns into the woman (Viola) and the now recognised woman (Viola) turns into the man (Sebastian). Shakespeare's 'master-mistress' of my passion is rea-lised in dramatic terms.

There is no reason to suppose that once their voices had broken the boys ceased playing female roles. We can turn to the famous and oft-quoted outburst of Cleopatra when she shudders at the idea of being taken captive by Caesar and carried in triumph through Rome:

54: Drag

The quick comedians
Extemporally will stage us, and present
Our Alexandrian revels; Antony
Shall be brought drunken forth, and I shall see
Some squeaking Cleopatra boy my greatness
I' the posture of a whore.

Curiously, this comment has often been interpreted as decisive proof that the boy actors did indeed 'squeak' in some unpleasing way – including Cleopatra herself presumably. But this need not be a reference to the male actresses of the adult companies, but to the gross satirical carryings-on of the children's troupes and the kind of ribaldry that brought them into disrepute (the play is dated around 1608). In *A Midsummer Night's Dream* we are given a comic glimpse of an amateur group putting on a play which hardly presents Pyramus and Thisbe with the sensitivity they usually attract. Cleopatra may have had this kind of venture in mind as well.

Cleopatra is probably Shakespeare's greatest female creation, demanding a wide range of emotional highs and lows as well as passion, poetry, playfulness and petulance. Whoever tackled the role must have possessed the technique, self-confidence and command to pull it off. Her voice would certainly not squeak. Commentators who assert that a man's voice emerging from Cleopatra – not to mention Lady Macbeth, Margaret of Anjou, Mistress Quickly, Gertrude and the rest – must have been embarrassingly inappropriate (unless 'sexually neutral' of course) overlook the simple fact that just as we tend to see what we expect to see, we also hear what we expect to hear. The sound emerging from what appears to be a woman will be interpreted as that of a woman's voice. Nor does the breaking of a boy's voice automatically render the new, adult sound unsuitable for female roles. Baritones and basses would inevitably present problems, but this still leaves a considerable range of much lighter male voices.

Few female impersonators working today make any effort to alter the pitch of their voices. When preparing to play the drag part of Dorothy Michaels in the film *Tootsie* the actor Dustin Hoffman found that using his natural voice was much more effective than

trying for some falsetto effect and discovered that by assuming an accent other than his own (he chose a Southern drawl) his own acquired an effortless 'feminine' lilt which was all he needed to complete his constructed persona.

During his stage act, the impersonator Danny La Rue, after making his appearance as a spectacularly gowned and made-up woman, would approach the footlights and shout 'Wotcha mates!' to his audience, presumably to assure doubters that he was a real man underneath and it was all a huge joke, really. Ironically, in order to project what would be heard as a 'masculine' voice, La Rue had to produce a coarse bass noise quite unlike his natural voice, which is a pleasantly light and lyrical Irish tenor.

Chapter four

Swinging Arden

THEATRE historians and commentators who have baulked at the idea of a male playing Cleopatra or Lady Macbeth, base their critique on the unquestioned idea that the actor would be a pre-pubescent boy with a clear treble voice. Along with this goes the assumption that although the boy may have looked and sounded like a girl he could not, at such an early age, have either the technical nor emotional experience to handle such complex roles convincingly. However, if we recognise that an adult 'female voice' very rarely equates with 'the unbroken voice of a choirboy', then there is no reason at all to suppose that the heroines of the Jacobean stage were played by inexperienced boy puppets. Older actors would, of course, have acquired those valuable assets of technique and emotional weight.

Audiences had to watch as well as listen, and the physical appearance of the heroines had its importance. Today we are used to the drag queen being larger than life – indeed, we expect it. She will be quite over the top in the way she dresses, makes up, does her hair, delivers her material. It would be a mistake to imagine that the female impersonators of Shakespeare's day behaved in such a way – on the stage, at any rate. But all indications are that productions by the adult companies were quite splendid to watch, with often elaborate costumes and accessories. We also know that plays were presented in the costumes of the day irrespective of whether their actual location was supposed to be ancient Rome or a wood near Athens. Within the plays themselves there are frequent references to clothes which support this,

probably the most famous being Cleopatra's request to have her lace cut – that is, her stays loosened.

The main suppliers of stage clothes were the servants employed by aristocratic families. Whenever a certain style of dress went out of fashion, the lords and ladies who had worn the garments passed them on to their employees. The strict codes relating to what individuals of certain ranks could wear usually prevented a lady's maid from wearing a lady's gown – so it was sold on to the actors. Shakespeare's queens and countesses would appear in clothes appropriate to their fictional – but not private – status. The effect was certainly splendid, with the full apparatus of high-class Elizabethan costume on display – its hoops, huge skirts, slashed sleeves, jewellery, ruffs and boned collars.

During the last few years a considerable amount of research into the significance of clothes on the Elizabethan stage has been done. Marjorie Garber, for example, argues that in *Twelfth Night* Malvolio's attempts at upward mobility through his apparel was probably more shocking and had a greater impact on the audience than the transvestism of Viola. But what concerns us here is that the male actresses must have looked pretty impressive. The dresses had, however, one drawback which would have affected the acting style. The clothes of upper class and aristocratic women in this period (and indeed of every period up to the present century) carried the message of wealth and leisure and, with their wide skirts, yards of material, corsets and laces, rigidly boned collars, seemed designed to restrict free and spontaneous movement. Perhaps the only vigorous physical activity women were allowed was dancing. The movements of the male actresses playing grand ladies on stage would, by necessity, have been formal and stately. Only when the heroines were allowed to disguise themselves as men was a greater freedom of expression possible. From this perspective the first meeting of the Countess Olivia and the boy Cesario in *Twelfth Night* – the one stately and veiled, the other anxious and jumpy – would offer the audience of the time a dimension which eludes us today.

If, as I believe, the male actresses looked convincing and sounded appropriate, what of the other criticisms and expressions of disbelief commentators have offered. The suggestion that Shake-

speare and his contemporary dramatists viewed the need to have their heroines played by males as a limitation, a major difficulty, is to misunderstand the conditions of the period. Shakespeare may have been a genius, but he was not Nostradamus and could hardly have foreseen a time when women would be allowed onto the stage any more than he could have predicted electricity, revolving stages or light-projected scenery. He worked with the resources to hand. His technical demands – for ghosts, storms, vanishings and so on – are modest and within his theatre's limits. One might speculate how much verse might have been lost if he had even Wagner's technology with which to create realistic pictures on the stage rather than in the imagination of his audience.

The alleged limitations of the boy players have been cited as the reason why Shakespeare's female roles are shorter than those of the male characters. But is this actually so? In terms of basic word-counting the girls don't come off badly at all. In three plays the heroines have the longest parts – Portia, Helena (in *All's Well That Ends Well*) and Rosalind. Juliet comes second to Romeo, Helena (in *A Midsummer Night's Dream*) has the third longest role as does Viola (with Olivia the fourth) and Desdemona. Cleopatra has the second longest part and Lady Macbeth is second only to her husband. In many other plays the leading ladies carry a dramatic impact quite disproportionate to the number of speeches they are given: Adriana in *A Comedy of Errors*, Isabella in *Measure for Measure*, Hermione in *A Winter's Tale*, Beatrice, Kate the shrew and those merry wives of Windsor are immediate examples.

Jan Kott's observation that though there are plenty of young girls in Shakespeare's plays and several much older women, there are few representatives of women in the full bloom of sexual maturity because boys couldn't play them similarly fails to stand up to scrutiny: Gertrude in *Hamlet*, Cleopatra, of course, Hermione, Lady Macbeth, the Mistresses Ford and Page, Lady Capulet and Margaret of Anjou are all roles that demand the confidence of sexual maturity.

Finally there is the charge that there is a striking lack of physical demonstration between the sexes in Elizabethan and Jacobean drama. The implication is that had real women been available the playwrights would automatically have given us passionate

embraces, bedroom scenes, nudity even. This is, of course, nonsense – even the most liberal-minded playgoers would have rebelled at the very idea. In fact, such episodes are virtually non-existent in the whole span of English dramatic literature from Congreve to Shaw.

Today directors can find many opportunities in the Shakespeare canon to show us characters making physical love, and have given us at times a nude Desdemona and a nude Cressida. But these are additions, and do not emerge from the text itself. What does emerge from many of the texts is a strong strain of sexual debate, of moral dispute, of sexual imagery used for both comic and serious purposes. There are scenes of sexual flirtation which do not need to be acted out literally in order to make their point. When, later in the seventeenth century, real women were allowed on the stage the first demand made on them was that they be glamorous and sexy. They were encouraged to flaunt their legs, flash their breasts and exploit their sexuality in a way which would have been repulsive, if not mystifying to audiences of sixty years earlier.

As far as Shakespeare is concerned, in those plays which are primarily based on male-female relationships there is no sense that the dramatist is deliberately holding back when writing for the leading ladies. In other plays – the histories, some of the tragedies and those concerned with male power struggles – women have by necessity a smaller role to play. We might also bear in mind that by and large it was the men, the male actors, who carried the audience: Tamburlaine, Hamlet, Macbeth, Falstaff, Shylock, the Henrys, Jonson's *Alchemist* and *Volpone* were continually topping the charts. *Twelfth Night* was also played frequently – but was by popular consent known as *Malvolio*!

These were authentic female impersonators; actors playing women with skill and finesse, relying on no collusion with the audience but accepted precisely for what they were playing. It has been suggested that Shakespeare contrived to put several of his heroines into male costume to somehow make it easier for the male actors. But this argument misses a few points, a major one being that it is far more difficult for a real man to play a woman disguised as a man with no assistance from skirts, wig or feminine accessories. The effect would be that of what we today might describe as an 'effeminate' youth (to the Elizabethans 'effeminate' meant something like

overdressed in a self-indulgent way rather than sexually dubious). Another point is that in disguising themselves as men Viola, Rosalind and the others were (in the context of the dramas) breaking the biblical dress code which stated that one sex should not wear the clothes of the other. Awareness of this gives an extra sense of tension to the plight of these women which only works if the characters are accepted as real women. As we have noted the stage gave males permission to wear women's clothes, but the parallel freedom (to wear men's clothes) was nowhere available to women. So when Viola is finally allowed to resume her woman's clothes and Cesario disappears; and when Ganymede disappears and Rosalind returns the audience feels a twin relief – that the heroine is happily united with her proper partner, and that the dangerous period of disguise is over. Everything is back in proper order.

All of which is why experimental productions of Elizabethan dramas with all-male casts, though offering perhaps new insights into textual complexities, can never get very close to the physical impact which these performances must have possessed. We have to lose too much baggage about sex, about actresses, about the stage as a visibly erotic playground which have accrued over the subsequent centuries.

There have been various attempts over the years. An important pioneer was William Poel, who died in 1934. During the eighteenth and nineteenth centuries traditions of producing Shakespeare had evolved which distorted the plays, obscuring them with unnecessary excrescences. Visual spectacle was regarded as important and the plays had been edited – or chopped up – into short scenes, each demanding a new setting. Productions were also garnished with elaborate musical scores by such modish composers as Sullivan and Mendelssohn. With a new set for every scene, and lengthy musical interludes (however attractive) it is easy to see how Shakespeare's 'two-hour traffic of the stage' could be extended indefinitely, or how the text would have to be drastically slashed, in either case removing the pace and tension from the dramas. In 1881 Poel went back to basics and began experimenting with productions which presented Shakespeare in a style which he deduced to be as near to their original form as he could manage. He introduced the now almost automatic requirement of a permanent set, he re-

stored contemporary (ie Elizabethan) dress and for a *Hamlet* in 1900 used an all-male cast.

Poel was responsible for encouraging the young Edith Evans to begin her stage career and in 1912 she appeared as Cressida in his productions at Stratford and at the King's Hall, Covent Garden. A curiosity of this production was that he cast another young actress, Elspet Keith, as the 'crooked scurrilous clown' Thersites, which she did so effectively that few members of the audience realised she was a woman. Poel claimed that the speeches of Thersites were often so foul that 'a man could not be trusted with the part' – a curious remark, but one which suggests he had an unusual awareness of the drifting sexual ambiguities of this, and other, plays.

Jan Kott's essays in *Shakespeare Our Contemporary* were, as we have noted, an important signpost in the mid-sixties, indicating new and different ways of interpreting Shakespeare's plays. He was the first commentator to suggest that the use of males to play female parts added another dimension to the realisation of the texts. His work appeared at a time when the rigid sex roles, imposed from the post-war years (women back to the kitchen, men out hunting and gathering) through the 1950s were coming under scrutiny and beginning to dissolve, superficially in such popularist concepts as unisex, more seriously in the debates which would eventually burst out as the women's movement and, a little later, the gay movement. He argued, for example, that in Viola Shakespeare invented the most perfect hermaphroditic figure, a figure that has persisted and attracted in art from Homer's time to the present day. Rosalind too is a similar example. She elects to call herself Ganymede and Ganymede is the classical symbol of pederasty. All this, Kott argues, recalls a mysterious paradise in which there is no division between the sexes.

His work was largely theoretical, but stimulating to directors working at that time, and was initially responsible for the all-male production of *As You Like It* that the National Theatre sprang on a largely mystified London in the autumn of 1967. The relevant chapter from his book, called 'Bitter Arcadia', was quoted extensively in the programme, but the director Clifford Williams actually made a point of disassociating himself from its precepts.

'This production is not designed to demonstrate specific ideas advanced in that essay,' he wrote. What he was looking for, he said, 'was an atmosphere of spiritual purity which transcends sensuality in the search for poetic sexuality'.

The production was given symbolic, rather than realistic, settings and the costumes were in a style that derived from the current 'swinging London' fashions of the King's Road and Carnaby Street, executed in plastics, man-made fibres and synthetic furs. If sensuality was being rejected, so was pastoral identification – we were being pointed towards outer-space, courtesy Courrèges. Disguised as a boy, Rosalind (played by Ronald Pickup) looked like any lath-like model girl demonstrating a trouser suit with cap and floating scarf. His fair, boyishly flopping hair gave him a widely noted resemblance to Twiggy, a popular young model of more than common angularity and boyishness (later to become an engaging musical comedy actress on Broadway). *The New York Times* noted 'an identity of spirit between the men playing the women's parts and the long-haired boys and short-haired girls in the pit'. In the same season a production of *A Midsummer Night's Dream* was also on view in London and its director Frank Dunlop introduced a sly joke on the transvestite theme by putting his girls in modern trouser suits and their lovers in the flouncing kilts of the Greek army.

Critical response to *As You Like It* was generally positive with most commentators confessing that their original doubts were swept away as the play proceeded. W A Darlington in *The Daily Telegraph* suggested that 'it does not matter what sex the player of Rosalind belongs to, so long as she or he can act'. In *The Times* Irving Wardle described Pickup's Rosalind as 'a blank that comes to life under the stress of intense platonic feeling' and in *The Sunday Times* Harold Hobson decided that the casting 'puts eroticism, whether ambiguous or straightforward, out of the theatre altogether'.

The popular press were mostly careful but it was *The Daily Mail* that summed up the production's quality best. Peter Lewis wrote: 'The moment at which we were watching in fact Ronald Pickup playing Rosalind playing the boy Ganymede pretending to be the girl Rosalind passed as smoothly as a dreamer glides through

layer on layer of different dream personages.' One dissenting critic was Ronald Bryden who in *The Observer* described the production as 'a bard for this season's King's Road silhouette of girlish boyishness. (Clifford Williams's) production is an essay ... in the contemporary cult – here we go again – of Camp.'

My own notes at the time suggest that camp was one quality notably absent from the production; in fact the whole event was, if anything, just a bit too po-faced. But a point was made. None of the four men playing women's parts attempted actually to impersonate a woman in the familiar drag tradition (with affected mannerisms, mincing walk, exaggerated use of accessories). What they did was to latch onto the characters and reveal them, allowing female qualities to emerge as and when they would. In an interview at the time Ronald Pickup described how he and Charles Kaye (who played Celia) were looking for something – a gesture, a style – which would suggest femininity without resort to obvious camp. They realised that women tend to touch each other more than men do and when they tried holding hands, the characterisation began to fall into place.

As You Like It was a notable and, for its period and place, a quite bold experiment. But it set no trends, nor did it cast any incidental light on Elizabethan playing. It did, however, support the view that Shakespeare and his contemporaries wrote their female roles straight and expected them to be played straight with no allowances made for the male actors nor with any expectations of virtuoso mimicry from them.

One may wonder if a search for 'spiritual purity which transcends sensuality in the search for poetic sexuality' meant much to the groundlings who packed the playhouses. Did they, too, long for a paradise where there was no division between the sexes? It seems unlikely – power struggles, battles and murder were more to the public's taste. But perhaps the Jacobean chattering classes had other preoccupations. It seems certain now that *Love's Labour's Lost, Twelfth Night, A Midsummer Night's Dream* and *As You Like It* were celebration plays, written not for the public playhouse but specially commissioned for private events. Jan Kott suggests, for example, that *The Dream* was created for the wedding of the Earl of Southampton's mother Mary Browne when she married, as

her second husband, Sir Thomas Heneage. A L Rowse, in *Shakespeare's Southampton*, is in tacit agreement that the play was written for some special Southampton occasion, but is not definite about which. Kott suggests that the play originally possessed meanings particularly relevant to the first audience but which elude us today, in-jokes at the expense of the assembled courtiers and nobles that would set the guests rippling with knowing laughter. All four plays have also been related to Shakespeare's relationship with the Earl of Southampton, the gestation of their heroines linked to the sexual ambiguity of the sonnets. It seems to me irrelevant to try and guess whether the poet was homosexually involved with the Earl – it seems as easy to find evidence that he was as it is to find evidence that he was not – but they were definitely involved as patron and playwright.

Certainly these plays seem more intimate and more sophisticated than others of the Shakespeare cannon, and they have an edge as well as a particularly intense poetry that might well have been blown to the winds on the open stage of the Globe. They seem private works in both subject and construction. Records show that *As You Like It* was not successful with the general public (at least there are no references to its being repeated by public demand). *Twelfth Night* was frequently played, but as we have noted, it was known as *Malvolio* – a significant change of emphasis. It is also worth noting that in those other plays where Shakespeare uses the girl-disguised-as-boy device, it is used as a plot mechanism rather than being centralised as a theme.

Chapter five

Onnagata and Tan

WE have noted how several theatre historians and commentators have suggested that the technique of the Elizabethan male actress may have had some similarity to the acting style of the female impersonators of the Chinese and Japanese theatres. This is a tempting theory but one which I find it difficult to accept. Many observers, not only enraptured orientalists but also disinterested Westerners, have regarded these Asian actors as representing the ultimate in perfection on the stage. This may have been so – but only within the context of their own unique theatre which, with its highly defined rituals and formality, seems to me to be diametrically opposed to the full-blooded gusto and surging realism of the English stage – even though certain powerful and often-used motives are common to both dramas – notably violence, use of the supernatural and the relentless process of revenge.

In fact, so stylised and refined are the techniques of the Asian theatres that to call their female impersonators 'drag queens' does seem inappropriate. And yet, despite the very evident differences of approach, the one thing they did have in common with the English male actresses was that they were practising what I have called 'real impersonation', that is playing women with no layer of ambiguity either of the purely comic kind or to create that textual androgyny now seen in those plays of Shakespeare we have discussed. And whereas the authentic female impersonator was banished from the English stage by the end of the seventeenth century and thus changed for ever our perception of the art, in China and Japan that tradition lasted unaltered until well into the present century.

The origin of theatre in Japan, and particularly in China, is more difficult to document than that of their English counterpart, but it is interesting to note that all three demanded that women's roles be played by men and that they all reached a certain peak of maturity at roughly the same time – in the late sixteenth and early seventeenth centuries. Also both legend and documented history suggest that the Asian theatres developed from acts of worship specifically associated with fertility and re-birth.

We have seen that the first English dramatisation of a peak-religious moment was the Resurrection. In Japan the first hints of a theatre have been associated with a dance, performed by one Princess Ame-no-Uzume, to entice the brooding sun goddess from her cave. Similarly Chinese theatre (which we in the West tend to call 'opera') traces its origins back to the songs and dances which celebrated religious ceremonies. Peter Ackroyd makes an interesting point when he suggests that those theatres which use transvestites have their origins in sacred rituals which involve fertility.[1]

Japanese theatre developed out of dancing and neither grew into a separate art, so theatre means dance and dance means theatre. To this was added music and singing or chanting. Japan has three main forms of theatre: first came the classic Noh drama which began in the fourteenth century and later became cross-fertilised with importations from Asia and the South Pacific to evolve into Kabuki and Bunkaru, the puppet theatre which does not concern us here.

And yet Kabuki was not, at the very beginning a transvestite theatre, as it was a woman, O-Kuni of Izumo, who is credited as being the first to articulate the dances which would eventually become Kabuki. She was a Shrine Virgin at the shrine of Izumo on Honshu and her style was initially informed with the techniques of what were called prayer dances. But she added other elements including some from the Noh theatre, comic interludes, rustic dances and erotic innovations of her own. Apparently she first performed on the dry river bed of Honshu's capital Kyoto attracting an enthusiastic following. This was clearly popular entertainment, very different from the aristocratic austerities of Noh. Her repertory was expanded and her troupe of dancers increased after she had married a man from a Samurai family called Sanza Nagoya who seems to

have taken over as manager and promoter. The dates of this development are imprecise but fall between 1586 and 1603.

Legend has it that Sanza Nagoya danced with O-Kuni on the river bed when he first met her and, while he was masterminding her career men did dance together with the women. After her death it seems that Kabuki became an all-female theatre and was known as *Onna Kabuki* or Women's Kabuki. And here again we find a parallel with that period in England when women first appeared on the stage – the association of female players with prostitution. As we shall see, English audiences of the Restoration rather relished this scandalous connection and the actresses survived triumphantly. In Japan the Women's Kabuki, associated with prostitution and political immorality, was banned in 1628. There was a short period when, in an attempt to clean up their act, the women brought men back into their company and each sex played its appropriate role. But eventually women disappeared from the stage altogether and did not return until the late nineteenth century.

The eventual consequence of the 1628 ban was a complete reversal and the formation of all-male troupes, *Wakashu Kabuki* or Young Men's Kabuki. But once again corruption and immoral practices became rife and since the dancers were now attractive young men homosexuality was the chief offender with too many Samurai falling for the charms of the female impersonators. In 1652 the *Wakashu Kabuki* was banned in its turn. At the same time the authorities also banned music and dancing from the stage.

The result of this was the creation of a different kind of all-male Kabuki called *Yaro Kabuki* which means Male or 'Mature' with its message that the actors were no longer fledgeling queens but grown-up men who knew how to conduct themselves. Short haircuts were the order of the day and foreheads were shaved high over the head – presumably to make the men less attractive. Respecting the ban on music and dance, they concentrated on speech and drama, but dance was so ingrained in Kabuki that the actors managed to retain this vital element by creating a kind of mime to music which could be regarded more as acting than dancing. This was the final form Kabuki took and it has remained in place to the present day. The Westernization of Japan has meant that popular theatre is no longer unisexual and that all-girl revues are popular.

Modern interpretations of Kabuki, popular and accessible, can be seen played by mixed casts, but when Noh and Kabuki are presented in traditional form they offer what is perhaps the only opportunity in the world today of seeing a female impersonator using real disguise: the *onnagata* or 'woman impersonator'.

But how 'real' was 'real' one wonders. All the evidence suggests that the *onnagata* symbolised femininity rather than impersonated it in what a Western audience would see as a realistic way and is, on the stage, distanced from the women in everyday life. This is expressed well by A C Scott in his book *The Kabuki Theatre of Japan* when he writes: 'He (the actor) must play to an audience that knows the rules of the game and which is primarily interested in the way he recreates a stage character in a traditional, accepted mould. At the same time his performance must contain an individuality beneath the unchanging conventions, his symbolism must be something more than imitative repetition.'[2]

Analogies are dangerous and eventually they usually break down, but perhaps the closest one in modern Western theatre that comes to mind is with classical ballet. Every Aurora and Odette has had her physical movements rigidly set down for her from the moment the roles were created by Petipa or Ivanov. The delight and excitement a ballerina brings is exactly that 'individuality beneath the unchanging conventions'. As in classical ballet the theatres of Japan and China possess a wide vocabulary of prescribed movement and gesture that always indicate certain things whatever the context. The Asian theatres have always been reluctant to change. Even when bearing in mind certain concessions made to a modern audience in the presentation of Noh drama (notably simplification and abbreviation) one can be sure that a performance today would be comprehensible to an audience of two hundred years ago. An Elizabethan audience would, on the other hand, most likely be bewildered by our contemporary productions of Shakespeare and Jonson. Another technical parallel which may help to clarify this point is that of the D'Oyly Carte Opera Company which continued to perform the Savoy Operas of Gilbert and Sullivan exactly according to the original production notes laid down by Gilbert himself, and amateur productions were forced to copy them. Audiences loved the mechanical repetition of movement and

gesture but a feeling grew that such routine preservation of a dated style was mummifying a series of brilliant English musicals instead of revealing them afresh, with all their sparkling wit and melody, for a new generation.

When the works finally came out of copyright in 1962, the Sadler's Wells Opera Company (now the English National Opera) and others offered new, inventive productions with considerable success but the D'Oyly Carte continued for several years in its own original style and only recently has the (now reformed) company begun to revise and refresh the works themselves. This response to popular taste did not happen in the same way with Noh and Kabuki – and one hopes that Gilbert's notes will never be lost. In fifty years an authentic production of, say, *The Mikado* done exactly as it was when it was first seen in 1885 would have more than archaeological interest, just as Noh and Kabuki performances have today.

As we shall see, after the Restoration the female impersonator in the West was forced to abandon her reality and became the comic drag queen. The Kabuki theatre's resistance to change prevented this happening to the onnagata. 'Noh went beyond the limits of time and space to lay bare the human soul and sing its longings,' wrote Prince Takamatsu and despite its more popular appeal Kabuki's aims were also high. In his book *Theatre East and West*, Leonard C Pronko writes: '(the *onnagata*) stands ... as a profound symbol of the mystery of metamorphosis, which is the mystery of the theatre. He seems to join two totally different worlds, not only in his double identity as actor and character, but in his dual role as man-woman. The *onnagata* is a dynamic and gigantic archetypal figure possessing, beyond his theatrical dimension, a metaphysical dimension. Whether the spectator is aware of it or not, the *onnagata* stirs in his unconscious a dim memory of some perfection partaking of both masculine and feminine, the great Earth Mother who is creator and sustainer, the divine androgyn in whose bisexuality both dark and light are harmonised. To approach the *onnagata* is to draw near to the secrets of existence, embodied in human form through the art of the Kabuki actor.'[3]

As with the interpretations of Jan Kott, discussed earlier, this rather philosophical passage implies that the audience's aware-

ness of the real sex of the performer is integral to the appreciation of his art. And yet evidence suggests that the *onnagata*, in pursuit of his art, was forced to go to great lengths to distance himself from his natural maleness. But the superficial imitation of a woman's mannerisms was not nearly enough. The rules of dress, deportment, gesture, make-up and costume were so rigid and became so bound into the whole ritual of Kabuki that had a real woman undertaken an *onnagata* role then the effect, on stage, would have been exactly the same as if it were a man. For, as Pronko points out, 'were a woman to attempt to play a Kabuki female role she would have to imitate the men who have so subtly and beautifully incarnated woman before her.'[4]

The stage female in Kabuki, then, is a male-created artefact. 'If an actress were to appear on the stage she could not express ideal feminine beauty, for she could only rely on the exploitation of her physical characteristics, and therefore not express the synthetic ideal. The ideal woman can only be expressed by an actor.' These are the words of a famous eighteenth century *onnagata*, Yoshizawa Ayame, who is credited with formalising the necessary techniques required by the impersonator. He lived between 1673 and 1729 and occupies a place in Japanese theatre history something of the position of his near contemporary in England, Edward Kynaston (who we shall meet in the next section). Ayame recorded his theories and principles of acting under the title *Ayamegusa* and this became the source book for all succeeding *onnagata*. It is not suggested that Ayame invented the *onnagata*'s techniques, but that he used his own genius to refine and perfect already established traditions.

Another of his precepts is: 'You cannot be a good *onnagata* unless you are like a woman in daily life.' He adds that if someone refers to your wife, the *onnagata* 'must appear so embarrassed as to blush', and 'no matter how many children he may have he must not lose his innocence of mind'. The assumption here is clearly that the *onnagata* is a heterosexual, probably married, man – the *Wakashu* Kabuki a thing of the past.

An *onnagata* was the central character in what was critically regarded as one of Kon Ichikawa's more outstanding films, *An Actor's Revenge*, made in 1963 and which appeared in Britain in

1967. In it Kazuo Hasegana played Yukinojo a female impersonator in eighteenth century Japan who sets out to wreak a fiendish revenge on three men he holds responsible for the death of his parents. It is a cool, formal but gripping film and its reconstruction of a Kabuki theatre was a frustratingly brief moment. Nor did it get a lot of mileage from the fact that the actor was living and behaving as a woman even off-stage, but there were some striking episodes, such as when bandits attack what they assume to be a woman only to find themselves confronted by an expert swordsman. The scenes in which the *onnagata* – still in female guise – makes love to a real girl have, at least for Western audiences, a nice sexual frisson. Interesting here, is that Yukinojo finds himself teaching the girl how to be a graceful woman, supporting the precepts of Ayame.

Just as the *onnagata*'s demeanour and manner were constructed to represent a symbolic ideal of womanhood, so were his looks. His face had to be the right shape: a broad, round face could bar an actor from taking female roles regardless of his other talents. The ideal was a fine oval, dead white with fine eyebrows and a tiny mouth. Young girls were indicated by a touch of pink on the cheeks; matrons and married women blackened their teeth and shaved off their eyebrows (as was the custom in Japanese society). Wigs and clothes were elaborate, huge and heavy and the clothes of the man playing a high-ranking courtesan (*oiran*) would be further embellished – or hampered – with lacquered clogs eight or ten inches high, which would force him to balance by holding onto the shoulders of attendants. This must have made for some spectacular entrances. In fact we learn that playing an *oiran* was every impersonator's ideal – so maybe the the spirit of the high-glamour drag queen was lurking there in eighteenth century Japan after all.

The history of the theatre in China is long and complex, mainly because different kinds of drama developed in different areas of the vast country, often with very little in common and appealing to specifically local audiences. Scholars have traced the origins of the theatre back as far as dance entertainments given in 1050 BC and each subsequent dynasty seems to have had an effect on the presentation and appreciation of drama. But by the nineteenth century the dominating and most popular form of theatre was that known as *ching hsi*, which means Peking drama, the

formative elements of which can be traced back to the thirteenth century. The use of men to play women's roles was the result, as in Japan, of a ban on women imposed by the authorities for moral reasons.

This happened during the reign of Ch'ien Lung (1735–96). Until then actresses had appeared but were regarded socially as courtesans and seem to have behaved as such. Ch'ien Lung enjoyed the theatre so his ban on women did not, as might have happened with a less worldly emperor, result in a total ban on all stage activity. It did, however, put managers in difficulties and the solution was the female impersonator, or *tan* actor. Originally these men were chosen for their looks and ability to appear feminine in women's clothes, but drama became stronger and more popular until, during the nineteenth century, the *tan* had become a vital component and his art had become so complex as to leave the initial problem of just looking pretty as a low priority. Actresses were beginning to be accepted on the Chinese stage from 1912, but had to contend with a lot of prejudice: they were not allowed to appear alongside male actors and even as late as the 1930s one of the older theatres in Peking refused even to admit female theatre-goers.

Reactionary and anti-feminist as this certainly was, in a curious way it was also a tribute to the power and popularity of the *tan* actors themselves who had, by then, dominated the stage for more than a century. As in Japan, the female roles were purely male creations which women themselves had later to imitate. And again we find a detailed and rigid vocabulary of costume, movement and gesture. A random example is the technique of sleeve movements. In *The Classical Theatre of China*, A C Scott lists 107 different movements alone. Of these thirty-nine are peculiar to the *tan* actor, the rest to all characters. There were similar lists of hand, arm, leg and foot movements to be mastered, not to mention a seemingly infinite and detailed code conveyed by robes, masks and make-up.

There were six categories of *tan* actors, each with its own specific demands: the faithful wife, modest woman, obedient daughter role, for example, required a good singing voice and demure, graceful movements. The glamorous, seductive leading

lady was not required to sing but had to be a good actor with a range of effective facial expressions and gymnastic ability. Other characters included the malicious evil woman (which could also be a comic role); the old woman and the vigorous maiden who could ride and fight which meant skill with sword and lance. Most *tan* actors would tend to specialise in one category, but many were admired for their versatility.

One of these was Mei Lan-fang who could probably justify the title of the World's Greatest Female Impersonator. His grand-father was Mei Ch'iao-ling who was born in 1841 and when a boy was sold as an apprentice to a theatre company in Peking. He became a popular female impersonator admired for his portrayal of grand aristocratic ladies. He had two sons, both of whom followed him into the theatre. One as a musician, the other, Shao-fen, became a *tan* actor but died before his reputation peaked. However his son, born in 1894, was Mei Lan-fang who was the inheritor of a strong family tradition, a responsibility he carried with great dis-tinction.

A C Scott writes that Mei's stage technique was 'unsurpassed in its unity of gesture, expression, and exquisite grace and delicacy of line. His voice has purity and quality ... but only strict training and discipline have enabled him to retain his vocal powers so long'.[5] (Scott was writing in 1957 when Mei would have been sixty-three years old.) During the twentieth century, Mei was heaped with honours, voted China's most popular actor in 1924 and during the 1930s toured Russia and America with great success. He conquered everyone he met and was admired by Stanis-lavsky. During the Japanese war he retired and grew a moustache to emphasise even further his divorce from the stage, but found no problem in making a sensational come-back after the war was over. He created new plays, improved technical presentation and intro-duced forms of dancing based on ancient styles. His techniques were followed, not only by other *tan* actors but by the rising gener-ation of actresses. Later in life he produced a few films of his plays. His death in 1961 after a career that had linked the distant past with a technological future marked the end of an era.

Notes

1. Peter Ackroyd, *Dressing Up: Transvestism and Drag, The History of an Obsession* (New York: Simon & Schuster, 1979).
2. A C Scott, *The Kabuki Theatre of Japan* (London: George Allen & Unwin).
3. Leonard C Pronko, *Theatre East and West* (University of California Press, 1967).
4. Ibid.
5. Scott, cited above.

Chapter six

Western Approaches

THE arts of Asia have been reflected in Western culture since the eighteenth century, but usually as decorative 'orientalism' – furniture, wallpapers, wood block prints, ceramics and one-off architectural frolics such as, in England, the pagoda in Kew Gardens and the Royal Pavilion in Brighton. During the last few years the cuisines of India and China have extended from restaurant to the domestic kitchen, with that of Japan not far behind. The lyric arts, however, have not been colonised to anything like the same extent. Though they may initially find the sound exotic and atmospheric, Western audiences seem able only to offer a short attention span to the timbre of the voices and instruments. Some stage techniques have found their way into Western productions – the use of black-clothed, and therefore invisible, stagehands to change sets in view of the audience is one example. The use of yards of rippling silk to represent water is another device.

In the 1950s and 1960s when troupes of Noh and Kabuki actors and the Peking Opera toured Europe our drag queens had never been further away from the *onnagata* and *tan*. For a brief period during the seventeenth century, they may have had something to say to each other, but no longer. Western theatricalisation of Asia has mainly concentrated on the superficial: coy decorative effects and the idea of 'barbaric' and 'exotic' spectacle, for example, exemplified in Puccini's opera of the *Turandot* story. The received notion of the Asian woman as passive and obedient, even fatally so, clearly appealed to Puccini's sexual sadism as we see in his treatment of Liu in *Turandot* and of course in Butterfly herself. Other Western artists have taken a more serious interest, notably Brecht,

and in 1956 the composer Benjamin Britten made a journey to the Far East where, in Bali, he heard gamelin music for the first time and in Tokyo saw the Noh theatre. Writing about this he commented: 'The whole occasion made a tremendous impression on me ... the economy of the style, the intense slowness of the action, the marvellous skill and control of the performers, the beautiful costumes, the mixture of chanting, speech, singing which, with the three instruments ... all offered a totally new "operatic" experience.'

The result of this impact came seven years later when Britten asked William Plomer if he could create a libretto from the Noh play *Sumidagawa*. Eventually this became *Curlew River*, the first of three 'Parables for church performance' which are, in fact, chamber operas. Although the story of *Curlew River* follows the Noh original very closely, the drama is moved from medieval Japanese Buddhist to medieval English Christian and the music is based on plainchant. The parable is presented as being acted out in a monastic community: the Abbot, monks and instrumentalists process onto the stage and from them the characters who will act in the play are drawn – including any female characters. The central figure in *Curlew River* is The Madwoman who, in the original performances and on record, was sung and acted by Peter Pears, and Britten composed wonderfully eerie music for his friend's high, flexible voice.

Curlew River is an authentic transformation of Japanese theatre into Western terms, the inspiration coming from within rather than applied as superficial decoration. Its first production given by the English Opera Group in 1964 was directed by Colin Graham who fifteen years later was to direct an operatic version of Kon Ichikawa's film *An Actor's Revenge* which he had seen while in Japan studying Kabuki technique. The film impressed Graham so much that he approached the composer Minoru Miki and the poet James Kirkup with the idea of making it into an opera.

An advisor, Kinnosuke Hanayagi, ensured the basic authenticity of the production's Kabuki model but Graham heightened the effects a little. 'It is not an imitation but a gloss on the real thing, stylized and slightly distanced from actual Kabuki.'[1] The music combined Western instrumentation with Japanese sounds in a

further attempt to make the work accessible. As the opera begins, Yukinojo – the actor – is now a monk and narrates his story of revenge as a kind of monodrama. This is acted out by another actor as his younger self when an *onnagata*, using mime. 'There is a tremendous dichotomy,' Graham comments, 'he must be this quiet, delicate woman on stage yet off-stage he is expected to be macho.' In the London production the young Yukinojo was played by Stephen Jeffries, a particularly masculine dancer. 'While never giving the impression of being a man in drag (Stephen Jeffries) nevertheless managed to look too like a man – and a European man at that,' I noted in my review of the piece. This operatic version of *An Actor's Revenge* was a worthwhile attempt to fuse the theatrical languages of East and West. It had a limited run in London during the autumn of 1979.

In the last twenty years there have been two notable theatrical attempts to bring the techniques and resonance of Chinese and Japanese theatres to a popular audience, one wider than that which attends the opera. One was the 1976 show *Pacific Overtures* written by John Weidman with music and lyrics by Stephen Sondheim and directed by Hal Prince, which used the narrative and musical traditions of Kabuki to tell the story of the Westernisation of Japan.

How the production evolved and, not without difficulty, eventually reached the form which was seen at the Broadway premiere in January 1976 is described in detail in Craig Zadan's *Sondheim & Co* which is essential reading for all Sondheim students. Casting was one of the problems. An all-Asian company was required and this proved hard to achieve. Zadan records that nearly a third of the eventual cast were non-professionals of various nationalities including American-born and naturalized Japanese, Chinese, Filipinos, Hawaiians, Burmese and Koreans. Sondheim used oriental instruments to create mood and his lyrics essayed the poetry of the Japanese *haiku*. But the important aspect here is that Kabuki was not used simply as an exotic location or as a kind of decorative overlay to the musical, but was integral to its form and function. Stage techniques, make-up, costumes and movement were all employed to deliver an epic story covering many years. Moving screens, the *hanamichi* – a curved runway used for ceremonial

processions and the appearance of important characters – stage-hands 'invisible' in black and a 'Reciter' who told the story, commented on it and sometimes participated in it were some of the authentic Kabuki conventions employed. Another, of course, was that female roles were played by male actors (until the final scene when a celebration of the commercial success of modern Japan brings real women onto the stage).

This 'American Kabuki', as Hal Prince called it, allowed for many layers of disguise beyond the obvious one. In a scene which includes one of the show's more conventional songs three Cockney sailors mistake a virtuous girl for a *geisha* and politely bid for her favours ('Pretty Lady'). And we have the spectacle of Asian actors playing English sailors courting an Asian man playing a Japanese girl. These unnerving double-takes seemed to touch a troubled nerve here and there: 'even the Americans are played by Asians', the theatre historian Gerald Bordman noted. Critics were divided, a few hailing the production as a landmark musical, but most finding it a puzzling bore. But nobody, apparently, questioned the presence of the male actresses. Production photographs suggest that the apparatus of Kabuki movement, makeup and costume provided that distance between audience and actor which removed any sense of the drag show.

There are, in fact, very few female roles in the drama – and the two who are required to play young, straightforward women are non-singing parts and present themselves through silent movement. Two important vocal roles go to the Shogun's mother who poisons her ineffectual son, and to the Madame of a brothel preparing her girls in excited anticipation of an invasion by American sailors. Both are scenes of high comedy; both women are given some of Sondheim's most ingeniously witty verses to sing; both could so easily tip the scales towards the obviousness of the self-referential drag queen. But again the artifice of Kabuki style creates a safe distance: the scenes are funny, but for what they are rather than for how they are executed. That the original Asian players were physically suited to the costumes and style of the piece also helped.

Revivals of *Pacific Overtures* inevitably add yet another layer of disguise in that getting a completely Asian cast together is

probably impossible and while a company might include a few Asians, inevitably a majority of performers will not be. The result is that a white, Western man is required to play an Asian man playing a specifically Japanese woman. Again costume and performance style help, but now physique becomes a liability rather than an asset. This was particularly evident in the English National Opera's 1987 production which, despite lavish production and superlative musical standards, did not become the expected box-office success. This was partly because somewhere along the line someone forgot that *Pacific Overtures* is essentially a Broadway musical propelled by brash energy, and not a solemn opera. The *onnagata* players were obviously hefty, European male opera singers uneasy in their kimonos and all too scrutable in make-up and gesture. The temptation to camp it up was only just resisted.

The other interesting experiment in exploring East-West tensions using, at least in part, the vocabulary of Asian theatre was the play *M Butterfly* by David Henry Hwang which was first seen in New York in 1988. It was based on a real event which created an international scandal when it was revealed in 1986. Twenty years earlier, a French diplomat called Bernard Boursicot had fallen in love with Shi Pei Pu, a star of the Peking Opera, without realising that Shi was in fact a female impersonator.[2] The case came to court when Boursicot and Shi were charged with spying and passing information on to China. Their treason was trivial – only unimportant documents were leaked – but what caused the sensation was the question of how a man could live with someone, and have sexual relations with them, for twenty years without realising that the person was not a woman.

Inevitably the sexual aspect of the case was the one which fascinated the press and caught for a while the public's prurient imagination. But probing this particular mystery was not David Hwang's chief objective, he was more interested in exploring the wider implications of the sexual balance of power between Eastern women (submissive) and Western men (imperialist) and to criticise the assumptions drawn from them. At the end of the play, Song Liling (the Chinese opera star) discards his kimono and wig, Gallimard (the French diplomat) puts them on, thus changing their roles visually as well as emotionally.

The English director John Dexter won a Tony Award for his Broadway production. Already distinguished as a director of opera in Europe and at the Metropolitan Opera House in New York, Dexter made extensive and decorative use of the ritual movements and martial arts associated with the Peking Opera. The play enjoyed a modest run and was later seen in England (Leicester and London), Italy and Japan. Amusingly, the cast lists for both productions identified the actor playing Song Liling with initials only (B D Wong in New York, G G Goei in England), and the programmes avoided any give-away pronouns in their biographies. Thus, until Song Liling strips in the play (at the end of the second act), an audience would have no idea that 'she' was really a man (unless of course the story was known beforehand). Exposure of the genitals is the ultimate revelation of the female impersonator, sometimes used as a shock tactic in transvestite cabaret but also used as a powerful way of reversing an audience's comfortable assumptions. Here it gives what begins as a story of espionage and East-West relations an astonishingly sexual dimension. In his film *The Crying Game* Neil Jordan used the device similarly to transform what begins as a story of IRA activism and Anglo-Irish relations into a sexual-emotional dilemma of far wider relevance. Exposure of the genitals had no place in Asian theatre, any more than it did in the Elizabethan and Jacobean theatres of England, and if it carries, in *M Butterfly*, anything more than shock value it is to bring home to a Western audience the authenticity of the Chinese male actress's skills in illusion and reveals something of the glamour and allure which the *tan* actors possessed at the height of their fame. A Chinese audience would take it for granted: the sexually unsophisticated Western audience needs it demonstrated.

Peking Opera survived the establishment of the People's Republic of China in 1949 and for a while became a national asset and made several tours in the West in the 1950s and 1960s when Shi Pei Pu (the impersonator on whom Song Liling is based) was a star. But the Cultural Revolution of 1966 changed all that. Madame Mao herself reduced the repertory of all China's acting troupes to eight plays – wooden, one-dimensional propaganda pieces. Moreover only actors personally approved by her were allowed to perform – the rest were put to hard labour, imprisoned

or executed and with them centuries of tradition and techniques carefully passed down the generations began to disappear in a pogrom more thorough than anything Cromwell could have imagined. After the death of Chairman Mao there was a suggestion of more freedom with relaxed censorship and China is once again sending its theatre abroad, but the emphasis now is on spectacle and pretty girls – the real sort.

Notes

1. Roger Baker, 'Hero/ine' (London: *Gay News*, September 20th-October 3rd 1979, p XIII).
2. Joyce Wadler, *Liaison* (Harmondsworth: Penguin Books, 1993) offers a fascinating account of Bernard Boursicot and Shi Pei Pu's relationships and was written with Boursicot's cooperation.

Chapter seven

The Male Actress Takes Early Retirement

DURING the twenty-five-year reign of Charles II, the period generally known as The Restoration, English stage practice underwent a radical transformation. The inherited traditions of the Elizabethan and Jacobean theatre were abandoned: dramatic writing, acting style, methods of presentation and even the architecture of the theatres themselves were virtually re-invented. Here we can see, in embryo as it were, the form of theatre that today's audiences would recognise. For the first time women appeared on stage and, in the early years at least, were defined as sexually attractive objects to be showcased for the pleasure of men, a continuing theme in all branches of showbusiness. Inevitably, one of the first casualties of the old style was the male actress whose artistry had, by the end of the century, been transformed into burlesque, and become the drag queen of low comedy.

The actual identity of the first woman to make a professional appearance on the English stage is still a matter of argument among theatre historians and today is probably only of interest to them. One contender is Anne Marshall. She, and her glamorous sister Rebecca, would soon emerge as among the most popular of the new actresses.

Another – who seems to get the most votes – is Margaret Hughes. She was the mistress of Prince Rupert and admired by the King, which suggests that she probably had some clout in the matter. But whoever the actress was, the character was Desdemona

and the occasion was a performance, in December 1660, of *The Moor of Venice*. This was Shakespeare's play *Othello* somewhat reorganised for Restoration tastes and given a special prologue by one Thomas Jordan. The sensational nature of the production is made clear:

> I come unknown to any of the rest
> To tell you news: I saw the lady drest:
> The woman plays today; mistake me not,
> No man in gown, or page in petticoat.

But the male actresses did not retire without a struggle; there was, for a few years, an overlap. Many actors who had specialised in women's roles were still around, waiting for the moment when they would reclaim their stage.

The Puritan grip on England had been tight. Attempts were made to abolish the public celebration of Christmas; pleasure gardens were closed, maypoles (those symbols of the phallic thrust of Spring) were banned, bear-baiting and cock-fighting outlawed. All the simple pleasures of ordinary people (whatever we may feel about bears and cocks today) were stamped upon, particularly the consumption of alcohol – which led to the emergence of the coffee house and its attendant culture. In September 1642, parliament issued a decree killing 'public stage-playes' which would not agree with 'the seasons of Publick Humiliations'.

In 1648, actors were deemed liable to punishment so after these edicts, as far as the general public was concerned, and the actors, writers and managers, the theatre ceased to exist. Some later historians have seen this break as beneficial. W Bridges Adams, for example, asserts that 'the drama was tired out, whatever the actors may have thought; it had spent itself prodigally.' Through the opening years of the seventeenth century, the argument goes, the strong vitality and freshness that had characterised the work of Shakespeare and his contemporaries had diminished. Sadism, incest, murder, suicide and all kinds of bloody horrors were trivialising a once noble theatre in repetitive and uninspired verse.

But this sounds suspiciously like someone being wise a couple of centuries after the event, ignoring as it does the many

other influences that affect an audience's taste and the theatre's response. A massive social upheaval like the Civil War and its aftermath would inevitably create change without any need for the theatre to be banned completely. In any case, there is evidence to suggest that the Puritan clamp-down was a political gesture rather than a private reality.

Though, with theatres closed and actors scattered, no plays were performed in public during the eighteen years of the interregnum, private entertainments continued, some enjoyed by Cromwell himself, and in 1656 a production which would be regarded as a landmark in theatre history was mounted by Sir William Davenant at his home Rutland House. Plays were printed while Cromwell was in power and he made no move to stop the established Elizabethan tradition of plays being performed in schools as a legitimate part of their curriculum. Some theatrical creativity continued and the formal acting techniques of the pre-war theatre were not entirely forgotten.

After the decree of 1642 the actors were, of course, immediately out of work. Some joined up and died fighting in the Civil War, taking up the Royalist cause partly because the Puritans had robbed them of their livelihood, partly because King Charles I and Queen Henrietta Maria had enjoyed and actively encouraged the theatre. One who survived the war was Charles Hart, believed to be a descendant of Shakespeare's sister Joan. He had been a specialist in female roles and returned to playing them after the Restoration. A contemporary journalist noted that many actors 'lingered under the heavy yoke of poverty and fed themselves and family with hunger, sighs and tears'. Some took to the road as freelance entertainers, offering illicit performances by the wayside or in friendly taverns. Others went abroad and joined companies in France and Germany. A few tried their hand at other jobs.

One was John Rhodes who had been a member of the stage crew at the Blackfriars Theatre as prompter and wardrobe master. He opened a bookshop in Charing Cross and kept his head down, drawing no special attention to himself. He was, however, keeping in touch with his former colleagues and, it is thought, gave clandestine acting classes to his apprentices and any other interested youngsters. He was clearly waiting and preparing for the moment

when the theatres would re-open, and made sure he would be perfectly prepared to take on a significant managerial role when that great day arrived.

It is perhaps difficult for us, more than three hundred years later, to appreciate the impact that the restoration of the monarchy made on the social texture of London. In many ways it seems as though the pendulum swung from repression to licence more or less overnight. Charles II's journey from Dover in May 1660 was a procession of triumph with bonfires and feasting all the way. He entered London on his thirtieth birthday, a handsome young man wearing his own shoulder-length hair. Then, as now, long hair worn by a man suggested a rejection of authoritarian values in favour of a more laid back attitude. This message was quickly picked up across the social scale. The Palace of Whitehall, with its parks and gardens, tennis courts, bowling green, royal and aristocratic residences, became the political and social focus of the capital.

A pleasant coach ride or even just a stroll away, London's entertainment district lay bordering the Strand, the thoroughfare that connected Westminster to the City of London. Here the narrow, teeming streets of Covent Garden with their markets, pie stalls, brothels and inns were suddenly enjoying a festive bonanza. It was here that the theatres would become re-established. 'Shaftesbury Avenue' is the internationally recognised shorthand for London's theatreland, but the greatest concentration of theatres is still in the Covent Garden area where they began.

Before long London became famous for 'lewdness and beggary', for its pretty women, for its lively hedonistic atmosphere. Tourists flocked in from continental Europe, attracted by the promise of available girls. During the last thirty years or so we have seen Copenhagen, Amsterdam, Hamburg and Bangkok each take its turn as a centre of sexual tourism, but London, it seems, achieved that dubious distinction first. And the women on the stage were among the main attractions.

The King himself is sometimes credited with the responsibility for introducing actresses onto the stage. An anecdote is told by Colley Cibber, the poet and dramatist, in his autobiography. He relates that one afternoon in 1660 Charles arrived early for a per-

formance, discovered that the actors were not ready to begin and wanted to know why. 'Upon which the master of the company came to the Box, and rightly judging that the best excuse for their default would be the true one, fairly told His Majesty that the Queen was not shaved yet; the King, whose good humour loved to laugh at a jest as well as to make one, accepted the excuse, which served to divert him till the male queen could be effeminated.'[1]

Amusing as he may have found the episode at the time, it is not improbable that the assertively heterosexual monarch with his strong sexual appetite, found the idea of watching grown men dressed up and acting as women not only irritating in itself, but also the loss of a good opportunity for talent spotting. One of his more famous mistresses would be the actress Nell Gwyn.

When he issued the Royal Patents for the creation of theatre companies, the King specifically included permission for women to play women which would 'add to the harmless delights and useful and instructive representations of human life'. Which effectively spelled the end of the male actress, though not at once.

The men in whose hands the restoration of the theatre rested were two theatrical entrepreneurs, Sir William Davenant and Thomas Killigrew. Each was granted a Royal Patent licensing him to set up performing companies, which had the effect of giving them a monopoly of the stage for several years. Both had courtly and showbusiness backgrounds.

Davenant – who was rumoured to be the natural son of Shakespeare – was a playwright and poet. He had devised court masques for Charles I (working alongside Inigo Jones) and had supported him in the Civil War. And it was he who, in 1656, evaded the ban on stage-plays by mounting a production in the seclusion of his own home, for which he was given permission by the Commonwealth government. This was *The Siege of Rhodes* and is recognised as one of the earliest attempts at an English opera. Davenant wrote the piece himself and sold it as an 'Entertainment after the manner of the ancients' which meant dialogues of debate – the first about public amusements and then about the merits of London and Paris. These were accompanied by songs and instrumental passages and were followed by the play itself which was a 'story sung in recitative music' composed by Charles Coleman and

George Hudson. Among the people involved in this production was Mrs Coleman, who becomes another contender for the title of first actress to step on the boards.

Thomas Killigrew had been a page to Charles I and was a friend of Charles II. In 1640 he had written a farcical comedy, *The Parson's Wedding*, which he would later revive to a mixed reception. From the start Killigrew's enterprise had the edge on Davenant's. He managed his company efficiently, encouraged young playwrights (including Dryden), obtained the rights to all Ben Jonson's plays, those of Beaumont and Fletcher and to one or two comedies by Shakespeare. The King was patron of the company and – perhaps most importantly – he had the best actresses. He built a theatre in Covent Garden – on the site now occupied by the Theatre Royal, Drury Lane.

Davenant's patron was the Duke of York (later James II). His company was led by Thomas Betterton, regarded as the greatest actor of this period. Davenant had the rights to Shakespeare's major tragedies – *Hamlet*, *King Lear* and *Macbeth*, in all of which Betterton triumphed. Davenant's charter was for a theatre in Lincoln's Inn – a converted tennis court – but was later transferred to Covent Garden.

These new, purpose-built theatres represented a major change from the old style Elizabethan arenas; a proscenium arch replaced the open stage; the pit had benches and plenty of room for the audience to wander and gossip, and around it were raised boxes. The problem of lighting had not been solved so although the stage and boxes were roofed, the pit was covered by a glass dome which notoriously let in rain. And along with these improvements came the greatest technical innovation of all – movable painted scenery. Davenant's sets were particularly admired for their design and colour.

Yet despite the weight of his core repertory, the reputation of his leading man and his glamorous stage pictures, Davenant's house was less popular than that of Killigrew and the reason for this seems to be that he was, initially at least, reluctant to include the new actresses in his productions.

A likely reason for this was that, once he had been given permission to found a company, he went into partnership with the

bookseller John Rhodes who was already busy chasing up his old contacts and preparing to form a company. As an old stager from way back, Rhodes instinctively thought in pre-Commonwealth terms and – perhaps naturally enough – expected things would be done in the good old ways and this included allocating female roles to young men and to the boys he had been surreptitiously training. He probably assumed that putting women on the stage was just another aspect of the general loosening up of morals which was happening in society and would prove a passing fad. Whether Davenant agreed with this or not, he needed Rhodes' experience and contacts.

He would certainly remember, as indeed would Rhodes, a disastrous attempt to introduce real women onto the English stage almost thirty years earlier. Both King Charles I and Queen Henrietta Maria supported the public theatre and it is likely that the Queen occasionally acted alongside her ladies in court masques. It was under her patronage that a company from France appeared for a season at the Blackfriars Theatre (where Rhodes worked) in 1632. In the context of the period this was a bold experiment, but also a recipe for the disaster it turned out to be.

On one side there was mounting Puritan disapproval, on the other a typically reactionary English audience then, as now, resentful of innovation. Contemporary accounts of this event are couched in complacently gleeful terms and one records that the women were 'hissed, hooted and pippin-pelted from the stage'. Another critic expressed surprise that from what he saw of them they seemed to be almost as good as men. The arch-Puritan William Prynne called them 'unwomanly and graceless' and his treatise raging against both female actresses and the performances of boys was interpreted as a direct insult to Henrietta Maria and for his pains Prynne lost his ears. Theatre criticism was a dangerous profession in those days.[2]

A memory such as this might have made Davenant and Rhodes wary, but whatever the reason for their initial reluctance to use women this allowed the professional male actresses one last fling. Inevitably, many of those recruited for the company were no longer young and one contemporary commentator remarked that they 'had grown out of use, like cracked organ-pipes, and have

faces as old as our flags', which does not create a particularly alluring picture.

The continuation of Thomas Jordan's prologue to *The Moor of Venice* seems to underscore this impression:

> In this reforming age
> We have intents to civilise the stage.
> Our women are defective and so siz'd
> You'd think they were some of the guard disguised.
> For to speak truth, men act, that are between
> Forty and fifty, wenches of fifteen;
> With bone so large, and nerve so incompliant,
> When you call Desdemona, enter Giant.

Whether this represents an accurate assessment of the situation or is a satirical sideswipe at a rival company we shall never know, but Davenant's company included Edward Kynaston, often cited as the greatest male actress of all time, as well as James Nokes, another *travesti* expert who was also admired.

But there was more going on here than a question of the convincing interpretation of great drama. In fact the quality of the new plays being presented in these early years seems to have been pretty low, attempts at heroic sagas or trivial and suggestive farces with romantic complications. Although George Etheredge's first comedy (*Love in a Tub*) was produced in 1664, it would be several years before the golden years of what we call 'Restoration comedy' would open up, with the arrival on the scene of Congreve, Farquhar, Vanburgh and Wycherley, who between them defined and set the future pattern for the English comedy of manners.

At this time it was the spectacle of women on the stage rather than the material they were dealing with that fascinated audiences. And Killigrew astutely responded to this appetite by going straight in with the women, fielding two who were soon to be among the most popular of the new stars – Margaret Hughes and Anne Marshall. There seems to have been a great deal of repartee between pit and stage and the actresses took every opportunity to flirt with their audiences. Prologues and epilogues were specially written for them to deliver, and in comedies situations were con-

trived to reflect an actress's off-stage relationships with rival lovers, often high-born chaps from the Palace of Whitehall. Actresses were not held in high moral repute. Many were attractive, ambitious girls hauled while still in their early teens from the streets of London. Rather like today, showbusiness was one route a no-hope teenager could take to achieve wealth and some kind of distinction. Many did just that, the most famous being of course Nell Gwyn.[3]

That solemn diarist John Evelyn, who never claimed to enjoy the theatre, noted this. In 1666 he wrote: 'Women now (and never 'til now) are permitted to appear and act, which inflaming several young noblemen and gallants, became their whores, some to their wives.' Clearly these are the precursors of the Stage Door Johnnies who similarly bedded and occasionally wedded the stars of variety and musical comedy two hundred years later.

On-stage rivalry between individual actresses added spice to some dramas. In a 1664 production of Sir William Killigrew's play *The Siege of Urbino* the adventurous heroine Celestina was played by Anne Marshall who had to dress in men's clothes, as did her maid Melina played by the then fifteen-year-old Nell Gwyn. Mrs Gwyn's legs were judged to be superior to Mrs Marshall's – which led to considerable tension between the two women. On another occasion one actress actually stabbed her rival on stage, though not fatally.

Thomas Killigrew clearly relished all this intrigue, this gossipy, sexy mix of courtiers and feisty young women, and never missed an opportunity to exploit his actresses. Once he went too far. In 1664 he revived his 1640 comedy *The Parson's Wedding* with an all-female cast. But it was not a success this time, partly because he had introduced too much bawdry and partly because he offended public taste by treating the plague, just then becoming a serious threat, as a joke. The general revulsion backlashed onto the women who took part and Killigrew did not repeat the experiment.

Against such competition, the male actresses of tradition stood little chance of survival, but for a few years the stages accommodated both. Even Killigrew retained one or two in his company, Charles Hart (he who was reputed to be Shakespeare's nephew) becoming a London favourite. He had experience of playing female roles before the Civil War, so must by this time have been quite

mature.[4] But he was particularly admired for his performance as the Duchess in a revival of James Shirley's 1641 play *The Cardinal*. He was, however, soon being given leading male roles (perhaps because of his age), including Othello. Hart's other claim to fame was his role as Nell Gwyn's lover and promoter of her stage career.

Despite the growing success of the actresses (albeit as a sexy novelty rather than as a new dimension to serious drama), the basic laws of supply and demand assisted the retention of the male actress for a number of years. Not enough women could be found and trained for the stage immediately; the actress had no history, no teaching had been handed down to her. She virtually had to make it up as she went along. And many did. Mrs Coleman confided in Pepys that she didn't know her lines when she made her debut. Anne Oldfield was plucked from behind the bar of the Mitre and thrust onto the stage when she was sixteen, and less than a year later was playing leading parts. Actors, managers and writers cruised the pubs and brothels, looking for likely lasses. Many of the girls were illiterate (there is no evidence that Nell Gwyn could read or write) and so had to learn their parts parrot fashion, by listening and memorising. Other skills – voice projection, dancing, deportment – they had to pick up as best they could.

Meanwhile plays were in demand, going to the theatre was an important social event and the show had to go on. Hence the male actresses were given a few years grace before their final eclipse.

Davenant's star female impersonator, Edward Kynaston, was much younger, probably in his late teens or early twenties. A contemporary portrait shows a sweet-faced androgyne, lips parted, eyes sliding in a suggestive glance, soft fair hair falling gracefully about his collar, small delicate hands poised in a graceful gesture. Much of our information about him comes from contemporary diarists and from the gossipy Colley Cibber.

Samuel Pepys records a visit to the theatre where he saw a performance of Ben Jonson's play *The Silent Woman* in which Kynaston starred: 'He appeared in three shapes, first as a poor woman in ordinary clothes ... then in fine clothes as a gallant; and in them was clearly the prettiest woman in the whole house: and, lastly, as a man; and then likewise did appear the handsomest man

in the house.' Another contemporary playgoer observed: 'It has since been disputable among the judicious whether any woman that succeeded him so sensibly touched the audience as he.'

Pepys' comments could lead us to conclude that Kynaston was using Jonson's play as a vehicle for his own expertise in transformation, as an excuse to appear in a remarkable series of sensational impersonations.[5] Several impersonators in this century have had productions created for them in which they could demonstrate a similar versatility.[6] But the information that Kynaston could 'sensibly touch the audience' gives the lie to this. Pepys clearly saw a straightforward production of what Dryden considered the most perfectly plotted of comedies and Kynaston was certainly acting legitimately and those who attended his performances would barely give a moment's thought to his being a male until, perhaps, it came to a comparison with the performance of a real woman at another theatre. And for Pepys, who had a lively taste for attractive women, to describe him as 'the prettiest woman in the house' argues a lifelike simulation of the female and not a knowing caricature.

Kynaston was, apparently, just as convincing and alluring off-stage. Cibber writes: 'Kynaston was at that time so beautiful a youth, that the Ladies of Quality prided themselves on taking him with them in their coaches to Hyde Park, in his theatrical habit after a play; which in those days they might have sufficient time to do, because plays were then used to begin at four o'clock. Of this truth I had the curiosity to inquire, and had it confirmed from his own mouth in his advanced age.' Like his Elizabethan colleague, Richard Robinson before him, and like many a drag queen since, Kynaston enjoyed showing off his ability to pass as a woman in collusion with other women. Others were not so amused. Another diarist wrote: 'Kynaston, the most beautiful youth who figured in petticoats on the stage, having been carried about in his theatrical dress by ladies of fashion in their carriages. This was an unseemly spectacle, and we can forgive the Puritans for objecting to see "men in women's clothing".'

In his later years, Kynaston began to take on male roles which he apparently performed with credit, though it was remarked that his training for female roles had somehow affected

the quality of his voice though how, precisely, is not clear. Cibber again: 'To the last of him, his handsomeness was very little abated. Even at past sixty his teeth were sound, white and even as one would wish to see in a reigning toast of twenty. He had something of a formal gravity in his mien, which was attributed to the stately step he had been so early confined to, in a female decency. But even that, in characters of superiority, had its proper graces; it misbecame him not in the part of Leon in Fletcher's *Rule a Wife*, which he executed with a determined manliness and honest authority well worth the best actor's imitation. He had a piercing eye, and in characters of heroic life, a quick imperious vivacity in his tone of voice that painted the tyrant truly terrible.'

Kynaston died in 1712, leaving a considerable fortune to his son. His career spanned perfectly this age of transition. When he first went onto the stage the idea of women acting was regarded as a passing phase, just another example of fashionable excess that would fade. Yet when he died there were no men left still playing women's roles on a serious level.

His contemporary, James Nokes, also turned eventually to male roles. He was a versatile and highly regarded comic actor and right up to the end of his career was still playing the nurse in *Romeo and Juliet* – in fact his nickname was 'Nursey Nokes'. Cibber tells us that 'he scarce ever made his first entrance in a play but he was received with involuntary applause ... and by a general laughter, which the very sight of him provoked and nature could not resist ... and sure the ridiculous solemnity of his features were enough to have set a whole bench of bishops into a titter. ...'

That such a popular, elderly actor could play successfully Juliet's garrulous nurse, and not jar with the real actresses on stage, is a proposition we can take on board today. The adaptation used then was by Thomas Otway and, given that improvisation was expected in the Restoration theatre, Nokes may well have created a rather different character than that we are used to today, perhaps even a kind of pantomime dame figure.

Until this time there was no particular tradition of dame-playing in English drama, the social and dramatic contexts in which a dame can flourish had yet to evolve. But we can discern the possible beginnings of the form at this time. As we have seen the

male actresses gradually took on the male repertory; those that didn't were getting older, their style of acting was no longer required, the roles they were given got shorter and were easily turned into burlesque. John Lacy (who along with Hart had trained Nell Gwyn for the stage) was throughout his acting life a brilliant mimic and parodist, satirising popular successes and well-known individuals. Comic female characters were among his creations.

James Nokes died in 1692 and the last of the serious actors who specialised in female parts is assumed to be Abraham Ivory whose fame as an impersonator was overtaken by his fame as a lush. *The Rehearsal*,[7] a play that satirises individuals and the heroic drama of the Restoration, includes a joke at Ivory's expense. A player informs the impatient director: 'Mr. Ivory is not yet come, but he'll be here presently. He's but two doors off.' This would raise an easy laugh from a knowing audience that realised there was a pub two doors away. This play, generally attributed to George Villiers, Duke of Buckingham, but probably written in collaboration by several people, was performed at Drury Lane in 1671. In just over a decade the male actress had been marginalised to a quick joke.

Notes

1. *An Apology for the life of Mr. Colley Cibber, Comedian* was published in 1740. Gossipy and entertaining, the playwright's autobiography gives a lively picture of theatrical life during the Restoration and later. He was born in 1671, so was writing some time after the events he describes.
2. Prynne's sentence (1634) also included life imprisonment and a fine of £5,000. Additionally he was branded on the cheeks with the letters S L (seditious libeller). He was released by the Long Parliament in 1640, his sentence declared illegal.
3. The actresses called themselves 'Mistress' (Mrs) since, at that time the title had dignity, being used by married women. 'Miss', on the other hand, was less respectful. Ironically 'Mistress' soon took on the meaning it has today (a married man's lover), while 'Miss' acquired a new dignity.
4. One theory is that there were two Charles Harts, father and son, both actors and both specialists in female parts. It does seem unlikely that the Hart who played female roles before the Civil War

was the same Charles Hart who loved Nell Gwyn and became a star of the Restoration theatre.

5. This is the play *Epicoene* in which Nathaniel Field, the Elizabethan boy actress scored such a hit. The story concerns the fooling of a rich old bachelor, Morose, who is persuaded to marry an apparently silent and humdrum woman. Once wed, however, she turns into a strident shrew. When Morose is released from his contract (by parting with some cash), the silent woman is revealed as a boy who has been trained for the part. This final twist is intended to be a surprise to the audience as well.

6. The American female impersonator Julian Eltinge toured for many years in plays specially written to demonstrate his versatility. In 1966 Danny La Rue starred in a musical play *Come Spy With Me* which enabled him to change his frocks and appropriate behaviour a dozen or so times.

7. *The Rehearsal* set a fashion for theatrical burlesque which culminated with Sheridan's *The Critic* (1779) with which it is sometimes confused.

Fantasies, Fairies
and Follies

Chapter one

Diplomats in Dresses

IN 1702, the newly-crowned Queen Anne made her cousin Edward Hyde, Lord Cornbury, the Governor of New York and New Jersey, a post he held for six years. To the astonishment and bewilderment of both his colleagues and the general population he persistently dressed as a woman. This was not private or closet transvestism but assertively public. He opened the Assembly in women's clothes, government business had to be delayed until he had completed his lengthy *toilette*, he would stroll through the streets in his skirts and dozens of people gawped at him every day.

There are at least two alleged representations of Hyde. One is a formal studio portrait showing a jowly male (but with delicate arms and hands) in a fashionable dress of the period. The other is a more informal sketch showing him walking alone through the street stopping several pedestrians in their tracks. There is the same strong face and graceful arms, but here he sports a small moustache, and he wears a dress remarkably similar to that in the portrait plus a large hat.

Between 1698 and 1709 the publican and writer Edward Ward wrote a series of sketches purporting to be a country boy's experiences of being shown city life by a resident Cockney. They were published in *The London Spy*. In one essay he reports:

'There is a curious band of fellows in the town who call themselves "Mollies" who are so totally destitute of all masculine attributes that they prefer to behave as women. They adopt all the small vanities natural to the feminine sex to such an extent that they try to speak, walk, chatter, shriek and scold as women do, aping

them as well in other respects. In a certain tavern in the City ... they hold parties and regular gatherings. As soon as they arrive they begin to behave exactly as women do, carrying on light gossip as is the custom of a merry company of real women. Later on, one of their brothers – or rather "sisters" – (in their feminine jargon) would be dressed in a woman's nightgown with a silken nightcap, and thus representing a woman, bears a "child" (a dummy being to hand for the purpose) which is afterwards baptised, while another man in a large hat plays the part of a country midwife, a third that of a nurse, the rest of them acting as unseemly guests at a christening. Each had to discourse at length and with great impropriety of the pleasures of a "husband" and children, and praise the virtues of the former and the wonderful talents of the latter. Some others, in the role of "widows", lamented the deplorable loss of their "husbands". Thus each imitated the petty feminine faults of women gossiping over coffee, in order to disguise their natural feelings (as men) towards the fair sex, and to encourage unnatural lusts.'

Sixty years later, London society – from the lowest to the highest – was gripped by a wonderful guessing game: was the Chevalier D'Eon, First Secretary to the French Ambassador to the Court of St James, a man or a woman? The arguments grew to such proportions that bets were laid at White's and Brook's clubs and gambling policies of insurance on the Chevalier's sex were issued. Though he denied the rumours strenuously and actually set about beating his offenders with a stick and making personal appearances at the Stock Exchange to challenge disputants, the rumours did not abate and the Chevalier was reported to have received many offers of hard cash to reveal the truth.

D'Eon was an interesting character – diplomat, spy, Captain of Dragoons, formidable swordsman and a cross-dresser. There was even a story that in 1755 he had been sent to the court of the Empress Elizabeth in St Petersburg to act as a spy, dressed as a young woman calling herself Madame Lia de Beaumont. But now, in London, his behaviour alienated the French Ambassador and Louis XVI sent his envoy, the playwright Beaumarchais, to get him back to France. D'Eon persuaded Beaumarchais that he was really a woman forced to wear men's clothes to serve his country. As a

result D'Eon was induced to renounce male attire and dress as a woman for the rest of his life, on which demonstration of his 'true sex' his pension would depend.

In the August of 1777 he made a public appearance wearing 'an elegant sack with a head-dress of diamonds'. Another report of the time describes him as 'a lusty dame without the least beard who was dressed in black silk with a head-dress in rosed toupet and a lace cap. She wore a diamond necklace, long stays and an old-fashioned stomacher.' Many portraits of the Chevalier exist, some straightforward representations of him as a man or a woman, others cruel caricatures. The most famous shows a figure dressed half as a man, half as a woman – an image which has been imitated many times, notably by sculptor Andrew Logan who for the Alternative Miss World events he hosted through the 1970s always had a similarly half-and-half costume created for himself.

In 1786, the German writer Goethe made a formative visit to Italy where he came across the carnival in Rome. He noted: 'The masks now begin to multiply. Young men, dressed in the holiday attire of women of the lowest classes, exposing an open breast and displaying an impudent self-complacency, are mostly the first to be seen. They caress the men, allow themselves all familiarities with the women they encounter, as being persons the same as themselves, and for the rest do whatever humour, wit or wantonness suggest. Among other things, we remember a young man, who played excellently the part of a passionate, brawling, untameable shrew, who went scolding the whole way down the Corso, railing at everyone she came near, while those accompanying her took all manner of pains to reduce her to quietness.'

Meanwhile, one of Europe's most famous bisexual adventurers, Giacomo Casanova, was also enjoying the street life of Venice and Rome.[1] In a café he mistook the famous *castrato* Bepino della Mamana who was sitting there in women's clothes, flirting with all the available men. 'The impudent creature,' he writes, 'looking fixedly at me, told me that if I liked he would prove that I was right, or that I was wrong.'

An English lord ... a French diplomat ... an Italian opera singer ... and bunches of screaming queens from all over the place:

images randomly selected from within a period of a hundred years. We shall be looking more closely at each example, but the interesting point here is the suggestion that it was during the eighteenth century that drag went public, became a matter of record. It is also at this moment that a direct connection between drag and homosexuality is perceived. It is almost as if once the female impersonator had been banished from the stage for good her anarchic sister the drag queen reappeared: men no longer able to get the vicarious pleasure of projecting themselves onto the male actresses in the theatre were now doing it themselves both solemnly and hilariously.

But the public appearance of drag queens was not unknown in England. The playwright Thomas Middleton, for example, in a book published in 1599 describes a meeting in the street between his narrator and a beautiful woman who, when he presses his attentions on her, turns out to be a man 'in a nymph's attire'.

This character appears to have been a transvestite using his charms to earn financial rather than sexual favours. The streets of London, the narrator moans, 'are full of juggling parasites with the true shape of virgins' counterfeits'. We can turn to Ben Jonson's play *The Devil is an Ass* (1616) for another example, this one specifically related to the theatre. It is a description of what happened when Richard Robinson, a male actress with the King's Men, was taken to a 'gossips' feast' dressed 'like a lawyer's wife'.

> But so see him behave it
> And lay the law, and carve, and drink unto them
> And then talk bawdy, and send frolics! O
> It would have burst your buttons, or not left you
> A seam.

Robinson is described as 'an ingenious youth', to which the reply comes: ' . . . and dresses himself the best, beyond Forty of your very ladies.' The exact nature of this incident is unclear: were the other women unaware that Dicky Robinson was a man, which would mean a game of some sort was being played on them; or were they all in on the joke? It is a common observation that some women

find the company of drag queens charming and amusing. We recall that the Restoration star Edward Kynaston, in stage costume, was often driven around Hyde Park in an open carriage by fashionable women who delighted in his extremely convincing appearance. This is probably the kind of entertainment Robinson was giving the assembled gossips.

These examples are all, of course, directly related to the stage – even if the incident Middleton describes was reportage of authentic street life he would reconstruct it with a dramatist's sense of form. By the beginning of the eighteenth century the theatre could no longer be used as an outlet or excuse for an exuberant drag queen. But there are other reasons why cross-dressing seems to have become more apparent at this time. One is that society itself was changing, it was becoming much more self-analytical. There was a much higher degree of literacy so people were writing – and reading – more. This was the time when the first magazines appeared, when the novel was taking on the form we recognise today. Autobiographies were being written – such as that of Colley Cibber from whom we learn so much about the theatre of the Restoration. Sketches and vignettes of everyday life were popular (like Edward Ward's *The London Spy*) and detailed social observation underpinned works as different as Pope's *The Rape of the Lock* and Cleland's *Fanny Hill*. In such a context it is inevitable that the Molly Houses and public figures like D'Eon would come under close scrutiny as public curiosities.

That 'elegant sack' which the Chevalier was seen to be wearing was not a designer hessian bag such as that Marilyn Monroe posed in. The sack was a fashionable dress which, at the back, fell straight from the shoulders to the hem, spreading out over the wide panniers worn under the skirt. The drag queen likes to be in fashion, to celebrate the beauty of clothes or, sometimes, to satirise the idiocy of extreme fashion and over-the-top couture. The eighteenth century offered plenty of opportunity for this simple pleasure. In previous centuries, what people wore had more to do with rank and status than with merely being 'in fashion', as we noted when discussing Elizabethan dress codes.

During the Restoration years and the reigns of Queen Anne and the Georges fashion began to assume its modern meaning,

signifying a person who was the leader of the pack, smarter, ahead of the others. The right place to be, the right people to mix with, the right vocabulary to use were now important to an in-crowd composed less of the aristocracy than of a mix of *parvenus*, social climbers and newly rich merchants and their wives. This theme threads through the satirical comedies of the period. And, of course, fashion had its more reactionary critics. One commentator, writing in 1749, was quite distressed:

'I must admit that no age ever produced anything so perverse as the clothing of the men of the present time who call themselves "pretty fellows". Their coiffures require nothing more than a row of hairpins to make them look completely feminine. It is easily realised why they always take great care to be as "pretty" as possible when they meet their companions, and all manliness is diametrically opposed to this unnatural behaviour. Consequently they try their best to imitate the mannerisms and dress of the opposite sex. ... I am told that some of our tip-top "beaus" wear frilled bonnets to give them a more womanly appearance, so that Master Molly has nothing to do but put on his frilly little bonnet and he will pass for a lady, except for his deplorable face. But even this can be remedied by means of powder and paint. ... There is nothing more amusing than their new "joke" hats of the latest fashion which are ridiculously dandyish. But to see them at balls or in evening dress – in silk jackets of many colours – revolts me beyond all measure. They had much better put on real women's dresses and petticoats instead of doing things by halves.'

The tone, attitude and even vocabulary of this outburst will be familiar to anyone who lived through the Flower Power years of the late 1960s or the brief appearance of the New Romantics in the early 1980s. It is the angry outrage of the person who finds his signals have been confused, that what has always seemed appropriate, and only appropriate, to women has now been adopted by men. It is unlikely that the Georgian fashion victims that scared him so much were either gay or transvestite. Their intention was not to dress as a woman, to pass as a woman or to be mistaken for one. But to describe a man as being 'like a woman' is the deepest insult he can offer. In the 1960s the term 'Master Molly' might have been replaced by 'camp' or 'nancy boy'. This commentator's authority as

a balanced and accurate description of mid-century fashion is doubtful; as usual it is a small but visible group that collects the greatest attention. However, the eighteenth century dandy did sport nipped-in waists and full-skirted coats, well-powdered wigs, lace ruffles and pretty buckled shoes with raised heels. One group, known as the Macaronis, affected high-rise wigs decorated with fruit and flowers just like those adopted by fashionable women. Such exuberance of personal display might have attracted the interest of a beady-eyed drag queen, but for the moment her attentions were concentrated elsewhere.

There were other changes too, changes which affected the relationship between men and women and which would, as these things do, help to define the future shape and function of the drag queen. For a clue we can turn again to the theatre and look at a couple of comedies separated by 100 years – Shakespeare's *Twelfth Night* (*c.* 1601) and Congreve's *The Way of the World* (1700). As the comedy develops it is quite clear that Shakespeare's play happens in a typical Elizabethan manor house with its hierarchy of servants, below-stairs hi-jinks and formal gardens. But we are told, from the beginning that this is not England, it is a mythical country called Illyria. So while Sir Toby Belch, Maria and the other broadly comic characters are living somewhere in Warwickshire, the quartet of lovers (Orsino, Viola, Sebastian and Olivia) inhabit a different world – somewhere romantic and apart, where love must struggle through illusion to achieve its realisation. In the other transvestite plays Rosalind and Portia undergo similar rites of passage in dream-like settings – as do the lovers in *The Dream* itself.

The effect of this separation (mythical Illyria/realistic England) is that when in the final act the disguises are dropped and the journeys end in lovers meeting we have no clear idea of what the married, domestic life of Orsino and Viola or of Olivia and Sebastian might be like. The resolution is satisfying and therefore cheering, but the characters' future could be seen as one of boundless, but unspecified, opportunity – or as just an optimistic blank.

The Way of the World offers a quite different view of life. Again, it is about two lovers weaving around the barriers that separate them and finally coming together. But the play is set firmly in a realistic contemporary London with its coffee houses and

pleasure gardens, its gossips and rivalries. No mystic illusions surround Millamant and Mirabel, they live and operate in a real world. And to bring about their marriage they have to negotiate and exchange a few hard facts. The couple lay down their pragmatic demands of each other in a scene which suggests that marriage is a matter of hard-nosed contractual agreement and proposes a future that will have to be worked at rather than drifted into to the sound of a heavenly choir. Clearly something very radical has happened during that hundred years which the theatre was reflecting: domestic life, and its expectations, have come into focus. Virtually all the great Restoration comedies deal with this, in one way or another. We enter a world where male/female relationships are much more closely structured. Their plots deal with infidelity, defloration, the rape of innocence, with inheritance, social climbing, the affectations and treachery of city life contrasted with the purity – but dullness – of country living. Women are sharp-tongued and manipulative as well as alluring and self-possessed. Viola and Orsino are seen as being equals in spirit and intention (even if she is a bit brighter than him); Millamant and Mirabel are also equals, but within that equality lies awareness of the roles they will be expected to play within marriage and Millamant knows that her independence and assertiveness will probably have to be toned down a little. They will have to become friends.

This concept of companionate marriage was evolving during these years: love and friendship were becoming valued above the assumption that women were little more than the silent property of their husbands and the legal receptacle of male lust. Enlightened as this may seem (and, indeed, was), it was not entirely liberating since here were sown the seeds of a different kind of imbalance, one which Millamant spotted when she agreed that she might 'dwindle into a wife' – the allocation of specific roles (social, domestic) to men and to women.

If this had the effect of organising an increasingly urban and mercantile society it also created rebels and critics, and among these was the anarchic drag queen, ever ready to create unease and generate laughter at structures and strictures. Two things seem to have been at work here. If companionate marriage gave heterosexual men and women a different model for their relationships, then it

actually created one for men whom today we would call homosexual. It seems no accident that gay historians have seen the birth of a gay subculture, recognisable as a distant template of today's, as happening in the early years of the eighteenth century.

Secondly, and connected, the reported activities in the Molly Houses[2] – mock weddings, honeymoons, christenings – can be interpreted as criticisms of the new social/sexual order, a gleeful parody of an evolving suburban uniformity and predictability. As we shall see, the Molly Houses and similar establishments existed until well into the nineteenth century. Their denizens often paid a price for their exuberance; clubs were frequently raided and the drag queens hauled through the streets in open carts while the jeering crowds would pelt them with anything to hand. On one occasion when a particularly notorious club was busted, dung, rotten fruit, stinking fish and brickbats were actually sold in the streets for ammunition. Magistrates were not kind and the pillory, sometimes the gallows, waited.

The drag queens provoked social outrage – as much for their apparent contempt for the comforting rituals of heterosexual domestic life as for their homosexuality or transvestism. Today's critics of drag queens frequently charge them with satirising, and therefore oppressing, women. At first glance this might seem to be the case, but what they are actually doing is criticising those social structures – the rigid division of roles between the sexes and the heterosexist values that ensue – which make women and men behave as they do. The drag queen is not deriding the ordinary lives of real women, or individual women as such, but society in general. And, it must be remembered, men do not escape the acid probe. This is as true today as it was in the 1700s.

Notes

1. John Masters, *Casanova* (London: Michael Joseph, 1969): 'He was a man of the theatre. He saw French comedy at Berlin, and *opera bouffe* at St Petersburg. He knew by sight every major figure of the stage, and he probably made love to half of them, of both sexes. . . . Now, Casanova as *Casanova*, Don Juan; first, How many women? Various devoted actuaries of sex have drawn Casanova's recorded copulatory output onto graph paper; but he must have had women

he does not enumerate, and we suspect that some of the affairs he does describe are imaginary. ... There is no list of the male lover, but I would bet on the Balletti brothers and of course the three dear old patricians. ...' p 288.

2. See Rictor Norton's *Mother Clap's Molly House: The Gay Subculture in England 1700–1830* (London: GMP, 1992).

Chapter two

Squalling Cats

SAMUEL Pepys commented that Edward Kynaston – the last of the true female impersonators on the English stage – had 'the loveliest legs that ever I saw in my life'. Within a few years, however, heterosexual men were relieved of the curious need to admire the legs of another male as if they were those of a woman. Real women, with their own lovely legs (not to mention breasts and hips) were now available on the stage, ready and eager to display their charms to an increasingly lecherous audience. And to display themselves the better, the new actresses were swift to seize opportunities to dress as boys on the stage and the 'roaring girl' – the actress in breeches – became a popular figure in the silly comedies and romantic interludes devised for her. But she was definitely down market. As the new wave of Restoration dramatists sharpened their satirical pens, the first generation of serious actresses conquered the English stage. Mrs Barry, Mrs Rodgers and Mrs Bracegirdle (who created the role of Millamant in *The Way of the World*) were given plays worthy of their skills. The drag queen had already lost her sacred function, now she had resigned her dramatic authority. Peter Ackroyd has observed that 'when cross-dressing ceases to be stylised, preserving a cool arena of illusion between performance and artist, only the grotesquerie remains'. Which is what happened to the drag artists during the eighteenth century. The established theatre now had no place for serious impersonation and when men did drag up it was for a comic diversion. The roots of pantomime, as we understand the form today, can be traced back to harlequinades of this period. John Gay's play with ballads, *The Beggar's Opera*, was first seen in 1728 and became perhaps the biggest single hit of the century, so popular and

familiar in fact that more than fifty years later it was given with all its roles sexually reversed. (Can we imagine a cross-dressed *Sound of Music?*) Charles Bannister made a hefty Polly Peachum, and the *St James Chronicle* described the event as a 'ludicrous' inversion. In a male-dominated society, with sex-roles increasingly defined, for a man to dress up as a woman was barely tolerable even as a joke: it was irrational, threatening.

There was, however, a corner of showbusiness in which the real female impersonator was able to hold his own for a few more years. In a performance of *Andromache* a man played the title role and a diarist wrote about the final scene and notes him dying 'in snow-white gloves, disappearing amid the immensity of a most sumptuous guard-infanta, and overshadowed by a vast wig adorned with feathers, flowers and birds'. On another stage an actor playing Julius Caesar was stabbed 'shod in elegant ox-tongue shoes with blood-red heels and paste buckles, silk stockings with flowers embroidered in colours up the sides, olive-green knee-breeches with emerald fastenings and an incipient rain of ringlets falling all about his face'.

This was opera, that 'irrational and exotic entertainment' as Dr Johnson, not it seems without reason, described it. The dying Andromache and the somewhat over-dressed Julius Caesar were both *castrato* singers, once pre-adolescent boys with remarkable voices who were then castrated to preserve the quality of the sounds they made. But the adult *castrati* did not, apparently, simply retain cool choir-boy tones; they remained sopranos or altos but maturity produced much greater volume, range and dexterity. The result was definitely a mature voice, but unlike those of women or men, a sound which is almost impossible to imagine today.

The *castrati* originated in Italy, the curious progeny of religious intransigence and musical evolution. St Paul's injunction that women were to remain silent in church was, in the West, responsible for all-male drama. In Italy it meant that women were not allowed to sing church music and so, in medieval times, castration was seen as a solution – eunuchs presumably being more acceptable in the eyes of God than women – and the *castrati* or *evirati* ('emasculated men') became integral to Italy's musical tapestry.

Despite the religious origination of the *castrato's* art, and the church's covert tolerance of castration, the Italians were not, it seems, particularly proud of their invention. The eighteenth century English travel writer Charles Burney describes his attempt to find out exactly where the operation was performed and he is passed on from town to town, each place in turn denying any knowledge. At one time Italy tried to put the blame on Spain. But it happened and went on happening, despite the operation being illegal (anyone found participating was punished, but not the subject himself). The inducement was money; high fees were paid for a *castrato* and it was most frequently the poorest families who grasped at financial salvation by sacrificing their little sons to the knife.

By the beginning of the seventeenth century all the arts were breaking away from church domination and in Italy – particularly Venice – secular opera was developing fast with the rich and glorious works of Cavalli and Monteverdi. But the church still forbade women to appear on the stage – licentiousness and potential prostitution were the all too familiar reasons. Women sopranos existed, of course, but they were restricted to private performances and did not appear on the public stage in Rome until the end of the eighteenth century. It was during these years that the *castrati* flourished so magnificently, taking on male leads as well as female roles. It has been suggested that in the eighteenth century no less than seventy percent of all opera singers in Italy were *castrati*.

It was an age of travel and the opera was a focus of interest to all visitors to Italy. Goethe, as well as Casanova, Burney and others, seems to have been favourably impressed, yet they probably saw some extraordinary spectacles. As they grew older the *castrati* usually became extremely plump, sometimes developing breasts, and the sight of a singer such as Marianino, already a sturdy six-footer, sweeping across the stage like some vast, flower-bedecked galleon must have been something to remember. As we have seen in the descriptions of *Andromache* and *Julius Caesar*, operatic productions paid no visual heed to the time and place of the supposed action of the piece. Whether we are in ancient Rome or a mythological Greece, stage clothes were elaborate, over-stated versions of prevailing fashions – gloriously over the top drag in fact.

Off-stage the behaviour of the *castrati* seems to have been

equally exuberant and challenging. They earned large salaries and seem to have been vain, quarrelsome and often remarkably stupid (the behaviour of some of our contemporary pop singers and football players, similarly projected from unpromising backgrounds to fame and fortune, comes to mind). Like other female impersonators through the years, the *castrati* were adored by women (of all ages), were highly feted wherever they went and enjoyed exploiting the teasing ambiguity of their sexual status. Medical experts today suggest that a *castrato* would not be able to consummate a sexual encounter with a woman, though some of the singers did take wives and others were reputed to have affairs with their female admirers whose husbands, of course, saw them as 'harmless'. The *castrato* Tenducci (who, it was said, carried his testicles around with him in a red velvet purse) married Dora Maunsell, a girl from Limerick, and claimed that his wife's two children were indeed his (though that marriage was later declared null and void).

Like the Japanese *onnagata*, some *castrati* lived as women off-stage, though contemporary reports suggest that this was not so much in dedication to their art, but rather to delight in the sheer fun of being a drag queen for whom the rules of society can be bent or ignored. Casanova's run-in with Bepino della Mamana has been noted. In another passage he described his visit to the opera in Rome when another celebrated *castrato* was singing the leading female part. 'He was the complaisant favourite, the *mignon* of Cardinal Borghese, and supped every evening *tête-à-tête* with His Eminence'. He elaborates on the scene at the theatre:

'In a well-made corset, he had the waist of a nymph and, what was almost incredible, his breast was in no way inferior, either in form or beauty, to any woman's; and it was above all by this means that the monster made such ravages. Though one knew the negative nature of this unfortunate, curiosity made one glance at his chest, and an inexpressible charm acted upon one, so you were madly in love before you realised it. To resist the temptation or not to feel it, one would have to be cold and earthbound as a German. When he walked about the stage during the *ritornello* of the aria he was to sing, his step was majestic and at the same time voluptuous; and when he favoured the boxes with his glances, the tender and modest rolling of his black eyes brought a ravishment to the heart. It was

Minor emendations have been made where appropriate – but I have not interfered with Roger's text unless it was absolutely necessary.

Although this book is sub-titled 'A History of Female Impersonation in the Performing Arts', it is by no means comprehensive and encyclopaedic. 'I don't want to compile a laundry list,' Roger told me on one occasion – and both Richard Smith and I have stuck to his general principle of giving an overview – a background with representative figures in the foreground. For more exhaustive accounts of drag in the cinema, or on the gay scene, see Homer Dickens' *What a Drag* and Kris Kirk and Ed Heath's *Men in Frocks*.

Peter Burton
Brighton, 1994

Notes on Contributors

Peter Burton, who contributed the chapters 'Glamour Girls and Terrifying Termagants' and 'Hollywood and Bust', is Features and Reviews Editor of *Gay Times*, Commissioning Editor of Millivres Books, author of *Rod Stewart: An Authorised Biography, Parallel Lives, Talking To* ... and co-author of *The Boy From Beirut* and *Vale of Tears*.

Richard Smith, who contributed the chapter 'Frock Tactics', is a freelance journalist. Publications he has written for include *Melody Maker, MixMag, The Guardian* and *Gay Times*. He is the author of *Forbidden Pleasures: Drug Culture and Gay Culture*, and is currently working on *Other Voices: Gay Men and Popular Music* to be published by Cassell in 1995.

Acknowledgements

Peter Burton thanks the following for providing assistance, support, information or photographs: Tim Anscombe and Paul Webb of A&W Productions (Hinge & Bracket photograph), Adrians Video for prompt delivery of videos, Sebastian Beaumont, Colin Bourner (Dame Edna Everage and Danny La Rue photographs), Peter Burgess, Bryan Connon, Quentin Crisp, Ceri Dupree and Sebastian Jones Productions (Ceri Dupree photograph), Fenton Gray and Patrick Hayes (Regency Opera's *The Mikado*, production photograph), Ed Heath (Boy George and Kris Kirk photograph), Michael Lowrie, Patrick Newley, Christopher G Sandford, Ira Siff, Andy Simmons, Tony Warren, George Williams, Faith Wilson, Mark Winstanley and The Bradford Players (*La Cage Aux Folles* production photograph. (Unless otherwise stated, illustrations from the collection of Peter Burton).

Richard Smith thanks Jayne County, RuPaul, James Maker, Sexton Ming, Julian Clary, Boy George, Nick Raphael, Paul Fryer and Jean Paul Gaultier for agreeing to be interviewed, and for providing additional information or help, Tom Sargant, Tony Warren, Warren Heighway, Elvina Flower, Michael Tomkins and my boyfriend, Seb.

Introduction

WHEN, in 1965, I first started making notes and collecting information and anecdotes for a possible book about female impersonation in the theatre my intention was no more than to produce an entertaining paperback which could be a useful addition to the literature about the stage. It was, I felt, an area which had never been properly explored and since, in those years, drag was being flashed more frequently in popular entertainment then such a book might have a slightly racy, fashionable appeal. I did not see female impersonation as a major element in theatre history but rather as a sometimes dazzling, sometimes unnerving but only occasional skill coming from the same part of the woods as acrobatics or conjuring, a comfortable corner in which to delve. I knew it was a corner that would extend back to the theatres of ancient China and Japan, would include medieval mystery plays and Shakespeare's boy actresses as well as opera, ballet, cabaret and pantomime.

My own experience of drag in its various contemporary forms was quite limited. There were distant memories of pantomimes seen in childhood, their shape and content almost forgotten. In my early teens I had been pressed into service at school to play a couple of Shakespeare's girls, Hermia and Bianca, before my voice broke and flashy male leads came my way. There was another memory. My parents began taking me to the theatre when I was about ten and there were regular trips to the D'Oyly Carte and Carl Rosa Opera Companies when they came to the Theatre Royal in Nottingham.

After one Saturday matinee I remember studying the front of house advertisements for an upcoming attraction and asking if we could go and see it. My mother took one look and briskly announced that the show would be quite unsuitable and whisked me away. I wondered why – after all, the idea of a musical revue

performed entirely by men in what looked like quite remarkable dresses struck me as being both shivery and alluring. The show was one of the ex-forces troupes, probably *Soldiers in Skirts* or *Forces Showboat*, that toured in the immediate post-war years.

So from the beginning the idea of a man dressed as a woman was connected with social embarrassment; it would be some time before I realised that the popular assumption was that female impersonation equals homosexuality. But even some time later, when I had finally identified myself as queer (the term used until the late 1960s) and was becoming socialised into the gay circles of Nottingham and London, seeing anyone in drag – either on the stage or at private parties – was comparatively rare. When it did appear it was parodic, self-mocking – absolutely nothing to do with real women – and I began to understand it as a part of that vocabulary which criticises the mundane and everyday by transforming them into a glamorous, satirical frivolity; a process generally identified by the term 'camp'.

There were good reasons why drag took such a low profile in the 1950s (and I shall identify them in the appropriate place) being virtually restricted, as far as the general public (as opposed to gay insiders) was concerned to the dame figure in annual pantomimes. But by the early 1960s it seemed that drag was staging a tentative comeback. A young female impersonator called Danny La Rue had moved from being an off-beat cabaret attraction at one nightclub (Winston's) to open his own club in Hanover Square and was collecting enthusiastic audiences. In 1965 there were more than thirty nightclubs in central London offering dinner, dancing and cabaret of a high standard. They catered mainly to an aspirant middle-class clientele and competition was sharp. So Danny La Rue's career move was seen by many as evidence that drag was working its way from cult to establishment and becoming acceptable entertainment for respectable audiences.

Nightlife of a different kind was to be found in the noisy, smoky, crowded pubs of South London and the docklands where drag acts of a rather different kind (raucous and rude) were joining the singers and local comics in the line-up of entertainers for a Saturday night. Although timid posses of gay men from up west would pay discreet visits (and sometimes score, not always danger-

ously), these pubs were by no means what we would understand these days as gay: the customers were predominantly working-class families, local heroes and their birds who – like the thrust of the drag queens' jokes – were assertively heterosexual.

There were other events. An extremely large, middle-aged Canadian called Jean Fredericks hired Chelsea Town Hall, put on a dress which once belonged to Florrie Ford (he said) and, using a strong soprano voice, gave a recital which started with straight lieder and slowly developed into a parody of the whole genre – with trombone interludes. Another impersonator, Chris Shaw, who had an entrepreneurial turn of mind, was busy promoting Old Time Music Hall shows and all-male pantomimes. He also ran Fancy Dress Balls which provided a valuable – and safe – opportunity for drag queens and transvestites to make a public appearance. His first was staged in 1964: within three years there was enough confidence around for these events to be advertised quite frankly as Drag Balls, and under various managements they became regular dates for several years.

These were scattered signals patched into the general buzz of London's cultural explosion. As if to prove that drag was not confined to low bars and the mere fringes of theatre, in 1967 the National Theatre presented an all-male production of *As You Like It* which had to be taken as a serious attempt to offer a new interpretation of Shakespeare. I had seen the work of the Azuma Kabuki dancers from Japan when they visited London some ten years earlier. That company included some notable male actor/ dancers who specialised in female roles and the effect of their work was astonishing. So was the effect of *As You Like It* – but in a different way and this production, placed alongside the memory of those Japanese dancers, was to be a major influence on my specu- lations about the style of the male actress in the Elizabethan theatre. Later that year came Simon Gray's play of sexual exploration, *Wise Child*, in which Alec Guinness spent the evening disguised as a middle-aged woman. I was there on the first night when groups of people stormed out of the stalls shouting abuse at the actor, horri- fied that so distinguished a knight of the theatre should demean himself by appearing in drag.

So when my book appeared, in late 1968 I recall, it was a

response to, as well as a product of, a particular time. And – like all books – it was the product of a particular person at that particular time. Today, those years of the mid-to-late 1960s can be isolated quite clearly as a time of radical change in cultural, social and political attitudes, areas in which new approaches to, and different perceptions of, sexuality played an increasingly major role. We can look back and make neat lists of the important legal reforms affecting abortion, divorce and homosexuality, noting also the abolition of state censorship of the theatre. Even the language was changing as the word 'bastard' disappeared (except as a term of affection or abuse) and 'unmarried mothers' became 'one-parent families'. Sexual 'deviations' were being transformed into 'variations', and before long 'gay' would replace 'queer' as the accepted term for homosexual people.

Curious as it may seem now, I did not fully relate these wider political movements to the work in hand. Obviously I was aware that discussing female impersonation would inevitably bring up questions about sex, sexuality and sexual preferences, questions which I didn't feel equipped to deal with. Although, as I have indicated, I was enjoying a satisfactory gay social life at the time, as far as work, family and (with one or two exceptions) straight friends were concerned I was still firmly in the closet. The impact of the women's and gay liberation movements which brought the dialectics of sexual politics into the foreground was a few years away. I squirmed at the thought that readers of *Drag* might think that I myself was queer or a drag queen – or both! Today, my dear, I don't give a damn but yesterday was not without its personal tensions.

I reasoned that I could get round this problem by sticking firmly to the theatre, to the performers, their technique and style and their place in the evolution of showbusiness over the centuries. Since it was the received wisdom of the day that anyone who pranced about on the stage in women's clothes must be queer, I decided to try and step aside from the implications of this and be quite firm in the assertion that an artist's personal sexuality was irrelevant to his stage appearance. The private life of actors may be fascinating to gossip columnists, but not to the theatre commentator. In this way, the whole issue of homosexuality would be kept strictly at arm's length as an irrelevance.

But there was a great sequinned snorkydork waiting in the wings. I had published letters in the posh Sunday newspapers and in *The Stage* (the theatre paper) explaining what I was doing and asked if any readers could supply anecdotes, memories, information about drag performances, particularly relating to the all-male companies that sprang up for a few years after both world wars. I did get a helpful and generous response, but I was quite unprepared for the positive deluge of letters from transvestites.

Transvestism was an aspect of behaviour of which I had absolutely no experience or knowledge. Nor was I particularly interested. But it soon became clear, as the correspondence piled up, that many of them interpreted the work I was doing as intimately relevant to them. At last someone was going to write (presumably with sympathy) about a hidden group of people which was intrinsically harmless but victimised by the contempt of an ignorant society.

Some of the men who wrote to me did have nice theatre stories to tell; some had at one time or another, tried to legitimise their desire to dress up by attempting a stage career; others lent me programmes, newspaper clippings, rare books. But the main thrust of the letters was a desperate need for acknowledgement. Yet I could not see a discussion of transvestism fitting into my scheme.

At about this time a casual phrase from a recent conversation floated to the surface. I had been talking to what one may describe as an ordinary, no-nonsense straight guy who had spent his entire life in showbusiness, mainly as a producer. At one point he said: 'Well, it's obvious – a bloke's queer so he wants to dress up as a woman and the next step is a sex change.' Instinctively I knew that what he saw as a logical progress was totally wrong. And I was astonished that an experienced man of the theatre could make such an ill-informed assumption. But I lacked the ammunition – and vocabulary – to contest his opinion on the spot. I probably nodded thoughtfully.

And he had released yet another spectre from the bushes: what today we call the transsexual, but was then called simply a sex change. This was another complication in my subject which I could have done without. During later interviews with drag performers I was to discover (partly fascinated, partly horrified) that one or two

did use hormone implants to make minor changes to their bodies – including the development of breasts. But all insisted that this was just a device, not irrevocable, designed to add greater realism to their acts and that they would never wish to go the whole way and relinquish their male identity completely.

Although change-of-sex operations (which today the evolution of the language has transformed into gender-reassignment surgery) had been first attempted in the 1930s, the term transsexual was not widely used until the early 1960s, and I think it is safe to say that nothing was known by the general public about the process, from either the physical or psychological points of view. When news of a successful operation did become known it was treated by the newspapers as a major event to be handled with that familiar mixture of shock, horror, moral despair and, of course, sleazy prurience.

The most celebrated transsexuals at this time were Christine Jorgensen in Denmark and Roberta Cowell in the UK, both of whom underwent the operations – and survived torrents of publicity – in the early 1950s. After them, teasing sex-change stories started to become a regular feature of some newspapers. The French nightclub entertainer Coccinelle was also known, and in 1960 the beautiful April Ashley was crudely and cruelly exposed (one might say outed).

Suddenly my cosy little corner of theatre history was becoming rather crowded and complicated. I realised that before I could say 'Lights! Music! Action!' it would be necessary to open the book with an attempt to define these various categories of men who liked to dress up as women and try to sort them into discrete groups.

I interviewed no transsexuals, but here is the passage in which I introduced the transvestite:

> The voice on the telephone was certainly male: brisk, businesslike, decisive; in quality a baritone with a slight cold. We arranged to meet in the cocktail lounge of a well-known hotel in London's West End.
>
> 'How will I recognise you?' I asked, when we had settled the time and the place. He hesitated a moment, obviously considering.

7: *Introduction*

'Oh, of course – it will be Saturday evening,' he said at last. 'I know – I'll wear a green velvet evening coat and five-inch heels – there won't be any other women in the bar wearing heels as high as that!' There was a mixture of complacency and defiance in the last comment.

At the bar he was unmistakable; that is, if one had some idea of what to expect. Certainly the other customers, sitting on high stools or lounging in plush banquettes drinking martinis and nibbling olives had no idea that the tall striking woman standing by the bar was, in fact, a man.

If they took a second glance it was merely because of his height and bold sense of dress. But as there are any number of unusual women drinking alone in the West End, the interest aroused, if any, was only passing.

The green velvet coat was well-cut and expensive; it was mid-calf in length and swung loosely from the shoulders; it had wide, three-quarter length sleeves. With it he wore long, black gloves with a glittering bracelet, a diamond watch and a large, flashy dress ring over them.

He stood, completely at ease, one elbow on the bar the other on his hip, laughing with the barman. His grey silk dress was, again, of stylish design, draped across the bosom and cut fairly low. Though his exposed chest was smooth and white there was no rounding of breasts or hint of cleavage. His legs were long, well-shaped, and the heels of his black court shoes were certainly very high. He also wore – as I discovered later on during the interview – his own hair; auburn (presumably slightly tinted), brushed and back-combed until it framed his head in soft waves. It was then severely lacquered into position. He asked me to call him Pamela and was angry when I inadvertently referred to him as a man: 'When I'm in these clothes I'm a woman,' he emphasised.

We sat at the bar for a couple of hours or more. He crossed his long legs elegantly and talked freely in that husky baritone that didn't seem at all odd emanating from this feminine figure.

During the day he worked in an office as a clerk in con-

ventional surroundings and it seemed that his hair, when combed into a male style, was not really long enough to cause comment. He shared an inherited family house with an elder sister in a quiet suburb of North London.

Pamela, I gathered, had always had an urge to dress in female clothes for as long as he could remember though he managed to keep the instinct under control and only indulged privately. Not until the previous year had he begun to give parties at home, appearing himself in drag as hostess, and later to venture out so dressed. His age was virtually impossible to determine — perhaps around forty-five — but friends who had known him for a number of years, and who had only recently discovered his transvestism, felt he must be over fifty.

'I decided it was pointless trying to be secretive about it any longer,' he said. 'I felt those friends who wouldn't accept me in my dresses weren't real friends anyway.'

Some of them got a shock when they first saw him in feminine clothes on being invited to one of his parties. One woman, who had known him for years, didn't recognise him and asked his sister: 'Where is J — ?' Any initial awkwardness was soon overcome; Pamela retained his friends and obviously feels much happier and more relaxed about his situation.[1]

There were other similarly colourful vignettes describing different kinds of drag queen. Today these passages seem both obvious and under resourced. A surprising amount of the press comment about the book — articles and reviews — tended to fix on the variety of these rather simplistic categorisations, the tabloid press having a ball, predictably, with the 'lorry driver in torn fishnet stockings' angle. So presumably my attempts to clarify a complex area of behaviour must have been to a certain extent helpful.

Reviewers in the more serious newspapers and magazines acknowledged this background but concentrated on the meat of the matter with, to my great relief, general approbation. A detailed survey of female impersonation on the stage had never been

attempted before (nor has it, in quite the same way, since) and I was nervous about casting the book before professional authorities on the theatre, imagining myself pilloried by lists of grave omissions and devastating errors. But this didn't happen. Even the formidable Philip Hope-Wallace of *The Guardian* approved[2].

Re-reading *Drag* today for revision and up-dating, it seemed to me that a certain dimension was lacking. By trying to restrict myself exclusively to the stage I left many questions unexplored. In his review, Philip Hope-Wallace commented: 'How far is homosexuality involved ? We are left in doubt.' Another reviewer pointed out that the narrative sometimes did wander away from the stage – to discuss such significant transvestites as the Chevalier D'Eon for example – but that it left speculation tantalisingly suspended.

The reasons for these awkward moments are what I have been discussing – an unwillingness to confront the homosexual connection; a rather blinkered, even dismissive view of the domestic transvestite; uncertainty about the transsexual; a curious need to take up what seem to me now to be quite inappropriate moral attitudes and to make negative value judgements. I remember even having reservations about the title, feeling that *Drag* was too down market – I wanted to call it *The Male Actress*, which I find a useful phrase to describe those men who played female roles in the theatres of the sixteenth and seventeenth centuries. All this reticence gave the book an oddly solemn tone with little sense of the anarchic fun that drag creates.

I was also fairly negative about the future of drag. The last line of the book speculated that one day we might see an all-male production of the Broadway musical *Hello, Dolly!*. This was intended to be a mild joke and, indeed, it didn't quite happen. But some fifteen years later we did see a production in which the female impersonator Danny La Rue played Dolly Levi. Drag, I concluded, had no place in the legitimate theatre apart, perhaps, from the occasional experiment. I could see no future stars emerging either in this country or in North America. Australia wasn't even mentioned. Glamour impersonation had, I decided pompously, 'a dim future'.

How wrong could I get.

Within three years drag was going to get right out of its box and strut its stuff in the most unlikely places.

To suggest that our awareness of drag in its various forms is higher now than it was a quarter of a century ago is rather an understatement. Sometimes it seems that every time we glance at a colour magazine, watch television, go to the cinema or submit to a pop video we are confronted by some aspect of cross-dressing. There has been a great shift in both emphasis and perception. The cinema, for example, has traditionally used drag as either a vehicle for fairly conventional comedy or as an emblem of psychotic derangement. But in 1992 two films appeared which addressed the subject in a completely new way. One was *A Little Bit of Lippy*, ostensibly about a young working-class wife who accidentally discovers that her handsome and butch husband is a transvestite but which opened up to discuss much more than that – showbusiness drag, cosmetic prosthetics and the erotic power of fetishistic accessories. The other film was *The Crying Game* which brought the question of sexual identity into focus by asking what happens when a (presumably) heterosexual man discovers that the woman he is becoming drawn to is a (presumably homosexual) transvestite. One must also note the 1993 film of Virginia Woolf's novel *Orlando*. In the opening scenes the male Orlando (who does eventually change his sex) was played by the actress Tilda Swinton and Queen Elizabeth by a man, Quentin Crisp. No particular attention was drawn to this interesting casting.

Most notably, discussion of transvestism has moved from the limiting area of medical or psychiatric discourse into the wider field of general cultural studies. 'There can be no culture without the transvestite,' asserts Marjorie Garber, Professor of English at Harvard.[3] 'The drag queen has emerged in America in the Nineties as a symbol of our sexual crisis' insists Camille Paglia in her role of intellectual agent provocateur.[4]

There is a mass of material, ranging from medical to academic, available for those who wish to explore the meanings and conditions of transvestism. The bibliography of Annie Woodhouse's book on the subject *Fantastic Women*, for example, cites more than 100 sources – the majority of them written since 1970. Transvestites now have their own magazines, organisations and support groups, more social outlets than just an annual drag ball, studios where men (however large and hairy they may be) can learn

about makeup and the more suitable frocks. The transvestite fraternity (sorority ?) is receiving considerable, and not necessarily pejorative, exposure in newspapers and magazines. While all this has not made it any easier for the individual transvestite to come out in the shopping mall or disco, it means that the wider public is slightly more familiar with him and that the idea of an ordinary (ie not showbusiness) man in a frock may become less threatening.

Theoretically the transsexual has no need to come out, for if his transformation has been successful he simply re-enters society as a woman – though, again, this by no means alleviates the pain and suffering of individual adjustment, especially in the pre-operative phase. The examples of April Ashley and Roberta Cowell made excitingly unusual copy for the tabloids in the 1960s and there was a brief revival of interest ten years later when James Morris, the travel writer and member of the 1953 Everest expedition, became Jan Morris. At about the same time in America Dr Richard Raskind was on his way to becoming tennis star Renee Richards. Today the press and public are a great deal less excited by the 'sex change' than they used to be and only seem to take notice when the man has a celebrity connexion as in the exposure of the novelist Jeffrey Archer's gardener who otherwise, like countless others, may have undergone the operation in complete privacy. As with transvestism, transsexualism too has an extensive literature including several illuminating autobiographies[5].

In pornography – film, video, prose, graphics, live sex shows – items of clothing are used as erotic accessories. Sometimes they serve to focus the object of desire, such as the suspender belt, straps and stockings framing the female pudenda, or the black leather posing pouch which emphasises the male genitals by bunching and bringing them under control. When the bodies are, in effect, cross-dressed – that is when the man wears the suspender belt and fishnet stockings or when the woman wears the studded leather chaps an exchange of power takes place, the erotic charge is increased. Sexual identity is cast – albeit momentarily – into doubt; even gender identity can become an exciting mystery.

During the last two decades or so, this mystery has spilled onto the streets of centres of sexual tourism across the world, notably in Thailand and Rio where boys emerge from depressed

rural communities or the no-hope backstreets of big cities seeking a moment of glamour, a touch of financial independence by operating as beautiful young women, sometimes strolling the pavements unequivocally as prostitutes, sometimes working in a nightclub floorshow. Oral contraceptives soften the skin, round out the angles and give them breasts. Although apparently only very few seek the final cut, the *katoi* (ladyboys) of Thailand, the *waria* of Indonesia, the *travestis* of South America are essentially social conformists, wishing to live decorously in their created world of beauty and elusive eroticism. Theirs is not the world or outlook of the drag queen who challenges and disturbs. Originally there was little social disapproval of the ladyboys of the cabarets of Thailand because Asian performance artists have, historically, always been male, so for a youth to join an entertainment troupe as a female participant was not a matter of concern. Westerners, however, reacted with a mixture of horror and fascination and the rapid exploitation of Thailand as a holiday location began to distort the situation. There was much needed cash in gender confusion; the boys found they were equally sought after in both gay and non-gay bars.

Drag artists with hormone-adjusted bodies first appeared in the 1950s, usually at specialist nightclubs in Paris and New York. The French artiste Coccinelle was probably the most famous being a mistress of the art of self-promotion. In her autobiography April Ashley claims that Coccinelle had 'masses of silicone injections in her breasts ... five nose jobs ... a face lift ... an ear job ... electrolysis on her facial and bodily hair ...'[6] Later, as drugs became more easily available, the ranks of such creations increased and soon it would be difficult, if not impossible, to distinguish between a real woman and the *travesti* with her swelling breasts and suave hips. In the sexually *louche* years of the late 1970s, an American performer called Chrysis appeared in London as the star of a lavish cabaret show. Beautiful, elegant and feisty she captured the eye. The crisis of her act was a strip tease, revealing her luscious breasts, her long legs, her neat backside and – when the g-string was finally flicked away – her well developed male genitals.

Although the theatre (or cabaret) was the ostensible reason and ultimate showcase for this and other similarly dazzling, if alarming, transformations such acts seemed to me to have little to

do with the conventions or peculiar charm of the drag act. How far away were we, I wondered, from the bearded lady or hermaphrodite of the freak show and circus. Also, if denied the final revelation and an audience believes it is watching a real woman singer or dancer, then that tantalising slice of ambiguity is missing. The annals of the music hall and circus reveal a number of artists — tumblers, ventriloquists, musicians, conjurors — who appeared as women but were actually men (and the other way round, too). Their reasons for appearing in drag have been varied, ranging from having a better chance of getting a job (a woman ventriloquist would be unusual) to simply being a transvestite. But deceiving and then astonishing an audience with their true gender was not one of them.

In any discussion of drag the question of collusion between performer and audience comes up over and over again, at every point in history and in every context. By this I mean what an audience knows and how it uses that knowledge. For example, if an audience watching a skilful conjuring act performed by what appears to be a woman knows that the artist is a man in drag then there is a double-take: how convincing is the impersonation and how convincing is the magic. The two skills must be assimilated at the same time and therefore feed off each other. If, on the other hand, the audience does not know the magician is really a man, then concentration is on the act and the gender of the performer is irrelevant.

I remember in the days before television, when radio comedy had the mass audience, a person billed as 'Mrs. Shufflewick' would trundle on and deliver her depressed working-class monologues. It was several years later before I discovered that she was really a man dressed up as a woman, and I know I was not alone in reading her at face value. At that time female stand-up comics were not rare, there had been Elsie and Doris Waters playing 'Gert and Daisy': also at that time Beryl Reid and Hylda Baker were rising stars. A 'Mrs Shufflewick' was no matter for query. More recently one of the most delightful acts of the 1970s and 1980s has been the partners called Hinge and Bracket who emerged from the gay clubs and pubs to attract a wide audience through radio and television. There had never been any attempt to pretend they were other than

men in drag, yet at a live show at the seaside resort of Bridlington it was quite clear listening to interval chatter that a large percentage of the audience assumed they were watching two engaging and eccentric Englishwomen. The drag queen can tell the audience where to look, or he can leave a choice open.

These are some of the mysteries that surround drag and which sometimes give it an eerie magic, sometimes an unnerving sense of the ground moving beneath one's feet. It was an attempt to do a kind of surgery on the mystery that led me, in the original edition of this book, to itemise the various categories of cross-dressers. For the reasons I have outlined I no longer feel such compartmentalisation is either required or necessary. Theatre is central to our understanding of the world around us; it absorbs, analyses, presents, sometimes dictates, re-interprets and often disturbs. The transvestite, the transsexual and the hormone-modified ladyboys have their place on the stage alongside all the other manifestations and are acknowledged whenever they stalk from the wings.

There is, however, one distinction I made – or, rather, evolved – which seems to me as relevant as ever and which has governed the overall shape of this new edition. That distinction is between what I called 'real disguise' and 'false disguise'. Since disguise itself constitutes a deception, a falsity, these terms might appear clumsy: the one contradictory, the other tautologous. So I use them as convenient tools.

'Real disguise' is when the actor playing a woman is taken by the audience and by the other actors in the play or show as a real woman. This does not mean that the audience and the players are unaware of the actor's real gender. It means that this knowledge is irrelevant to the nature of the drama being played out, or to the effect of the actor's work. This, as I shall argue, is how the boy actors of the English Renaissance theatre were accepted by their audiences. And when Danny La Rue played Dolly Levi in *Hello, Dolly!* he was assuming real disguise since in the context of the musical the fact that he is a man had no relevance to the drama. Dolly is not Charley's aunt who, in that play, is known to be a man by the audience and several of his on-stage colleagues. From that device the comedy flows.

'False disguise' happens when there is no attempt by the performer to pretend he is anything other than a man playing at being a woman: he may use an unequivocally male name (such as Danny La Rue); he may give the audience direct clues with self-referential asides (jokes about his difficulties with high heels, for example) or – as La Rue does in his act – deliberately assume a masculine voice and attitude for a moment to remove any lingering doubts. With a high-profile performer such devices may be unnecessary – that Dame Edna Everage is Barry Humphries (or vice versa) requires no explanation and the duality is intrinsic to his (or her) spooky presence.

My argument is that only 'real disguise' can properly be called 'female impersonation' and that this disciplined and antique art disappeared from the English stage in the late seventeenth century when actresses were finally accepted on the boards. After that time all female impersonation was, in effect, what I have called 'false disguise'. This change, coming when it did, has a sense of historical inevitability and is much more than the result of a moment's royal irritation when Charles II decided he wanted to see real women on the stage. English society was in a state of upheaval, taking on the basic shape we can still discern today. Attitudes to marriage were changing, the roles of men and women were being redefined, the centrality of the family was being asserted. And for the first time signs of a specifically gay culture were becoming evident. Rather like the situation at the end of the nineteenth century – and indeed today – long-held assumptions and expectations were being called into question. And the drag queen was born.

I have allowed this distinction between 'real' and 'false' disguise to govern the plan of this new edition of *Drag* in that there are now two main sections. The first I have called 'The Rise and Fall of the Female Impersonator'. This traces the history of the male actress from the birth of public English drama in mediaeval times through to his forced retirement in the late seventeenth century. It includes a note on the theatres of China and Japan. All the historical material from the first edition has been retained with a few inaccuracies corrected and additional material added where relevant.

The other main section I have called 'The Rise and Rise of

the Drag Queen' and here we can relish the wide variety of female impersonation which blossomed through the later centuries as the theatre and other forms of public entertainment including the cinema, the musical and experimental drama, developed up to the present day. The original book ended, of course, in 1968. Since then there have been, as I noted earlier, many exciting and unlooked for manifestations of the man in a frock.

In between these two sections I have included a kind of interlude called 'Freaks, Fairies and Follies' which is an attempt to capture forms of drag, and its exponents, which while relevant to the basic theme of the book remain on the fringe of the main discussion: the *castrati* and other operatic oddities, some astonishing transvestites, a few notable amateur actors, cross-dressed streetwalkers and eccentric individualists. The chapter which discussed male impersonation was originally included as a token gesture towards completeness and amounted to little more than a laundry list of women who had impersonated men in the classical theatre and music hall. During the last twenty years a tremendous amount of work has been done, mainly by feminist writers, on the incidence and on the social and political significance of female-to-male cross dressing in both ordinary life and on the stage. This time, rather than corral male impersonators into one slim section, I have drawn attention to significant examples in the relevant place: Katharine Hepburn, Jessie Matthews and Barbra Streisand are thus seen in the context of the cinema. How the sexual messages transmitted by male and female impersonators differ is an important point of reference.

Finally, a word about terms is probably necessary. Already in this introduction I have used several different expressions to describe the male artists who dress as women, but for the sake of clarification:

Transvestite: the man who finds relief and personal satisfaction by dressing as a woman, being treated as a woman (or, rather, as he feels a woman should be treated), who hopes to pass as a woman in public but who has no wish to undergo surgical transformation. He is happy in his maleness and is generally heterosexual.

Transsexual: the person who, believing they have been born into the wrong sex, seeks the surgical 'sex change' or gender re-assignment

operation. Neither of these terms has any significance in a theatre context.

Male Actress: performers who use 'real disguise', who project authentic female characters rather than male-designed fantasy types, and is mainly confined to discussion of Jacobean and Asian theatres.

Female Impersonator: inevitably, an all-embracing term describing any male who entertains by dressing as a woman. However, as we shall see, there have been literally hundreds of actors and comedians who have made an impact by playing as women (Alec Guinness in the play *Wise Child*, Dustin Hoffman in the film *Tootsie*, Les Dawson in pantomime are examples) but who could hardly be categorised as female impersonators. This is an important distinction, especially when discussing the dame tradition in British theatre.

Drag: originally back-stage slang. Eric Partridge in his *Dictionary of Slang and Unconventional English* says it describes 'the petticoat or skirt used by actors when playing female parts' and suggests that the word derives from 'the drag of the dress (on the ground), as distinct from the non-dragginess of trousers'. He dates this reference back to 1887, but also quotes an earlier definition from 1850: 'Go (or, more general, flash) the drag is to wear women's clothes for immoral purposes'. *The Penguin Wordmaster Dictionary* (1987) simply defines the term as 'women's clothing when worn by men'. The word is, however, like a lot of theatre slang, associated with the gay world and gay slang. *The American Thesaurus of Slang* defines drag as 'the female costume of a male homosexual', and Bruce Rodgers' *The Queen's Vernacular*[7] offers more than twenty ways in which the term is used in gayspeak (some ephemeral and many peculiar to the United States). The use of the word to refer exclusively to men suggests that a woman dressed as a man cannot correctly be described as being in drag, but lacking any other term it is used in that context. It has also extended its reference in another respect and is now often used satirically to describe any elaborate or showy form of dress worn as a costume or even as a professional requirement. Thus one can refer to 'legal drag', 'clerical drag', 'leather drag', 'military drag' and so on.

Drag Queen: my own preferred term for full-time drag artists,

though possibly a contentious one in some quarters. Both words are part of the vocabulary of gay slang and when used together like this seem to be making a statement about the sexuality of the performer. Also some touchy or self-important artists reject the term because they see 'drag' as being tacky and downmarket and so degrading their 'higher art' of female impersonation – which is a queen's attitude if ever there was one. Others have even rejected 'female impersonation' as being too crude, preferring to be known as 'impressionists'. But be all that as it may, to me the phrase conveys perfectly the *chutzpah* and the self-confident, challenging abrasiveness of these powerful performers.

Other cultures where the convention of men playing female characters in classical theatre has lasted well into the twentieth century, have precise words to describe them: the *katoi* of Thailand, the *tan* of China and the *onnagata* of Japan. These terms allow no ambiguity and are used only in the relevant context – though ladyboy (a translation of *katoi*) is useful to identify those artists who have used hormones to acquire breasts and other secondary female characteristics.

Drag is about many things. It is about clothes and sex. It subverts the dress codes that tell us what men and women should look like in our organised society. It creates tension and releases tension, confronts and appeases. It is about role-playing and questions the meaning of both gender and sexual identity. It is about anarchy and defiance. It is about men's fear of women as much as men's love of women and it is about gay identity.

This book offers no Grand Theory of drag, I'm afraid. I don't like Grand Theories very much, they make me think of those ruthless *autobahns* that snake (or should I say ladder) from Holland across Germany – easy to get on, difficult to get off. And when one's sights are set rigidly on a single destination anything that doesn't fit in gets missed or lost on the way; castles remain unvisited, forests unexplored, streams unpaddled, bars untried, people ignored. I prefer, rather, to wander more gently, to spend time enjoying the curious and exotic creatures who will cross our path.

19: *Introduction*

Notes

1.   Roger Baker, *Drag: A History of Female Impersonation on the Stage* (London: Triton Books, 1968), pp 31–32, 34.

2.   Philip Hope-Wallace, 'On and off stage' (London: *The Guardian*, September 1968).

3.   Marjorie Garber, *Vested Interests: Cross-dressing & Cultural Anxiety* (New York & London: Routledge, 1992).

4.   Roger Baker reviewed both Camille Paglia's *Sexual Personae: Art and Decadence from Nefertiti to Emily Dickinson* (London & New Haven: Yale University Press, 1990) and her *Sex, Art and American Culture* (London: Viking, 1993) for *Gay Times* and this reference comes from the latter book, p 99.

5.   Amongst the most well-known transsexual autobiographies are Duncan Fallowell & April Ashley, *April Ashley's Odyssey* (London: Jonathan Cape, 1982); Julia Grant, *George & Julia* (London New English Library, 1980); Christine Jorgensen, *Christine Jorgensen: A Personal Autobiography* (New York: Bantam, 1968); Stephanie Anne Lloyd, *Stephanie: A Girl in a Million* (London: Ebury Press, 1991); Jan Morris, *Conundrum* (London: Faber & Faber, 1974); Tula, *I Am a Woman* (London: Sphere Books, 1982). Books of photographs of transsexuals include Barry Kay, *The Other Women* (London: Mathews Miller Dunbar, 1976) and Byron Newman, *The Ultimate Angels* (London: Hutchinson, 1984).

6.   Duncan Fallowell and April Ashley, cited above.

7.   Bruce Rodgers, *The Queen's Vernacular: A Gay Lexicon* (London: Blond & Briggs, 1972). Much pirated since the first edition, *The Queen's Vernacular* is a unique work of reference which includes gay slang from around the world. Rodgers is currently revising and expanding the book.

Part I

The Rise and Fall of the Female Impersonator

Chapter one

Out of the Chancel — into the Streets

SHE emerges from the mists of time and threads her way through the histories of all cultures and all nations. She is present at solemn religious rites and kicks up her skirts at anarchic celebrations which mock authority and challenge the status quo. In the high drama of ancient Rome and Athens she was there to facilitate the ceremonies of rebirth and fertility. In the low theatre of the common people she has leered and flaunted her sexual ambiguity. Among the Indian tribes of North America she has, as a berdache, been institutionalised as an awesome representation of a third sex, one gifted with magical powers and invested with divine authority, uniting male and female into the undifferentiated sexuality of the primal creative force.

The drag queen has two faces: the sacred and the secular. Her secular mask is comic and allows her to take on the role of court jester, with privilege to challenge the laws of society and to crash through the boundaries that separate male from female. It is a role that has existed across the centuries, from ancient folkloric festivals that marked the changing seasons to the pantomimes and cabarets of the twentieth century. When Lily Savage or Dame Edna Everage stalk onto the stage and fascinate their terrorised audience they are recreating for us one of the oldest of our totems, becoming emblems of the unseen but ever present tension between order and chaos.

Although her energies seem today to be channelled into the

theatre, the film and the nightclub the drag queen's unruly spirit still hovers unexpectedly over the popular festivities, the fairs and celebration days held in villages and small towns all over the country when men dress themselves as grotesque women with over-stuffed bras and suspender belts to play charity football matches or compete in High Street races. These are the remnants of an ancient communal transvestism, primitive and pagan, which the church could not eradicate and so, as with many pre-Christian observances, incorporated them into its own functions with the last day of Christmas (Twelfth Night) becoming associated with misrule and reversal of order.

The drag queen's sacred face is less familiar to us, but it was in this persona that she presided over the creation of drama in ancient Greece where masked actors played Hecuba and Clytemnestra and in the classical theatres of China and Japan. A strange unanimity in civilisations so isolated from each other by both time and geography, even though the dramatic arts of the Far East would evolve quite differently from those of the West. In England she crept into the developing theatre disguised as a choirboy.

When a civilisation is maturing, waking up and looking about and into itself, then drama emerges as a natural expression of the people and as a means of self-examination. The English, shaking off the shackles of the dark ages, built cathedrals, began to tame the countryside, wrote poems and started singing. Poetry and music are the basic tools of drama, a means of expressing intense emotion and were used on festival days or important occasions. For a pre-literate society they also served the function of story-telling, of preserving ancient sagas and passing on acquired wisdom – sung lyrics and rhyming verses are easier to assimilate and remember than lumps of prose.

Live entertainment – apart from games, sports and pastimes invented at home – was basically of three kinds: blood sports, the strolling players and – eventually – formal drama. Bear-baiting and cock-fighting were the first sport-entertainments to be outlawed. The second and third groups, which are basic to the theatre were both, for sacred and social reasons, denied the participation of women.

The strolling players represented the natural, untutored

instincts of the people – to dance when happy, to sing of love and war, to celebrate a birth or a good harvest, to devise ways of passing the winter darkness agreeably. These entertainers were the displaced persons of society. They could sing, dance, juggle and tumble. They carried the latest gossip and more weighty items of news from place to place. They might knock up their entertainment on the village green for a fair or market, or in the galleried court-yard of an inn. If they were lucky the great hall of the local castle or big house might be available: the arrival and treatment of the player troupe in *Hamlet* serves as a vivid illustration of what might have happened – though their entertainment would have been less sophisticated than that demanded by Hamlet.

This episode is evidence, too, of a continuity of the strolling tradition alongside the established professional theatre: *Hamlet* was written two centuries after the time of which we are speaking. At that period strolling players were officially classed as rogues and vagabonds and in many cases they probably lived up to that classifi-cation. The first royal patron the players received was Richard III, who died some seventy years before Elizabeth came to the throne. There are no women in the troupe who visit Elsinore – the Player Queen is identified as a boy – and it is likely that any woman who did travel with the players would be regarded as utterly shameless.

Formal drama came, literally, from the church, from the chancel into the market place. It all began as an attempt to make the liturgy of the church more intelligible to the largely illiterate congregations. First it was the most important parts of the mass which were dramatised in a very simple, basic way – initially by a plainsong response. It is generally agreed that medieval drama had its origins in the story of the resurrection, and it seems that the Easter mass was the first episode to be further elaborated with movement. Gradually over the years these incursions of sung dia-logue and movement became more elaborate until, to celebrate the major holy days, they eventually burst from the church altogether and were acted out before the west doors of the cathedrals. Le Corbusier reminds us that cathedrals were once white, the statues and carvings on their facades picked out in brilliant colours: one may imagine an impressive spectacle.

These pageants, reference to which can be traced back as far

as 1100, became very important to the public and a major attraction on holidays. The next step was privatisation as the various dramas were completely separated from the church and responsibility for them was taken over by the local Guilds, a form of trades union. Each Guild adopted and mounted one or two particular episodes most appropriate for the craft (or mystery) it represented. Thus the Vintners would perform the Marriage at Cana, the Shipwrights would present Noah and his Ark, while the Goldsmiths could use the Adoration of the Magi as a suitable excuse to display their precious products.

Once in the hands of laymen the plays began to take on a new, vital life of their own. More and more biblical episodes were dramatised and then expanded to include sub-plots irrelevant to the main story. Comic scenes were introduced. In this way the great cycles of what we now call the Mystery Plays were created. Each town had its own version of the plays, similar in basic shape and direction but different in treatment, stamped with the qualities of the town to which they belonged. The idea of a permanent stage was unknown at this time, so each Guild mounted its production on a mobile wagon which could be dragged through the streets, the play being performed before several different audiences during its circuit. Thus, on a special holiday for example, it was possible to settle in one spot and watch a succession of episodes as first one then another of these portable stages stopped to present its show.

Women played no active part in the services and offices of the church, so the original acting was done exclusively by men, choirboys assisting the clerks and playing women's roles when required. When the plays were divorced from the church, their religious content plus the influence of the church on the life of the people ensured that the all-male rules applied. It has been speculated that occasionally an amateur actress might have taken part, but tempting as it might be to imagine no real evidence exists. A fifteenth century miniature by Jean Fouquet showing a performance of *The Martyrdom of St. Apollonia* is often used as an illustration of how plays were staged at that time. It seems to be realistically brutal with the saintly lady tied up while her hair, and apparently her teeth as well, are being pulled by sturdy gentlemen with pointed hats and black beards. Fouquet has drawn the person who plays the

saint most definitely as a woman – shapely and well-formed – her long hair certainly attached to her head, which suggests that a real woman participated. But this may, of course, be the artist drawing what the audience was expected to imagine rather than the reality of what it actually saw.

The plays that have survived are vigorous, colloquial and racy but nonetheless illuminated with a simple simplicity, awe and tenderness. There aren't many outstanding parts for women in these stories – if we assume that angels are sexless: the three Marys are usually inactive and have few lines to speak, roles which a sweet-looking choirboy could carry off appropriately.

But the mystery plays were huge popular entertainments, associated with high days and holidays when work in the fields was a low priority, when relaxation and fun were the order of the day, times when cross-dressing traditionally added to the unbuttoned atmosphere. You can't keep a good drag queen down and it wasn't long before her secular face intruded on the scene to bring comedy and disruption to the sacred rituals.

A notable example is that of Noah's wife. All we learn from the story of the ark in Genesis is that Noah and his three sons each had a wife. There is no comment on the character or attitude of these women. For the mystery plays which tell the story of the deluge the character of Noah's wife is built up to provide a comic sub-plot. She is always represented as a nagging shrew, a busy gossip, disapproving of Noah's labours to build his ark and, at the climax, flatly refusing to board the boat. Her reasons are trivial but seem to her to be of vital importance. In some versions she is driven up the gangplank by her husband who has finally run out of patience, in another she is manhandled on board by her sons, always protesting noisily. In the Chester version she makes a stand for having her cronies accompany her. It is a good broad comedy role and not hard to see it as the forerunner of all the mothers-in-law and nagging wives who populate British working-class comedy through the years and are still present today, recreated by stand-up comedians in pantomime and variety shows, on television and sea-side postcards.

In contrast to the assertive presence of Noah's wife, the wives of Japhet, Shem and Ham are pallid subservient roles. It seems that

just as today every amateur drama group can produce one or two vivacious, extrovert actors, so could the medieval guildsmen. In these plays it is possible to detect the origins of some of the familiar characteristics of British proletarian theatre. The evil-spouting Lucifer was a popular character, and so was Herod whose part was enlarged to include great scenes of rage and bombast. The player would seize his fifteen minutes of fame and delight the crowds by leaping from the stage and hassling the audience – a precursor of pantomime's Demon King. And Noah's wife is, similarly, an early sketch for the pantomime dame – though at this time kept within the limits of the narrative with no improvised solo turns.

Strong comedy roles for husband and wife are cogently developed in the two Shepherds' plays which were performed at Wakefield in Yorkshire and can be found in the Towneley MS, which dates from the latter half of the fifteenth century. The second play has been called the first English comedy but might more realistically be defined as the first English comedy that has been preserved. Its biblical text is, of course, the Nativity but this seminal event is parodied by a parallel story concerning sheep-stealing – which refers, apparently, to a contemporary case. The problem is how to hide the stolen sheep which Mak (the sheepstealer) brings home.

His wife, Gyll, has an idea and she organises a deception:

> I shall swaddle him straight in my cradle;
> Were it a greater sleight, I could help still.
> I will lie down straight . . .

So the stolen sheep is wrapped in swaddling clothes to be nursed by Gyll who emulates the sounds of labour to foil the pursuers. She makes Mak tuck her up in bed and when he starts to panic bullies him with instructions:

> Sing thou Lullay fast
> When thou hear them at last,
> And but I play a false cast
> Trust me no more.

When the pursuing shepherds arrive they do a thorough search and Gyll lets rip with a storm of protest:

> Aiee! my middle!
> I pray to God so mild
> If ever I you beguiled,
> That I eat this child
> That lies in this cradle.

– a safe enough promise, under the circumstances. The deception is finally discovered by one of the shepherds:

> Give me leave him to kiss and to lift up the clout –
> What the devil is this ? He has a long snout ...

But Gyll persists in pretending that the sheep is really a baby: 'A pretty child is he as sits on a woman's knee.' A fight breaks out in which they all join until the Angel appears and the play ends with the Adoration of the Shepherds.

An interesting element in this treatment is that Gyll – played, of course, by a man – goes through the audio-visual mime of labour and childbirth. The audiences presumably accepted this as broad comedy (which it is), but one of the drag queen's functions has been to confront those female mysteries which exclude and so intimidate men, creating in them fear, uncertainty and a sense of apartness. She can do it in the high comic style of Dame Edna Everage, for example, or with the low comedy of that succession of male stand-up comedians from Dan Leno to Les Dawson. The targets are intrusive mothers-in-law, aggressive wives, the sexually assertive female often with the implied pendant of a timid, sexually inept or indifferent male. The knockabout comedy of the secular drag queen Gyll and her sheep helps to diffuse possible male fears surrounding childbirth thus allowing the sacred drag queen Mary her awesome moment of real mystery.

30: Drag

There is a border country legend which suggests that the drag queen who uses her power to diffuse fear made a strategic appearance in the Chester cycle of mystery plays (which includes the more vivacious version of the Noah story). Chester was an important town crucially placed on the Welsh-English border and as a result was continually terrorised by Welsh mountain fighters who made frequent pillaging forays into the town. Ultimately the citizens began to build their houses on sturdy stone pillars with stairs leading up to the living quarters. Heavy doors covered the stairs and they were closed and barred during a raid. This architectural feature remains today in the Rows with their galleries of shops above street level.

But Chester was an important market town and for economic reasons the Welsh farmer's wives had to be allowed in on market days. According to the old tales, the Welsh fighters would dress up as women and mingle with the crowds flocking into town. Once they had reached the market place they would get rid of their skirts and attack. How a burly and presumably bearded mountain brigand was able to pass himself off as a homely farm woman is not explained but it is believed that a character representing the disguised fighter was introduced into the plays – a grotesque female played by a man dressed up as a Welshwoman, complete with steeple hat. The idea was to persuade the population to ridicule rather than fear the invaders.

So at the very beginning of English drama the drag queen asserted her presence in both sacred and secular modes. And as plays took to the streets with the improvisation of the strolling players enlivening formal scripts, they became extremely popular entertainments. By the beginning of the sixteenth century troupes began to use the courtyards of public inns as a performance space with trestle tables forming the stage, the galleries providing vantage points for the audience. Alongside this Renaissance England was founding schools and creating bodies of choirboys not just for the cathedrals and churches but also for the private chapels of the great aristocratic families. The schools used drama – turning to Greece and Rome for inspiration – to teach the skills of public speaking and rhetoric; the choirboys began to add masque and mime to their repertory of song. A permanent professional theatre was on its way

and it would burst into full flower during the last quarter of the sixteenth century. But not without difficulty.

Despite its popularity with the ordinary people, the theatre had its enemies, notably the Puritans and – for slightly different reasons as we shall see – the civic authorities. In the London area plays were being performed in the courtyards of inns in Aldgate and Islington (records date the earliest of these performances as 1557) much to the chagrin of the authorities which, by 1574 had made it almost impossible for any kind of theatrical activity to happen within their jurisdiction. However in 1576 London's first permanent theatre was built – by James Burbage, a carpenter, then actor and the first showbusiness entrepreneur. He leased land in Shoreditch which was outside the jurisdiction of the Common Council and built there. The house was simply called The Theatre and had dressing rooms and facilities for producing serious plays.

Success was immediate and attracted companies of actors operating under wealthy patronage which in turn attracted an audience drawn from the upper classes. Standards of performance – and of writing – rose and though the Puritans were furious ('Venus palaces,' one called The Theatre) and a second theatre (The Curtain – named after the estate where it was sited) was built by Henry Lanman. Soon the two managers merged their companies, Shakespeare had joined Burbage's troupe, and other theatres followed: the Swan, the Rose, the Globe, the Fortune, the Cockpit.

By this time both the nature and subject matter of drama had changed: it no longer recycled familiar Bible stories but offered narratives of power and politics, tragedies of star-crossed lovers and comedies of romantic cross-purpose. Dramatists sought inspiration from the writers of ancient Rome and Greece and from the poets of Renaissance Europe. Plays were no longer inspirational tracts enlivened by moments of clowning, but gripping stories peopled by three-dimensional characters.

The secular drag queen found herself marginalised and ignored. There seemed to be no place now for her special brand of anarchy. She would retreat to the countryside once again and play havoc among more simple people for almost a hundred years until she spotted her chance for a comeback. The sacred drag queen had a different fate; she survived to undergo a remarkable transform-

ation. No longer just an inarticulate angel or modest virgin, she moved centre stage to become the theatre's leading lady, to articulate that remarkable gallery of heroines created by the new wave of dramatists. The presiding deity had become a working girl, a male actress, the first of the great female impersonators.

Chapter two

No Place for a Lady

THE Elizabethan playhouse was a rough and rowdy, unstable and often quite dangerous place. Going to a show would be quite different from today's experience of theatre-going; audiences did not sit in neat, docile rows silent and respectful as the drama unfolded – they would walk about, chat and argue, heckle the stage and express instant noisy disapproval if a performance failed to please. Every so often the Lord Mayor of London, prodded by the City Fathers, would make an effort to get the playhouses closed.

'They are a special cause of corrupting youth, containing nothing but unchaste matters, lascivious devices, shifts of cozenage and other lewd and ungodly practices,' he complained in a memorandum of 1597. This has a familiar ring, but he was not talking about television or video nasties, but what are now revered texts.

And if immorality was seen as being rampant on the stage, off stage were gathered it seems a fair selection of Elizabethan low life: 'They (the theatres) are the ordinary places for vagrant persons,' the Mayor says and offers an engaging list of vagabonds including 'masterless men, thieves, horse stealers, whoremongers, cozeners, conny catchers, contrivers of treason.'

The playhouses were blamed, too, for encouraging apprentices and servants to play truant from their employment. Presumably countless grandmothers were hastily buried on the afternoons when *Tamburlaine the Great* or *Macbeth* were being played.

To modern ears, perhaps the most immediately acceptable of the Lord Mayor's complaints was that the theatres were a breeding ground for disease, places where infection was easily transmit-

ted. And he ingeniously points out that convalescents who may think they are recovered will be tempted to rush to the theatre while unknowingly still carrying their germs – a neat touch that. The Elizabethans walked with a constant awareness of death. Life expectancy was short, a man might be recklessly killed in a tavern brawl (as it is believed Christopher Marlowe was) or be suddenly struck down by the ever-lurking plague. Theatres were automatically closed the moment there was an outbreak of plague, to the distress of and impoverishment of the actors and their families. For these were the common players, the nearest thing to our own understanding of the professional actor. In fact the emergence of acting as a full-time job derives from this period, a development that can be traced from around 1560.

But these continual attacks masked a far deeper unease which the theatre created. For in that highly-structured society, with its hierarchies and rules of behaviour and dress, the stage was a privileged space where things were allowed to happen that would be forbidden or penalised elsewhere, rather as court jesters had licence to approach treason. As we shall see, actors were given special permission to wear clothes that, off-stage, only certain well-defined members of society were allowed. And boys or young men dressing as, and impersonating, women flouted the biblical injunction expressed in Deuteronomy: 'The woman shall not wear that which pertaineth unto a man, neither shall a man put on a woman's garment; for all that do so are an abomination unto the Lord thy God.' Actors were given permission to violate these codes, and when the social codes are broken then the puritan imagination can run riot – usually into visions of sexual mayhem.

The various companies working the London stages were, of course, all male and each was under the patronage of some distinguished or aristocratic person as their names suggest: Leicester's Men, for example, and the Lord Chamberlain's Men of which Shakespeare was originally a member. When, in 1603, all the companies were placed under the patronage of members of the royal family, James I himself took on the Chamberlain's Men and so Shakespeare became one of the King's Men. Despite the apparent cachet of the troupes' titles, an actor's life was no soft option; when not out of work they were overworked and were constantly cen-

sured by the Puritan faction on moral and social grounds. To find a woman acting in the public playhouse would have offended not only on religious and moral grounds but also be seen as a shocking example of inappropriate behaviour.

The public's demand for drama was insatiable; if a play flopped it was dropped and replaced by another. Our contemporary theatre's expectation of a continuous run until takings fall below a break-even figure was unknown and several plays would be shown in a repertory system. The companies were quite large as the well-populated plays of the period suggest, even though doubling in the smaller roles would be usual. An additional responsibility of the actors was the training of young entrants into the profession – in stage-management as well as acting.

As a member of one of these companies, a young boy would lead a life which if not exactly glamorous was probably more interesting than most other options open to him at the time. He would have to be tough, quick-witted and self-reliant to survive the hurly-burly of the public playhouse on stage and backstage. If he had a suitable face and a slim body, then his first acting assignments would be in female roles. As I shall argue later, this was a highly specialised branch of acting requiring particular expertise in deportment, voice production, and gesture as well as make-up and the wearing of skirts. Rarely does Shakespeare, or the other dramatists of the period, introduce substantial parts for more than three women in any one play which suggests that there were few boys of adequate proficiency at any given time. Smaller female roles would be doubled by youths playing messengers, spear-carriers or all- purpose nobles. The apprentices were each put in the charge of an individual actor from whom he would learn the business, thus equating acting with other trades like building or brewing.

The use of the term 'boy' to describe the young actors may create some problems for modern readers. Today the term is used widely and loosely and, depending on the circumstances can refer to any male up to the age of around twenty. It is also used dismissively, a put-down, as seen in the way in which, until quite recently, black men whatever their age would be called 'boy' by arrogant whites, reducing them to the status of servants. And, of course, gay men

have also been referred to as 'boys' (as in *The Boys in the Band*) which is again a reduction of status from adult male (and therefore responsible) to rather naughty youngsters (and therefore of no account). In the context of the Elizabethan theatre, however, 'to boy' actually meant to play a female role on the stage irrespective of the actor's real age – and that is how I am using the term here. Scholars have disagreed (of course) about the exact age at which youngsters joined the companies, with suggestions ranging from ten years old to the mid-teens. Common sense suggests that an untrained ten year old would be an unlikely candidate for important roles, but bright children learn fast and perhaps some heroines were portrayed by twelve or thirteen year olds. The names of some of the actors, including the boys, have survived (notably those of the Lord Chamberlain's Troupe) and the assignment of names to particular roles has been a pleasant, if pointless, game for theatre historians. One scholar will produce an elaborate reconstruction of who played what, only to be challenged by other scholars. Certain apocryphal traditions have become established – that Shakespeare played the ghost in *Hamlet* and Adam in *As You Like It*, for example.

Thus the first Ophelia is thought to have been Nathaniel Field who ultimately became as famous an actor as Richard Burbage the great Elizabethan heavy. The first Desdemona may have been Richard Robinson, the first Lady Macbeth might have been Alexander Cooke and Rosalind is attributed to Willie Ostler. A young man called Robert (or Bobbie) Gough (or Goffe) is frequently named as the first Juliet, and also as the first Cleopatra. There are at least seven, possibly more, years between these two plays and if Gough did indeed assume both the nightgown of the Veronese nymphet and the robes of the Egyptian queen then he must have been properly adult by the time Antony hoved into view. Which would be evidence that not all the female roles were played by barely adolescent boys with beardless chins and unbroken voices. If young Gough spent half a dozen years specialising in heroines then his standard of impersonation must have been authoritative.

These common players were not the only acting companies around. Another group of companies consisted entirely of children.

Their existence – and they lasted on and off for just over thirty years – coincided with the establishment of the adult companies, but they were quite separate and at one time had every appearance of becoming a serious rival to them.

The history of these children is sometimes pathetic, one of descending status reflected in the cherry-stone rune: silk, satin, muslin, rags. It is, too, a story of abuse and exploitation. At the beginning the groups of boys were quite simply chapel choirs maintained by the households of the crown and the aristocracy. They sang at regular services and were expected to give more complex performances at the major religious feasts such as Easter and Christmas. During the reigns of Henry VIII and Elizabeth they sang some of the greatest English music with Tallis, Byrd – and the musical Henry himself – providing anthems and a capella pieces. Elizabeth had the boys of the Chapel Royal and the boys of the Chapel of St George at Windsor. There was another choir at St Paul's and at the chapels maintained by various noble families.

Since they were attached to wealthy households, the choirboys enjoyed lives of considerable privilege. They were well looked after – fed and clothed – and had special livery for their appearances in the private chapels. Selected for their voices and aptitude in the first place, their education was continued and they were carefully trained in the arts of music and rhetoric.

Gradually, as they became more proficient and their scope widened, the boys – and the Masters in charge of them – wanted them to be more than just choirboys. The talent was there for masques and secular entertainments and they would put together little shows for important occasions; in modern terms, perhaps, an after-dinner cabaret. Quickly these events grew into full scale entertainments – fanciful, allegorical pieces with emphasis on costume and music rather than formally constructed plays – and the Masters began to look for ways in which the talents of the boys might be enjoyed by a wider audience, outside the protective walls of castle and stately home.

This was achieved with a little smart dealing. The aura of privilege was important and had to be retained and there must be no chance of the boys' companies being regarded as in any way similar to the common players. By the 1570s two important boys'

companies were established in London. The boys of St Paul's had their theatre within the precincts of the cathedral, and the children from Windsor were set up within the Liberty of Blackfriars which also enjoyed the protection of the church. Both companies, therefore, were working in protected circumstances and were automatically immune from the Lord Mayor's incursions against the theatre.

The spaces in which they performed were smaller than the public playhouses and they were enclosed which gave an unusual sense of intimacy as well as that essential feeling of exclusiveness. Audiences, drawn predominantly from the upper and literary classes, were quiet and attentive.

Some indication of the refined atmosphere can be gleaned from a few lines in John Marston's play *Jack Drum's Entertainment* which mentions the boys of St Paul's when the character called Planet remarks:

> I'faith I like the audience that frequenteth there
> With much applause. A man shall not be choked
> With stench of garlic; nor be pasted
> To the barmy jacket of a beer-brewer.

This was written perhaps two decades later than the period we are discussing but no doubt the conditions – and certainly the attitude – had changed little. The boys' companies reached their peak of popularity and success during the 1580s when they attracted the attentions of several upcoming young playwrights, one of the most notable being John Lyly.

In 1578 he had published *Euphues*, a prose romance which achieved a hugely fashionable success, largely through its elaborate and self-consciously florid style which gave us the term 'euphuistic'. All his plays were written specifically for the boy actors to be performed before small, knowing and courtly audiences. Among them was *Campaspe* which was given for the queen on New Year's Day 1584 by a combined company drawn from the children of St Paul's and the Chapel Royal. It was another success for the thirty-year-old writer and, unusually for the period, ran into three editions within the year. The plot, a variation on the painter falling

in love with his model, is unremarkable. More interesting was *Galathea* in which two heroines must each disguise herself as a boy.

During the course of the action the two girls fall in love with each other, each supposing the other to be a real boy. As a solution to this complication the two girls are led away by Venus who promises that at their marriage one will be changed into a real man. How audiences were intended to take this curious idea – or, indeed, how the actors were intended to play it – must remain a matter of conjecture. But it is probably the earliest treatment of sexual ambiguity on the English stage and probably required all the flowery prose and verbal dexterity that Lyly could command to prevent knowing sniggers.

By 1590 the boys' companies had been closed down and they would be absent from the scene for ten years. One of the reasons for this was that their precocious talents were being exploited by writers and backers as weapons in the private feuds and rivalries that went on. Lyly, for example, never lost an opportunity to satirize the enemies of his patron the Earl of Oxford. Lyly also became involved in the Marprelate Controversy and used the boy actors to orchestrate his political abuse which was considered a lampoon too far.

But there were other reasons for the closures. During the frequent campaigns against the theatres the children's companies escaped direct censure because of their protected position. But nevertheless attempts were made to regulate their material. In one report Northbrooke ruled, for example, that the plays should contain no ribaldry and should be performed largely in Latin; that productions should be less frequent and be modestly clothed; the plays should not be put on for individual profit and should contain no love interest.

The inference we may draw from these demands is that the plays had begun to create some unease even among their sophisticated audiences. The 'ribaldry' could refer to sexual innuendo – or even more overt expression – and the suggestion that the material should be played in Latin may represent a desire to return the companies to their ecclesiastical roots. It may also be a tacit agreement that ribaldry could be acceptable if it were couched in a

language only the well educated would understand rather in the way that the translators of Latin or medieval erotic verse used to leave the quite unambiguous passages in the original language.

Modesty of dress would not refer to body-revealing clothes, but to the splendour of the companies' wardrobes. There seems to have been a good deal of conspicuous showing off. It is interesting to note that the inclusion of love interest in the dramas created unease. That women's roles were played by boys was accepted and unremarkable at this time and – as I shall speculate later – in the public playhouse at least did not affect the dramatic validity of those roles. But were the boys perhaps playing love scenes in a style that triggered an audience's awareness of a transvestic and homo-erotic undertow?

The closing of the boys' companies seems to have been, therefore, the result of a number of socially disquieting elements coming together at the same time and indicating that the troupes had wandered too far from their origins in worship. The days of silk and satin were over.

For ten years there were no child companies and the public playhouses gained in strength and popularity. But in 1599 the children of St Paul's (who had been disbanded in 1589) were set up again by the Earl of Derby, William Stanley, who was a keen theatre buff and, it was rumoured, had been writing plays for the adult companies under a pseudonym. The company enjoyed another six years of popularity with a repertory from the new wave of younger playwrights including Marston, Middleton, Beaumont and Ben Jonson. The atmosphere had changed; invective and malice were still to be heard emerging amusingly from the mouths of small boys, but the plays were now looking at society from a much wider perspective, making the glittering barbs of Lyly and his in-crowd a decade earlier seem trivial. Also there was no pretence that the boys were giving private performances any more and it wasn't unusual for respectable citizens to allow their sons – with no previous choral training – to become apprentices to the children's troupes, just as with the adult companies. The gap between the two was narrowing.

It wasn't long before the Children of the Chapel Royal were in business again. The venture was started by two men – Henry

Evans, who had been a colleague of Lyly at the Blackfriars Theatre, and Nathaniel Giles who now had Mastership of the Chapel. They quickly put together a company of talented boys using means that were often more foul than fair.

During the early years of her reign, the young Queen Elizabeth had delighted in the masques and entertainments devised for the royal choristers. Like her father she loved music and poetry and succeeded in making her court a great cultural centre where musicians, writers and painters could enjoy a relaxed and stimulating atmosphere. In this context the plays performed by the boys seemed appropriate and charming. Later, however – around 1567 – her enthusiasm waned and the companies lost her support. The choirs of the royal chapels continued to exist, of course, and by 1597 it seems that the supply of young voices was drying up so the Queen took dramatic measures to secure new talent. She granted Giles a power of impressment which, as Master of the Children of the Chapel, he was free to use. 'Our Chapel Royal should be furnished with well-singing children from time to time,' her proclamation went, 'and (we) do authorise our well-beloved servant, Nathaniel Giles ... to take such and so many children as he or his sufficient deputy shall think meet, in all cathedral, collegiate, parish churches, chapels or any other place or places, as well within Liberty as without, within this our realm of England, whatsoever they be.'

On the face of it this seems to be a straightforward permission to scout for voices with which to refresh the choir. Giles and his 'suficient deputy' Evans did create a brilliant company which included two boys who in different ways were to leave their mark on dramatic history. But it wasn't always easy going since, after the scandals of ten years earlier, being selected for service in the Chapel Royal was no longer seen as being quite so prestigious, nor was there the same distinction between a privileged Chapel boy and a common player.

But armed with the Queen's decree, and scenting commercial opportunism, the two men became arrogant and high-handed and their dubious methods were beginning to cause gossip. Then one day a thirteen year old schoolboy, Thomas Clifton, was walking through the network of streets between Christ Church and his home in St Bartholomew's when he was roughly abducted by Giles

and Evans. The boy's father, Henry Clifton – a wealthy landowner from Norfolk – demanded his son's release but Evans defied him, asserting that Giles' royal decree gave them authority to take any nobleman's son. In a rash act of defiance they produced the boy, thrust a script into his hand and made him learn some lines while his father looked on, seething and impotent. Clifton went straight to Sir John Fortescue, a member of the Privy Council, and the boy was released.

Clifton was disturbed by the whole incident, however, and initiated enquiries about the way Evans and Giles were operating and in 1601 laid his evidence before the Star Chamber. One of the points made by Clifton was that though the impressment was specifically designed to acquire singing boys, no such thing was required of them nor was there any indication that they were being taught this art. He also asserted that 'the base trade of a mercenary interlude player' was no life for his son. The result was that Evans was ordered to give up all rights to the theatre and the plays he had acquired, while Giles was censured and ordered to sever his connection with the stage. The affair caused a reverberating scandal and the Queen ordered that the children of her chapel should no longer participate in theatrical activities. She does seem to have protected Giles because he continued to round up boys for both the choirs and for the stage throughout the rest of her reign and through that of James I right up to 1626 when the parliament of Charles I flatly forbade him to continue his activities.

After the death of Elizabeth in 1603 the children's companies were given a new lease of life. Singers were completely separated from actors and the troupes of boys became, quite openly, common players. For a while they had tremendous success, even putting some of the adult companies temporarily out of business. This turn of events is referred to when Hamlet discusses the arrival of the travelling players at Elsinore with Rosencrantz who tells him about an 'aery of children, little eyases' who are 'now the fashion' and thus forcing the visiting company to go on tour. The children's reputation for putting on plays full of scurrility, satire and abuse continued and heightened. In his spirited defence of the stage, *Apology for Actors* (1612), the prolific playwright Thomas Heywood referred to writers 'committing their bitterness and

liberal invective against all estates to the mouths of children, supposing their juniority to be a privilege for railing.'

Finally they annoyed the King himself and after one particularly subversive performance some members of one company were put into Bridewell. Eventually the public too became jaded. The boys' brief period of fame had ended. Richard Burbage, the leading actor of the day, took on the lease of the Blackfriars Theatre and allowed the more promising boys to join his and Shakespeare's companies as apprentices; others went off in disreputable touring groups, their fortunes now diminished to muslin and rags.

Despite their unpopular methods of collecting children, Giles and Evans probably had an eye for potential talent. Young Thomas Clifton was released so we have no means of knowing how he might have made out on stage. But two of the 'Children of the Queen's Chapel' achieved fame in different ways. Salathiel Pavy did it by dying at the age of thirteen. Ben Jonson, who was writing and producing at the time, composed a touching valedictory lyric which gives us a clue to the talents of the child actors:

> Years he numbered scarce thirteen
>   When Fates turned cruel
> Yet three fill'd zodiacs had he been
>   The Stage's jewel:
> And did act (what now we moan)
>   Old men so duly
> As sooth Parcae thought him one,
>   He played so truly.
> So by error, to his fate
>   They all consented ...

The other boy, Nathaniel Field, was also thirteen when he caught the attention of Jonson who took him under his wing and taught the boy the essentials of both acting and playwrighting. Nathaniel was the son of John Field, a Puritan divine and a tirelessly vocal enemy of the stage. Fortunately for his son's future the father died when Nathaniel was barely a year old, which enabled him to pursue a distinguished career as an actor.

After joining the King's Men, and under Jonson's guidance,

Field's talents blossomed. Jonson gave him a leading role in his allegorical comedy *Cynthia's Revels* and later in *Epicoene*, a play which makes the greatest demands on the talents of a female impersonator and which became a showcase for Edward Kynaston, one of the last male actresses, some sixty years later.

In *Bartholomew Fair* Jonson inserts this exchange:

Cokes: Which is your Burbage now?
Letherhead: What mean you by that, sir?
Cokes: Your best actor, your Field?

This links Field with Burbage quite clearly and many authorities suggest that Field was Juliet, Ophelia and Desdemona to Burbage's Romeo, Hamlet and Othello – the Thompson and Branagh of the day perhaps. Field seems to have played female roles well into his twenties when he is described as having a 'peculiarly smooth and feminine look, with no whiskers'. Later he switched to leading male roles ranging from the swashbuckling romantic lead in Chapman's *Bussy D'Ambois* to the Moor of Venice himself when he was described as 'the true Othello of the poet'. He also found time to write plays (among them *Amends for Ladies* and *A Woman is a Weathercock*) and father five children before dying at the age of forty-six.

Other names associated with the playing of female roles surface through the mists, though with less documentation or contemporary reference than Field and Robert Gough. There is Alexander Cooke who Boswell decided must have been 'the stage-heroine' of the day playing all the principal female roles in Shakespeare's plays. Gough's son Alexander, who was born in 1614, also became a distinguished interpreter of female roles, being known as 'the woman actor of Blackfriars'. He was one of the dedicated actors who ensured that acting skills and performing traditions were not forgotten in the years between the Civil War and the Restoration by networking on the actors' underground and organising illegal performances in private houses. Such is the background to the 'boys' of the Tudor and Jacobean stages, the places where they performed and their management – sketchy stuff, often

Tony Curtis and Jack Lemmon in *Some Like It Hot* (1959): 'Billy brought in a female impersonator to work with Jack and me . . .'

Dustin Hoffman in *Tootsie* (1983). An entertainment with intellectual pretensions above its station.

right: Men in Frocks writer Kris Kirk with Boy George: The family's favourite pop star. Photograph by Ed Heath.

Garbo as Queen Christina (1933).

Tim Curry as Frank-N-Furter in *The Rocky Horror Picture Show* (1975) briefly echoes Garbo in *Queen Christina*.

In *Yentl* (1983), Barbra Streisand played a young Jewish woman who has to become a boy to get an education.

From the earliest days of silent film, comedians have donned dresses:
Charlie Chaplin in *A Woman* (1915).

Robbie Coltrane as 'Annabelle' in *The Fruit Machine* (1988).

Fenton Gray as Koko and Dame Hilda Bracket as Katisha in Regency Opera's production of *The Mikado* (1993). Photograph by Patrick Hayes.

above right: Ceri Dupree as Mae West: 'I want to be funny, but not cruel.'

Dame Edna Everage: A terrifying termagant. Photograph by Colin Bourner.

The American 'male actress' Charles Pierce as Bette Davis.

left: Jim Bailey creating an 'illusion' of Judy Garland.

Dame Hilda Bracket and Dame Evadne Hinge: Completely convincing characters.

La Cage Aux Folles has proved immensely popular with amateur operatic and musical societies; pictured, The Cagelles from The Bradford Players production, 1994.

La Gran Scena Opera Company, Ira Siff centre: 'You could use drag to heighten the drama and the comedy ...'

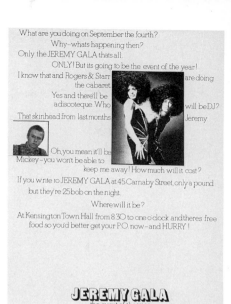

What are you doing on September the fourth?
Why–whats happening then?
Only the JEREMY GALA thats all.
ONLY! But its going to be the event of the year!
I know that and Rogers & Starr are doing the cabaret.
Yes and there'll be a discoteque Who will be DJ? Jeremy
That skinhead from last months
Oh, you mean it'll be Mickey – you won't be able to keep me away! How much will it cost?
If you write to JEREMY GALA at 45 Carnaby Street, only a pound but they're 25 bob on the night.
Where will it be?
At Kensington Town Hall from 8.30 to one o'clock and theres free food so you'd better get your P.O. now – and HURRY!

JEREMY GALA
the event of the year.

Barri Chatt, left, and Terri Gardner (*c.* 1947): Chatt was the inspiration for Captain Terri in Peter Nichols' *Privates on Parade*.

above right: An advertisement for the *Jeremy* gala (1970) at which the sophisticated drag duo Rogers and Starr did cabaret.

Danny La Rue:
The last
glamorous gasp
of British music
hall.
Photograph by
Colin Bourner.

David Raven (Maisie Trollette) and Douglas Byng: Two generations of drag artiste, in mufti, after Byng's penultimate performance, Brighton 1987.

Kazuo Hasegawa in Ichikawa's *An Actor's Revenge* (1963) which has an annoyingly brief reconstruction of a *Kabuki* theatre.

The Ascot scene from *Forces in Petticoats*, Danny La Rue is between the two men at the right of the photograph.

Jean Fredericks, musical satirist.

Splinters, formed after the First World War, consisted entirely of ex-servicemen.

Soldiers in Skirts toured throughout World War II and well into the 1950s.

Julian Clary: Dressing up was a tactic. Photograph by Peter Mountain.

Pieter-Dirk Uys as Mrs Evita Bezuiderhout: A brilliant deflation of the arrogance that shored up apartheid.

RuPaul: 'We're born naked and the rest is drag.' Photograph by Norman Watson.

obvious he hoped to inspire love of those who liked him as a man, and probably would not have done so as a woman.'

Casanova then observes: 'Rome, the holy city which in this way forces every man to become a pederast, will not admit it, nor believe in the effects of an illusion which it does its best to arouse.'

A link between theatrical drag and homosexuality is perceived and articulated, just as a link between private drag and homosexuality was made in the Molly Houses of London's Covent Garden. It is worth noting that, in both examples, it was not the drag itself which signified homosexuality, but the actions and manner of the men wearing it – and the effect of this on the witness. Even the bisexual Casanova was obviously a bit shaken by finding himself attracted to a man dressed as a woman: London's general public was not attracted to the Mollies in the same way, but was scandalised by men who could so blatantly flaunt convention and mock the very foundations of domestic society.

It may have been a lurking sense of sexual unease that prevented the *castrati* from being as popular in London as they might have been – considering that opera was a fashionable sport, and that Handel was there, composing operas with specific roles for his favoured singers. The diarist Evelyn had come across a *castrato* when he visited Venice in 1644. He went to the opera particularly to hear the reigning diva Anna Rencia, but noted 'there was a eunuch who, in my opinion, surpassed her'. In 1667 the ever adventurous Killigrew introduced three singers from Italy to London – one woman and two *castrati* – who were quite liked by those who heard them, including that great amateur of the theatre, Pepys: 'they sing indeed pretty high and have a mellow kind of sound but yet I have been as well satisfied with several women's voices and men also. . . .'

Though foreign singers were becoming fashionable by 1704 and society leaders flocked to subscription concerts to hear them, a reaction was setting in and people were already talking about 'a parcel of Italian eunuchs, (who) like so many cats, squall out somewhat you don't understand.' Resentment was fuelled by xenophobia and the fact that the words, sung in a foreign language, were incomprehensible. Also, the very idea of a eunuch touched deep chords of distaste. The flamboyant quarrels and rivalries – on and off stage – which went on between the imported and native singers, between the female sopranos and the *castrati* created a kind of ongoing opera war which delighted the audiences. Farinelli, considered the greatest of the *castrati* with his voice of 'honey drops' was 'ridiculously popular' and made so much money from his work that for his retirement back in Italy he built himself a superb mansion and called it 'The English Folly'.

By the 1780s Italian opera was fast losing its popularity and commentators were swift to get their knives in. 'In order to realise completely to what extent the prevailing taste has shrunk, it is only necessary to visit the magnificent theatre devoted exclusively to Italian opera – a monument of English extravagance. Lovers of this type of public entertainment find so much enchantment in the empty tones that some even sacrifice their masculinity to the god of music. The voice of nature and the expression of human passion appears here in the form of farcical trilling and warbling. . . .

'But that is not all. By supporting these emasculated foreign singers we are promoting general moral degradation and effeminacy, which is contagious like the pestilence and throttles in our young noblemen all nobility of feeling. Instead of presenting to them as examples the characters of patriots and heroes who have performed great deeds in the service of their country, we are shown a group of pitiable creatures, neither men nor women who, no matter how highly they are praised, lack all manliness and capacity for action which is, after all, the basis of dramatic expression.'

Once more we find a reactionary distrust of foreigners, dislike of opera and a confusion of dramatic and sexual values. By the end of the century it seemed that London had seen the end of the *castrati*, but twenty-five years later Giovanni-Battista Velluti arrived to sing in the premiere of Meyerbeer's *Il Crociato in Egitto*. There was a certain amount of interest since this was the first opportunity London opera-goers had to hear the music of the new composer whose spectacular style was already changing the face of opera. But it was the prospect of an appearance by Velluti that created a different kind of stir.

The Times thundered: 'Our opinion was that the manly British public and the pure British fair would have been spared the disgust of such an appearance as that of Velluti upon any theatre of this metropolis ... Humanity itself should rise against such a violation of decency – such an outrage upon feeling. But women! Can women too attend the scene? Can British matrons take their daughters to hear the portentous yells of this *enfranchise* of nature, and will they explain the cause to the youthful and untutored mind?'

In the event Velluti seems to have been a success, though opinions of his voice varied from 'luxuriant and highly expressive' in the *Morning Post* to 'the discordance of a peacock's scream, or that of a superannuated lady scolding her servants' from *The Times*, still determined to direct readers' minds to the singer's genital lack rather than his vocal prowess. Another paper, a Sunday called the *Telescope*, returned, if slightly indirectly, to the theme. 'Among the most enthusiastic of the applauders we observed a good many young ladies of fashion in the boxes: and indeed we do not know when we have seen so many delicate hands beating their snow-white gloves to pieces on behalf of a new favourite upon the boards.' Perhaps the 'British fair' were wiser than *The Times* imagined.

Favourite or not, Velluti was the last *castrato* to appear on the London stage. The *castrati* did leave a couple of legacies. One was the art of *bel canto* singing to be perfected by men and (real) women in the operas of Bellini and Donizetti. The other legacy would ensure that the ghost of the *castrato* haunted the operatic stage for as long as certain great works continued to be performed. This was his transformation into what is known as the 'trouser role', that is, a male character, usually a young man or an adolescent – written for a female voice.

As the greatest period of operatic composition dawned casting an opera was, to a certain extent, done irrespective of the sex of the singer. Thus a female part could be played by a man in drag or a real soprano and a male lead written for a high voice could be played by either a *castrato* or a woman. But with the disappearance of the *castrato* composers had either to transpose the parts or agree to having them sung by women. In his opera *Idomeneo* Mozart composed the role of the young prince Idamante for 'my *molto amato castrato* Dal Prato' as he referred to him. When this opera was 're-discovered' in the mid-twentieth century, the role was assigned to a tenor with a high *tessitura* which worked well. Such reassignment was often neither possible nor indeed desirable in many of Handel's operas which include soprano and mezzo-soprano voices singing princes and soldiers. During the height of the *bel canto* period, the sound of two female voices singing in thirds proved irresistible. Bellini got round the problem in *Norma* since her rival in love is also her maid which gives their two show-stopping duets dramatic validity. In his *Semiramide* Rossini cast the male role of Arsace for mezzo-soprano – at the premiere Teresa Mariani sang it with Isabella Colbran in the title role. It remained a very popular opera throughout the nineteenth century, and is still revived when two singers of sufficient calibre are to hand. Giulietta Simionato was Arsace in Milan in 1962, but the most notable exponent of the role in recent years has been Marilyn Horne – both she and Simionato sang opposite Joan Sutherland in the title role.

The complexities of confusions left by the *castrato* is nicely demonstrated by Gluck's great and mould-breaking opera *Orfeo ed Euridice*. For the first performances in Vienna in 1762 Orfeo was sung by Gaetano Guadagni, one of the most famous male con-traltos of the eighteenth century (Handel had assigned the contralto parts in *Messiah* to him). In 1774 Gluck made a second version of the opera for Paris, but this time writing Orfeo for the tenor Legros. This became the version generally used until 1859 when Berlioz, in a search for authenticity, transposed the tenor role to fit a female alto voice which gave Pauline Viardot-Garcia a major success. Since then the role seems to have been the exclusive property of the female alto: the almost baritone voice of Clara Butt, the plummy contralto of Kathleen Ferrier, the lighter supple tones of Janet Baker and the dramatic incision of Maria Callas suggest the variety of a wide range of approaches – bearing in mind that a female alto is not the equivalent of a *castrato* alto. And audiences find it disorientating when, as occasionally happens, a tenor appears in the role. Possibly the androgyny of Orfeo is as important as that of Peter Pan, also played by a woman and resented when in 1982 the Royal Shakespeare Company fielded a man in the role.

During the last twenty years the growing interest in original instrumentation and historically authentic sound has meant that in revivals of eighteenth century opera women's voices are being used more frequently. A performance of *Idomeneo* today, for example, is more likely to have a soprano rather than a tenor singing the role of Idamante. Also greater use is being made of the counter-tenor (again not an exact equivalent to the castrato but probably closer than a female voice). Some directors can have great fun with Baroque opera. P F Cavalli's 1651 Ovid-inspired *La Calisto* requires Jove to disguise himself as the goddess Diana in order to seduce her follower Calisto. While in this disguise, Jove is pursued by Diana's earthly lover Endymion and other confusions of identity follow. For his 1970 production of the opera at Glyndebourne, Peter Hall had the mezzo-soprano Janet Baker sing both Diana and Jove when disguised as Diana, while Endymion was sung by the counter-tenor James Bowman. To add to this confusion of delights, Diana's maid Lynfea – a crotchety old crone – was played by the extraordinary French tenor Hugues Cuenod who turned in a splendid drag performance. And a randy little Satyr who fancies Lynfea is played by who else but a soprano. This glorious production is now regarded as a classic of its kind, perfectly matching Raymond Leppard's perhaps over-glamorous realisation of Cavalli's score. The very nature of opera, with its heightened atmosphere where the credibility of the plot is less important than the intense emotions that plot releases, distances an audience from the nitty-gritty of humdrum 'reality' and creates a perfect arena for explorations of illusion, disguise and gender confusion.

In his book The *Castrati in Opera*, Angus Heriot emphasises the glamour that these eighteenth century singers possessed and suggests that their charisma was something similar to that projected by the great stars of Hollywood (he mentions Clark Gable and Marilyn Monroe), whose appeal to both men and women, it can be argued, has a certain androgynous quality. This combination of high glamour and sexual uncertainty confused the highly experienced Casanova; in his novel *Sarassine*, Honore de Balzac explores the possibilities that might result if an unworldly young man should make such a mistake. Sarassine is a young sculptor, ignorant of the facts of life, who falls in love with La Zambinella, a Roman opera singer, and only after several meetings does he learn that she is a *castrato* – a fact that is, of course, well known to all but him. We may be reminded here of the relationship between Fergus and Dil in

Neil Jordan's *The Crying Game* and the crucial revelation that pulls the whole question of sexual identity (and attraction) into focus. Fergus is inevitably confused but for Sarassine the results are fatal. In 1990, the writer and actor Neil Bartlett used Balzac's text for one in a series of theatre works designed to re-examine gay culture and gay history. In a fascinating variation (or perhaps elaboration) of the original story La Zambinella was played by three performers – the counter-tenor Francois Testory; a woman, Beverley Klein, who has a richer, musical-comedy voice; and the individualistic drag queen Bette Bourne who, deep and mellow, sounds more distinctly male. The songs ranged from eighteenth century opera through to modern vaudeville, opening up what might have remained a slightly remote literary piece into a relevant exploration of gender significance.

Those first audiences who saw Gluck's *Orfeo* in both Vienna and Paris did not have to look through, or ignore, the gender of the hero: tenor or male alto, he was still a male figure. The trouser roles that evolved during the nineteenth century were of decreasingly heroic proportions, most often adolescent boys who are either clumsy or love-struck or both, and the sight of a pretty girl in knee-breeches was a certain attraction. In terms of dramatic and musical function perhaps the most satisfying trouser roles are Cherubino in Mozart's *The Marriage of Figaro*, the page Oscar in Verdi's *Un Ballo in Maschera* and Octavian in Richard Strauss's *Der Rosenkavalier*. One should also note Isolier, another page, in Rossini's *Le Comte d'Ory* (an opera which also requires the male chorus to appear as nuns), Hansel in Humperdinck's opera of *Hansel and Gretel*, Hoffmann's companion Nicklausse in *The Tales of Hoffmann* and Prince Orlovsky in Johann Strauss's *Die Fledermaus*. As an amusing dramatic twist both Cherubino and Octavian are required to dress up as girls at one point: Mozart's opera makes little of this joke but it becomes a major farcical scene in the Strauss. Some trouser roles seem to have no particular dramatic function – the boy Siebel in Gounod's *Faust* is there merely to sing a couple of sentimental ballads (one of which is frequently cut anyway). These are all examples of what I have called real disguise – that is, we are expected to accept these characters straightforwardly as males. We rarely do, of course, at least on the level of basic drama. But music, which can induce us to overlook a middle-aged Salomé or an overweight Calaf, can also persuade us to overlook this point. Only Orlovsky – wealthy, bored, aristocratic – offers real possibilities for playful gender ambiguities. I have seen the role played by tenors and a counter-tenor as well as the more familiar mezzo-soprano, and the character can come across as an androgynous youth, a handsome man, a handsome woman in a man's evening clothes, or as a sardonic dyke – in any event, she is the ideal host for a party which focuses on disguise and mistaken identity.

Quite often in opera a heroine is required to dress as a man but this is usually just a plot device, that use of false disguise which draws irony or comedy from the fact that though the audience knows she is a woman, the other characters do not. The outstanding example of this is Beethoven's opera *Fidelio* in which the devoted wife Leonora disguises herself as a young man called Fidelio in order to try and rescue her husband – a political prisoner – from his dungeon. Here, the false disguise gives the role an unusual edge: a character so completely disguised by cross-dressing is very rare both in opera and on the dramatic stage. Inevitably the jailer's daughter Marcellina begins to prefer the gentle Fidelio to her regular boyfriend. It is so important that Leonora's true identity remain intact that she cannot reveal herself to Marcellina. No comedy is allowed to develop from this familiar situation; the difficulty is handled in such a way that it becomes another demonstration of the tenderness and integrity of the heroic Leonora.

Opera's other great *travesti* role is that of Octavian, which does present some difficulties, notably in the opening scene of the opera. *Der Rosenkavalier* was originally conceived as a light comedy, after the fashion of Mozart's *Figaro* but set in a fantasy eighteenth century Vienna. When first thinking about the project the librettist, Hugo von Hofmannsthal, wrote to Strauss: 'There are two major roles, one for a baritone and another for a graceful girl dressed as a man.' It seems that originally one of the main intentions was to recreate a Cherubino figure – hence the elaboration of the sequence where Octavian is disguised as a girl. Cherubino never actually makes it with anyone, but his twentieth century incarnation most certainly does and after a prelude which graphically describes a vigorous sexual encounter the curtain rises on the exhausted lovers – Octavian and his older mistress.

The stage directions ask Octavian to be kneeling beside the bed in which his lover is lying. She is hidden from sight except for her arm which lies outside the bed-curtains. This stage picture caused problems from the start and court censorship demanded something far less explicit for the Berlin premiere in 1911. Whether the objection was just to the unequivocally post coital message of the scene, or whether the fact that two women were involved was also influential, is not clear. But even today the episode is often seen as distasteful. 'It is seldom that the two actresses involved manage to avoid suggesting a repellent sort of Lesbianism as they hug and caress one another, crooning torrid endearments,' commented William Mann in his book on the operas of Strauss. And, of course, depending on the shapes and acting ability of the two sopranos the scene can also be hilarious. Clearly any Octavian must be skilled and confident if she is going to avoid either calamity. These days most do, aided by careful stage directors and a perceptible increase in opera singers' acting abilities generally. But, like the other less demanding trouser roles, Octavian can never be taken by any audience as a young man – even if she looks good, belief must be suspended the moment she opens her mouth. After that awkward opening scene Octavian becomes little more than a kind of high-class Principal Boy, and the episode in which he is dressed as a girl and flirts with the boorish Baron Ochs plays for easy laughs.

The sumptuous, soaring vocal lines of *Der Rosenkavalier* may have been 200 years away from the 'squalling cats' of the eighteenth century, but it is here that the *castrati* finally rest. The female impersonator became a male impersonator and trouser roles are no longer written. The drag queen has a small revenge.

Chapter three

Shame in the Ladies' Morgue

EXPOSURE of his genitals means a revelation of the drag queen's ultimate secret. When the Chevalier D'Eon died on 21 May 1810 the mystery of his true gender was finally solved and the information that he was a man came as a genuine shock to all those people who had been close to him in the last decades of his life. All that excitement about his 'real' sex, the bets placed in London clubs, the fashionable flurries of gossip and vicious cartoons were now nearly forty years ago. For thirty of those years the Chevalier – re-titled Chevalière – had lived and dressed as a woman, eight years in France and for the final twenty-five in England.

In order to earn some money, and also probably to escape for a while from the immobilising nature of women's clothes, the Chevalière had launched herself as a female fencer giving exhibition bouts in theatres and other public places. This adventure came to an end in 1796 when a severe (and neglected) wound forced her retirement. From then on she lived a quiet poverty-stricken life, sharing lodgings with another ex-patriot Frenchwoman, Marie Cole who cared lovingly for the invalid. Her spiritual and health needs were attended to by Father Elysée, a doctor-priest.

It was Father Elysée who made the momentous discovery while examining the body to determine the cause of death and the news caused a final flare-up of the old controversy about D'Eon's true sex, so much so that it was felt appropriate to obtain and publish certificates which would settle the matter for all time. His naked body was examined by surgeons and then exposed to priests, to French noblemen and to his recent companions. 'I found the male organs of generation perfectly formed in every respect,' stated the surgeon Theo Copeland. Her landlord at 26 Millman Street where she and Mrs Cole had lodged declared: 'I always believed him to be a woman. I declare further that having seen his body after death the result is that he is a man. My wife makes the same declaration.'

Marie Cole was shocked too. She and the Chevalière had been intimate companions, loving and supportive. The two elderly women were familiar figures in the neighbourhood, sometimes assumed to be mother and daughter. Despite their intimacy, Mrs Cole had never suspected her companion was a man. Whether any of the old bets were called in is not recorded.

A hundred and seventy years later, the friends and associates of another woman received a similar shock when the evolution theorist Dr Charlotte Bach was found dead in her flat at Highgate (North London) in June 1981. Born in Budapest, Dr Bach had arrived in England in 1948. She worked as a lecturer and as an Agony Aunt for a popular magazine and then set herself up as a hypnotherapist, collecting quite a high society following. Then she began to concentrate on writing a book about transvestism. This was rejected by all the publishers to whom the manuscript was submitted, but in 1969 she withdrew it because by now she had, from her work on transvestism and other sexual variations, developed a theory of evolution which she called Human Ethology. She had been a lecturer in philosophy and psychology at Budapest University and set about promoting her ideas. The first people to whom she showed her work were puzzled and sceptical, but by 1973 her name was beginning to be known and she was collecting quite a following. The writer Colin Wilson gave her guarded support and Bob Mellors (one of the two young men who started the Gay Liberation Front in London in 1970) found her an inspiration for his own developing theories of sexuality, and became a friend. Colin Wilson has described her as 'a broad-shouldered mammoth of a woman with deep masculine voice and a heavy Hungarian accent'.

After Charlotte Bach's sudden death, a post-mortem examination revealed that she had a penis and was, in fact, a man. Despite her size and deep voice, Charlotte had convinced everyone that she was a woman, so the discovery, naturally enough, created consternation among her associates and some of them – notably Bob Mellors – began to piece together the true story of this remarkable person's life. The personal history which she had confided to friends was found to be an elaborate invention – though certain elements were true and had been simply burnished and slightly adjusted to add colour to the new life story. His real name was Karoly Hajdu, his father a tailor. He had no academic qualifications. He came to England after the war and set up an accommodation agency adopting the title of Baron. He married an English woman and in 1956 he raised money to send British 'freedom fighters' to Hungary during the uprising but was then accused of embezzling the funds. At this time he changed his name to Michael Karoly and became a lecturer and journalist. For some time he had, under the name of Daphne Lyell-Manson, advertised himself as a spanking madame in contact magazines. 'You were most generous and kind to spend so much energy on my ugly backside,' wrote one satisfied customer. But his wife had died unexpectedly and this, combined with bankruptcy, provoked a severe nervous breakdown which finally turned him into Charlotte Bach – a full-time transvestite, living, working and passing as a woman.

In the examples of both the Chevalier D'Eon and of Charlotte Bach, the revelation of their true gender shocked their closest associates who had never questioned their friend's status as a woman. The Chevalier did, of course, have a history of sexual ambiguity but, having been officially declared to be a woman and he having apparently gone along with it, the old controversy was taken as settled and by the time of his death, virtually forgotten. Charlotte Bach had no known history of sexual ambiguity: she had deliberately recreated herself in mid-life and virtually started afresh. So the shock delivered to her closest friends on her death was equivalent to that delivered by the Chevalier. But with Charlotte, the revelation produced further implications on a quite different level because it brought into question the inspiration and value of her work. A female academic researching transvestism and developing a major theory of evolution from this is one thing: that the person turns out to be a male transvestite who, however widely read (and Charlotte was certainly that), had little academic training is something else again. Were her outpourings a desperate attempt at self-justification demonstrating a need to rationalise what he saw in himself as distressing compulsive behaviour? And then again, if this were the case, does it necessarily devalue her insights?

I am in no position to debate the point, but this particular conundrum does seem to me to be a good example of how the revelation of a drag queen's genitals can create shock waves reverberating out in ever widening circles. If, as in the case of Charlotte Bach (and apparently that of the Chevalier), the impersonation is unsuspected then the new information forces a reappraisal of all that has gone before – relationships, attitudes, behaviour. In Neil Jordan's film *The Crying Game* the discovery that Dil, the attractive hairdresser seductive in mini-skirts and high heels, is a man provides the emotional crisis and turning point. But it is important to realise that Dil does not strip and reveal his genitals to shock Fergus – she thinks he already knows that she is a transvestite and is prepared for whatever sexual encounter may happen. But Fergus is shocked – he reacts with gut violence – and so is the audience in the cinema. We are forced suddenly to rethink through a great deal – all the aspects of Dil's behaviour we have witnessed so far; her job, her relationships with other men and particularly with her boyfriend Jody, the (black) British serviceman whose murder by the IRA brought Fergus and Dil together in the first place. Fergus has to rethink Jody as well as himself. Dil, through Fergus's reaction, is also shocked and she in her turn has to reappraise Fergus. All of this must be absorbed and processed while the film is relentlessly pushing its narrative forward.

Catching a glimpse of the drag queen's cock can also provide a moment of low comedy as in Terry Jones' 1987 film *Personal Services* about a working class girl, played by Julie Walters, who is drawn into prostitution and eventually becomes a madam running a very specialist brothel in south London. The story was based on the actual career of Cynthia Payne, now an outspoken and vigorous proponent of sexual liberty. While working as a prostitute the Cynthia Payne figure acquires a maid to welcome her clients and look after her rooms. This maid is a middle-aged woman, efficient and knowing but a little shy and retiring. A moment arrives when the maid is accidentally stumbled upon in the lavatory and, with her knickers down, seen to be a man. The revelation provokes a hilarious climax to an already tense suburban wedding reception, but any shock value it may have is limited to the one incident. The maid (played by Danny Schiller) continues her job and can be seen to fit in nicely with her mistress's growing clientele of transvestites, uniform fetishists and bondage queens. Essentially, the maid's transvestism is happily taken on board, in keeping with the film's good-humoured atmosphere, which makes a case for the acceptance of unusual but harmless sexual needs.

The Chevalier D'Eon spent much of his life as a dashing and brave but ordinary, virile man, an expert fencer (as we have observed), seeing action in the army and eventually becoming a Captain of the Dragoons. But he did have occasional urges to dress as a woman and the entire confusion of his life was triggered when he made use of this for political reasons. In 1755 (when he was twenty-eight years old) he was sent to Russia to act as a spy at the court of the Empress Elizabeth at St Petersburg and while there he disguised himself as an attractive young woman, gaining the confidence of the Empress herself. There is a portrait reputed to be of D'Eon dating from this time in which he appears as a woman. It is a pretty face: he wears a lace cap and a fairly low-cut dress revealing a definite swelling of breasts. Round his neck is a band of ribbon, he wears drop earrings and a lace cap. The portrait is identified as being of 'Carola-Genoveea-Louisa-Augusta-Andrea-Timothea-D'Eon-de Beaumont', which is a clear feminisation of his given male names 'Charles Genevieve Louis Auguste Andre Timothee Marie D'Eon de Beaumont.'

The political background to this strange adventure is that Louis XV maintained a secret network of spies across Europe which implemented his own private foreign policy and which was supposedly unknown to his official ministers. The Chevalier became a member of this complex which was known as *Le Secret due Roi*, and his purpose in visiting St Petersburg was to persuade Elizabeth to act favourably towards France and to present the Empress with a letter from the King.

Whether D'Eon – who in one account was introduced to the

Russian court as Mlle Lia de Beaumont – actually did impersonate a woman at this time is still a matter of controversy among the many scholars who have researched his life. Although the Chevalier had been a well-known and interesting public figure for most of his life no serious biography appeared until 1885 when J Buchan Telfer's *The Strange Career of the Chevalier D'Eon de Beaumont* was published in London. Other books about him followed, but the story was clouded by the existence of a volume called *Memoirs of the Chevalier D'Eon* by Frederic Gaillardet published in Paris in 1836. Gaillardet asserted that his work was authentic, supported by letters, documents and diaries kept by the Chevalier himself. It is a vastly entertaining book. But that such a brilliant diplomat, devious spy, brave dragoon and formidable swordsman should be a secret drag addict presented Gaillardet with a problem. Such a hero needs a comparably impressive sex life and, blandly ignoring all the internal evidence that D'Eon had no sexual urges whatsoever, Gaillardet proceeded to give him some. His 'remorselessly truthful brush' paints D'Eon jumping on Madame de Pompadour, being fingered by a faintly glazed Louis XV, bedding down with Elizabeth of Russia and making off with virtually every pretty woman who crosses his path.

Thirty years later Gaillardet revised his book and admitted his inventions – of which there were many. But the damage had been done: there were enough red herrings, false trails and half-truths to establish some highly engaging legends and confuse scholars for many years. The question of whether he did present himself in St Petersburg as the pretty Mlle de Beaumont seems unlikely to be resolved. Discussing this particular question Marjorie Garber observes: 'Whether D'Eon actually impersonated a woman in Russia or not seems in a way less important than the desire ... to think he might have done so.'

And indeed, this particular desire – to make a man into a woman or, at least, into a drag queen – is not an unfamiliar response where sexual uncertainty is the issue. It can also be seen at work when certain newspapers or individuals try to finger well-known people as being gay. Partly it represents a need for certainty in the face of crossed signals or a response to the sense that something is slightly outside the regular order of things. Those young –

and not so young – men whose sexual orientation occasionally comes under sly or blunt scrutiny (the popular singer Cliff Richard, the Windsor scion Prince Edward and the actor Jason Donovan are recent examples) all have the appropriate credits for 'eligible bachelor' but all seem quite happy doing nothing about it. Such men who seem to avoid both marriage and a public sex life are, in our society, what I call 'outside the regular order of things' – whether they are actually gay or not is ultimately less important than the need to place them in some rigid pigeon-hole. But the truth is final and boring: a definite answer to such a question – like the exposure of the drag queen's genitals – removes the mystery and with it the excitement of a delicious uncertainty.

The delight in nourishing this sense of 'might have been' to which Garber refers is found in the folk legend that Queen Elizabeth I of England was actually a man. The story was unearthed, put together and published by Bram Stoker – he of Dracula fame – in his book *Famous Imposters*. It is important to understand that Stoker did not invent this story. The belief had enjoyed a local currency around the Cotswold village of Bisley for three hundred years. Essentially the legend has it that the twelve-year-old Princess Elizabeth was evacuated to the country to avoid an outbreak of the plague in London but then died suddenly just before her father, whose notorious temper always had a short fuse, was due to pay a visit.

A terrified governess decided to replace her with a suitable substitute. No appropriately aged or physically similar girl could be found so, in desperation, the woman used a boy who had been a playmate of the princess. He turns out to have been the natural son of the Duke of Richmond, himself the illegitimate son of King Henry – which at least kept it in the family. However, once the deception was in place it had to be maintained and so 'the Bisley boy' as he came to be called grew up as a princess and eventually became a queen. Stoker makes quite an exciting tale out of all this, feeding in a spot of gratuitous tension here and there, but also sorts through various questions about the actual likelihood of such an event, discussing the boy's complexion – he was pale with reddish hair, like Henry and as Elizabeth is portrayed, but unlike the brunette Anne Boleyn (the real Elizabeth's mother) – and noting the emotional distance between Henry and his daughter, which meant he would not expect or seek any intimate moments on his visit.

Were the story true it would explain many of the so-called mysteries and eccentricities of the Queen – her famous virginity, for example; the notion that there was some dark secret in her life known only to her childhood guardians, a nurse Mrs Ashley and Sir Thomas Parry; her dread of doctors and refusal ever to be examined even on her deathbed; that she went bald with age – hence her remarkable collection of wigs; her outbursts of temperament and, of course, the strong nature of her leadership and her assertive personality, which have always been seen as peculiarly masculine. Whether the story is true or not is – like that of the Chevalier D'Eon in St Petersburg – less important than the fact that it might be.

Which may be why the casting of Quentin Crisp as Queen Elizabeth I in Sally Potter's film of Virginia Woolf's novel *Orlando* became, in the event, so ideal. It seemed on paper a quirky and amusing idea. Orlando himself was being played by the actress Tilda Swinton – with good reason, since Orlando himself lives on over the centuries and in the course of time changes into a woman. Swinton made an elegant, androgynous boy not unlike a Hillyard miniature of an Elizabethan young man. To have the Queen a man in *travesti* would make a neat pendant. Crisp (who seems never to have had any particular interest in drag) plays what I call real impersonation: there was no suggestion that this queen was a man, we had to take the character at face value. And in fact he did seem a more likely Elizabeth than any of his predecessors – and they include such assertive (and therefore, according to sexual stereotyping, masculine) artists as Bette Davis and Glenda Jackson. Crisp's presence, a stately rustle of luxurious skirts, added a curious resonance to the sumptuous Tudor scenes. Perhaps there was a touch more historical truth there than anyone suspected.

These images of uncertainty, suggested by the examples of D'Eon, Charlotte Bach – and possibly Elizabeth I – lead us to the interpretation of the drag queen as a realisation of the 'veiled woman' – a phrase drawn from Freud's observation that 'the erotic life of women ... is still veiled in impenetrable obscurity'. These secrets wait to be unveiled by man – either literally in the process of seduction, or through the penetration of the male gaze, as when watching a strip-tease. But the veiled woman is dangerous; what will be revealed is the threatening spectacle of female sexuality. Freud associated this with castration fears, suggesting that when a boy first discovers that a woman has no penis the sight rises for him fears of his own possible castration, hence the concept of the *vagina dentata* – the vagina that bites and eats. When the drag queen unveils, or is unveiled, the man is confronted not with an absence but with a significant presence.

Perhaps the Western world's most famous stripper is Salomé, unnamed in the gospel story, but who became an inspiration for painters, poets, writers and dramatists from the Middle Ages to the French decadents of the nineteenth century, and later for several film-makers. She was given the shape and form we recognise today in the play by Oscar Wilde, who drew heavily on Flaubert's short story (which also inspired Massenet's opera *Herodiade*) and was, as well, influenced by the Salomé paintings of Gustave Moreau.

In Richard Ellmann's biography of Wilde there is a photograph which purports to be of Wilde himself in costume as Salomé. This image has been reproduced by several other authors though neither they, nor Ellmann, give any provenance for the photograph (apart from the credit: Collection Guillot de Saix, H Roger Viollet, Paris) so we do not know where or when Wilde assumed the robes of his own *femme fatale* – or even if it really is Wilde, or simply some amateur actor with pretensions who happened to look like him. There is a resemblance – the pronounced nose, sensual mouth – and the figure is well-fleshed.[1]

This Salomé is kneeling, looking down at the severed head of Jokanaan (seen from the back, so looking like a wig on a plate rather than an actual head) and reaching out her plump arms to seize the trophy. The drag is not particularly impressive; the skirt could be a curtain wrapped around his solid waist and it is stretched uncomfortably by an awkward pose. The 'barbaric' head-dress, bangles and jewelled belt have a distinctly home-made air about them. As we shall see, men played women in amateur theatricals frequently and with no comment at that time, so this may be a record of such an event – though a classical column in the background suggests a studio rather than a stage.

But Wilde or not, stage or studio, a point is made – that Salomé has a homoerotic sub-text and that the focus is not merely the exposure of a woman's body to the eyes of men, but on the mystery of sexual ambiguity. Salomé's final veil reveals that the men have been titillated not by a Jewish princess but by another male. Or have they? Such is the androgynous power of the drag queen that what lies behind the veil may represent reassurance as much as alarm.

Inevitably Wilde's play, which he wrote in 1891, ran into censorship troubles because it represented a biblical subject. An English translation (Wilde had written in French) by Lord Alfred Douglas with illustrations by Aubrey Beardsley, appeared in 1894 and the play was finally mounted in Paris by Sarah Bernhardt in 1896. It was played frequently in Germany and Russia, and various versions provided opportunities for actresses and dancers to scandalise the public, but the play in its authentic form was not seen in England until 1931. However, the power of the play, and its central imagery, was familiar to readers and to admirers of the suggestive Beardsley decorations. Opera-goers were luckier when Richard Strauss used Wilde's text as the basis for his opera *Salomé* (1905) and this version has a long production history. Unfortunately the title role and her dance created major problems since the part requires the physique of a teenage girl and the voice of a mature and experienced soprano. In some productions the dance was performed by a double, the real Salomé emerging at the conclusion. Strauss himself approved this solution saying he'd rather have a Salomé with two personalities rather than witness the horrendous spectacle of a hefty prima donna attempting the dance. Only in the last few years have we been lucky enough to discover sopranos who can both sing and dance the role – such as Josephine Barstow in the English National Opera's exotic production, and Maria Ewing who reveals herself completely naked.

Hollywood, inevitably, attempted to promote the story, first in 1922 with the notorious Alla Nazimova, who used the Beardsley illustrations as inspiration for the sets and costumes. Production stills indicate that the result was an essay in high camp, glamour styles of the twenties mixing with grotesque and decadent images drawn from Beardsley. It has been rumoured that all the men in the cast were gay. Yvonne de Carlo shed the veils in a 1945 version and Rita Hayworth had a bash in 1953 in a version that distorted the story to such an extent that the dance is performed in order to save John the Baptist! But however distorted and ludicrous the various accounts may have been, they have all perpetrated the notion that Salomé is basically a strip-show with politely decadent decoration if required.

The play, and its androgynous resonance, was rediscovered in the 1970s mainly through a version presented in London in 1977 by the Lindsay Kemp Company. Using Wilde's text as a basis, the show was a highly theatrical and stylised mix of dance, mime and drama. Kemp himself played Salomé wearing an elaborate head-dress of feathers, ropes of pearls and lavishly flowing robes. For the dance, however, he abandoned these glamorous accessories and presented his own lithe, male body. David Haughton the actor who played Jokanaan in the production, described Kemp's Salomé as 'the embodiment of lust and carnality. He'll be a cross between Rita Hayworth, a pantomime dame, Earth Mother and Bette Davis as Elizabeth I'. Salomé's mother, Herodias, was also played by a man (credited in the programme as 'The Great Orlando'), false moulded breasts exposed above vast skirts, peacock feathers springing from her cloak, eyes rolling, mouth slobbering in a hair-raising demonstration of skin-crawling evil. Elsewhere there were beautiful, almost naked, young men in jewelled jockstraps and the inscrutable Vladek Sheybal as a sinister Herod.

At the same time, Kemp and his company were also presenting *Flowers*, a similarly conceived entertainment based on Jean Genet's novel *Our Lady of the Flowers*, and again he elected to dance the role of the drag queen Divine. His first entrance, down a long ramp (reminiscent of the *hanamichi* of the Kabuki theatre) was an unforgettable moment – remorselessly slow, statuesque, elegant: a fur stole around his neck, one hand holding an open fan, the other delicately lifting his skirt. Once more the full armoury of decadent imagery was brought into action through costume, lighting, dance and – possibly for the first time – the extraordinary quality of Genet's prose was made visible. (The German director Fassbinder though using different means also caught the lurid, unreal power of Genet's heightened style in the look of his film of *Querelle de Brest* 1982.)

Kemp's productions of these two gay texts arrived in London during a period when gay and transvestite theatre seemed to be everywhere with startling groups from America and France, as well as home-grown ones, swishing onto the gender-bender cat-walk. As we shall see later, many of these theatre groups were a direct response to the impact of gay liberation. But while this general climate may have helped to make Kemp's productions seem appropriately topical, it would be a mistake to dismiss him as an opportunistic drag queen ('kemping it up' and similar variants on the pun were often used). His stated ambitions 'to be glamorous and to charm' went much further back. He started his career as a dancer with the Ballet Rambert and other contemporary dance companies, eventually touring northern working men's clubs where his classic clown in pink tights and chelsea boots offered an unex-pected contrast to the usual diet of strippers and low comics. He appeared in films for Ken Russell and Derek Jarman, always odd and quirky, often disturbing. He had also directed – and appeared in – a series of David Bowie extravaganzas when the singer was going through his own gender-bending phase.

If, in his assumptions of Salomé and Divine, Lindsay Kemp was looking into the mysteries of gender and androgyny it was just one part of his armoury of theatrical weapons. There were no street-level politics in his work, no sub-text about changing society for the better. He once listed those weapons of his as 'my music, my voice, my beauty, my humour and my body. I have never restricted myself,' he added, 'I simply want to do it marvellously. I'm going to pull out all the stops till they call the cops.' Kemp's range is impres-sively wide and his ability to concentrate passion into frozen moments, split-seconds of silent stillness transcends sexual specifics, until his creatures become figments of the audience's own imaginations. Kemp can now be seen as the precursor of artists like Neil Bartlett in his seeking out of gay texts, submitting them to fresh interpretation and giving them a new resonance.

It was film director Ken Russell (for whom Lindsay Kemp appeared in his *Savage Messiah*) who was responsible for the latest manifestation of Salomé on the cinema screen. In *Salomé's Last Dance* (1987) the play is presented as an amateur show put on to entertain the clients of a homosexual brothel with Wilde himself among them, which grounds the gay sub-text in a very literal fashion. At first, however, it seems as though Salomé's dance is going to be the conventional strip by a teenage lollipop-licking Lolita figure. But Russell, perhaps predictably, has it both ways. At the climax of the dance the last veil reveals a young man flaunting his buttocks and cock at the audience's gaze. However, this climax past, it is the girl we see again. The veiled woman has revealed her phallus and become a woman once more.

Note

1. Merlin Holland, grandson of Oscar Wilde, has proved that the photograph is *not* Wilde, dating it to 1908. See the book pages of *The Sunday Times*, London, 24 July 1994.

Chapter four

The Things That Are Done by a Nun

THE lifestory of the Chevalier D'Eon de Beaumont might have been invented by Dumas *pére* – or even perhaps Baroness Orczy – and the name of this most high-profiled of all transvestites remains with us. Havelock Ellis – the pioneer sexologist – coined the term eonism to define the transvestite compulsion; the word never became universally popular (unlike Ellis's other inventions such as 'auto-eroticism' and 'narcissism', which were taken up by Freud), but is still used now and then. And the London-based organisation set up to provide support and information for (hetero-sexual) transvestites called itself the Beaumont Society.

But D'Eon was not the only celebrated transvestite to come out of France during the seventeenth and eighteenth centuries. There was Philip, the Duke of Orleans, known as Monsieur. He was the brother of Louis XIV and the husband of Charles II's sister Henrietta who, however, died suddenly in 1670. Later he married Charlotte Elizabeth, Princess Palatine who described him as having 'a big thick nose, a very small mouth and bad teeth'.

Despite this unflattering description it was agreed that Monsieur resembled his mother (Anne of Austria) to whom he was significantly attached. It was said that she deliberately brought him up 'as a princess' so that he would not become a threat to his virile and dashing brother. Contemporary diarists portray him as always dressed like a woman, as delighting in jewellery, make-up, wigs and scents. He seems to have been a quite attractive personality, very popular at court where he was happiest advising young women and girls on the best way to do their hair, choose their clothes and then helping them to dress and adorn themselves. Once more we find the repeated theme of women unselfconsciously enjoying the company of a drag queen and creating for themselves moments of frivolous theatrical relief, in this case from the formality of the French court.

He would devise little songs which, dressed in his finery, he would sing for the amusement of the court. One such had this verse:

> *Suis-je une fille? suis-je un garçon?*
> *Ton-ton, tontaine, ton-ton*
> *Peut-être l'un, peut-être l'autre*
> *Voyez, voyez, si ma façon*
> *Convient à l'une ou bien à l'autre.*

One of Monsieur's greatest admirers was the vivacious Madame de Choisy, wife of Monsieur's Chancellor, who used him as a role model for the bringing up of her son Francois Timoleon – later known as Abbé de Choisy, who was born in 1644. In his *memoires* he recalls: 'My mother made me wear bodices that were extremely tight and this pushed up the flesh. ... I also took care of my neck, rubbing it every night with veal broth and a pomade of sheep's foot oil which makes the skin soft and white. My hair was done into large black curls. I had big diamond earrings, a dozen patches, and a necklace of false pearls.' He also remembers '... a bodice embroidered with natural flowers on a silver ground and a skirt of the same material with a long train. The skirt was fastened up on both sides with yellow and silver ribbons, with a large bow at the back to mark the waist. The bodice was very high and padded out to make it appear I had a bust, and as a matter of fact I had as much as a girl of fifteen.' He constantly took precautions to keep his skin white, wearing masks in the summer to shade his cheeks from the sun, a preoccupation he shared with Monsieur, of whom it was said that during battle he was more afraid of the sun and gunpowder smoke than of musket bullets.

Monsieur was a frequent visitor *chez* de Choisy and the two young men seem to have had a lovely time getting into petticoats and skirts, arraying themselves with diamond earrings (Choisy had his ears pierced) and face patches and then settling down to cards and canapés with the bevy of well- born attendant girls who tended to treat Monsieur as their private pet. Choisy was always attracted to pretty young women and, unlike D'Eon, enjoyed several liaisons during his youth and early middle-age. But he dressed exclusively in women's clothes throughout his childhood and adolescence, wearing those of his own sex for the first time at the age of eighteen when he went to the Sorbonne. The following year he obtained the Abbacy of St-Seine, but decided he would rather be an actress and got a job at a theatre in Bordeaux.

'During five months I played in comedy at the theatre of a large city, dressed as a girl,' he recalls. 'Everybody was deceived: I had lovers to whom I granted small favours, but was very discreet as to great favours, and had a reputation for prudence and virtue. I enjoyed the greatest pleasures that one can taste in this life.' Why this promising and clearly pleasing career ended so quickly we are not told – it might have been due to the intervention of his family, some members of whom were frankly embarrassed by his behaviour. Most of his friends, however, seem to have been fascinated and not at all disapproving.

De Choisy's subsequent career was, by any standards, extraordinary. For a while he attended to his duties as an *Abbé* in Paris; later he set himself up as a *Comtesse* in the village of Crespon where his neighbours assumed he was a real woman; he was sent to Rome for the election of the Pope and appeared at the coronation ball in spectacular drag. He continued to live in Italy for a few years (probably as a result of family pressure again) still dressing exclusively as a woman. As deputy Ambassador to Siam he appeared at a public function there 'gorgeously arrayed in a feminine evening gown, make-up and jewellery'. The Siamese, apparently, thought it was some weird European custom. It was about this time – de Choisy was forty-one – that he reluctantly set aside his female clothes because he realised they were no longer becoming. He applied himself to church activities and to his writing which included his two volumes of *memoires*. But the drag was never packed away completely and in his old age de Choisy couldn't resist reverting to his life-long delight in complete transvestism. His

History of the Church was written while he was wearing women's clothes. His biographer D'Alembert comments: 'to appreciate the literary value of these ecclesiastical annals it will perhaps suffice to call to mind the picture of an old priest, more than seventy years of age, dressed in a costume unsuited to his age, sex and condition, working on a history of martyrs and anchorites.' In his *Memoires*, Choisy attempts a little self-analysis which may today sound a touch naive, but it does reveal with unusual candour something of the delight he found in transvestism. 'I have tried to find out how the strange idea came to me of believing myself a woman. It is an attribute of God to be loved and adored and man – so far as his weak nature will permit – has the same ambition. It is beauty which creates love, and beauty is generally the woman's portion; when it happens that men have, or believe they have, attractions for which they may be loved, they try to increase them by putting on woman's attire. They then feel the inexpressible pleasure of being loved. I have had that pleasant experience many a time. When I have been at a ball or a theatre in a beautiful dress with patches and diamonds and when I have heard someone whisper near me: "There is a pretty woman" I have felt a pleasure so great that it is beyond all comparison. Ambition, riches, even love cannot equal it, because we always love ourselves more than others.'

Choisy may have been convinced that presenting himself as a beautiful woman was the only way to achieve the love of others but becoming a woman physically and attracting men was not part of his scheme. Despite those mysterious 'small favours' he granted (presumably male) admirers during his days as an actress, de Choisy was an assertive – almost predatory – heterosexual man and enjoyed a regular sex life well into middle-age. He seems to have preferred young, boyish women, particularly actresses, and he drew a particular pleasure from dressing his mistresses up as young men and living with them, each cross-dressed. The first time this happened was when de Choisy was living in Paris where he would take his mistress right into the public arenas of the theatre and the opera house, introducing her as Monsieur de Maulny. Later, when living as a woman at Crespon he formed a liaison with another young actress. Again the girl was induced to wear boy's clothing while Choisy referred to her as 'the little Count'.

Another transvestite is worthy of note. He was a contemporary of de Choisy and also a cleric: the Abbé d'Entragues. The story is that his mother, desperately hoping for a daughter, was bitterly disappointed when she gave birth to a son and promptly proceeded to bring the child up as a girl. He was dressed and treated as such throughout his childhood and when he reached adolescence his complexion was kept pale by regular bleeding. Having a white skin was clearly a matter of great importance to these seventeenth and eighteenth century beauties, and as well as being bled d'Entragues slept with his hands tied above his head to keep them, and his arms, white.

When he became an Abbé, D'Entragues wore the appropriate clerical dress but indulged his need for female attire at night. He habitually slept in a corset laced with ribbons, a woman's nightdress, a nightcap trimmed with lace, a top-knot and other decorations and with patches on his face. He was described as being tall and well-built and notable for his skill at conversation. He was popular at the salons of smart hostesses but his line in caustic wit made him several male enemies. The striking pallor of his face always caused comment.

He seems to have led a fairly dissolute life and at one point revolted against the vows of the church and became a Protestant. A period of exile followed but he later repented and returned to Paris where he seized every opportunity to get into full drag. He also spent a period imprisoned in the fortress at Lille when he had offended the Duchess of Orleans who decided he had become quite mad. He was well-treated in prison and allowed everything he wanted – including a number of dolls which he loved to play with. D'Entragues was eighty when he died.

Both de Choisy and D'Entragues were, of course, clerics, which has led to suggestions that there may be some link between transvestism and the vestments worn by priests; an idea that cassocks, stoles, albs and the other ceremonial garments, often richly embroidered and executed in luxurious materials, are essentially feminine and would therefore be attractive to men who have a leaning towards drag. This assumption has always struck me as either superficial or a wilful distortion. But that there has been some kind of connexion can be demonstrated by the fact that the word 'frock' was originally used to describe 'a monk's wide-sleeved garment'. *Chambers Twentieth Century Dictionary* lists this as the word's first meaning, with 'a woman's or child's dress' as the fifth. The expression 'to furnish with a frock' is defined as 'to invest with priestly office'. There is a survival of this meaning when disgraced clergymen are 'defrocked', and also in the term 'frock coat' which has a similar root. All this has, though, little to do with drag as we understand it.

Choisy, however, with his obsession for clothes, set about converting his boring regulation clerical wear into something entirely feminine. In his *Memoires* he describes this process. When he first became an Abbé he began paying social calls on the local priest, the churchwardens and distinguished families in the neighbourhood. 'At first,' he writes, 'I wore only a dressing gown of black cloth, buttoned down the front with black button holes to the ground, and a train half an ell in length, which was carried by a lackey, a small peruke, slightly powdered, very simple earrings and two large velvet patches on the temples.' This he regarded as modest attire.

The people he visited accepted his appearance without comment – one curé told him that it was 'much more graceful than that of other young abbés, whose long coats and little cloaks did not inspire respect'. Thus encouraged de Choisy went a few steps further for his next round of visits. He undid five or six of the lowest buttons of his dress to reveal that under it he was wearing 'a robe of spotted satin the train of which was not as long as my dress. I had also underneath that a petticoat of white damask which was not seen except when the train was carried.' He also stopped wearing 'small clothes' – male underwear – which he didn't see as feminine, and managed to modify his gown further so that he could offer glimpses of those beautifully white shoulders of which he was so proud. Later he observes: 'I thought myself really and truly a woman.'

All this has overtones of the city businessman who wears a bra and panties under his suit, but de Choisy, sly and witty, was clearly a much more determined queen. Today, the reason any alleged link between clerical garments and women's clothes seems to me often superficial simply derives from the commonplace observation that even at the most elaborate of religious ceremonies (like the Coronation, for example) when the priests and their acolytes are dolled up to the eyebrows they simply look like priests splendidly robed to signify their special proximity to occult mysteries, their authority to communicate them and their distance from the unenlightened congregation. They look no more like women than does a Scotsman in his kilt – one of the butchest of uniforms. This distinction has been made very clearly by the Culture Club singer Boy George, who made some of his earliest appearances dressed as a nun. He has also used elements of Jewish religious costume in his stage clothes. Contributing to Kris Kirk's survey of mid-1980s female impersonators *Men in Frocks* Boy George wrote: 'I dress in a similar way to a priest or an archbishop. I wear robes, not dresses, and to be a transvestite you must wear women's under-garments. I don't.'[1]

I have also suggested that linking priestly robes with women's dresses is a wilful distortion, a view based not on accurate observation but on a need to denigrate, ridicule or undermine the church itself. Priests can be seen as a quite separate class within society, part of a political and social power base, and as such may be feared, perceived to offer a threat or quite simply disliked for their teaching, particularly on sexual and moral issues. To diffuse these feelings of fear and unease, to undermine the group's power, it is necessary to taint or demonise it in some way. Gay people, transvestites, immigrants, Jews and people with Aids are among those groups whose validity is trashed by wilfully inaccurate labels. To assert that because of their robes, the priesthood is effeminate or camp or homosexual (irrespective of any participating individual who may be one or all of these things) is a potent way of doing this. There is a well-worn camp joke about a person seeing for the first time a fully accoutred priest swinging his censer in church and hisses: 'Adore the drag, but did you know your handbag's on fire!' (Marjorie Garber attributes this shaft to Tallulah Bankhead and she may be right, but over the years I have heard it attributed to other famous wits including Noël Coward and Coral Browne!) But the message is the same: to accuse a man of being effeminate is one of the most damaging insults in a society where sexism still rules.

A more precise example of this occurs in Linda Grant's

survey of the sexual revolution during the last half of the twentieth century.[2] In it there is a taut chapter which describes how human sexual needs allied to the advancing technologies of contraception and abortion have undermined the stranglehold of the Catholic Church on the Republic of Ireland. The title of this chapter is 'The country run by men in dresses' and in it she comments: 'A priest is no more than a man in a dress, and the priesthood a kind of sex-defying transvestite brotherhood. ...' In the face of the powerful evidence she offers of lives ruined by intransigent religious teaching (and bearing in mind also the Vatican's teaching on homosexuality) one must share both her distress and her distaste. But throwing in transvestism as the ultimate put-down seems as flip as Tallulah's remark. Ms Grant offers no explanation for her image or any analysis of why she used it. Maybe she takes it for granted that everyone will understand and hopes perhaps that the trivial abuse will raise a smile. (The image also seems to me to hold the gut dislike that many feminist and post-feminist women feel for the transvestite – something which will be discussed in a later section.)

Any link between the ceremonial robes of formal religious observance and drag comes from somewhere else. Mainstream drag artists – in the theatre, cabaret or nightclub – have not as a rule used clerical garments as part of their illusion. When, rarely, it does happen the focus is on the figure of the nun and tends to broad comedy. The idea that nuns are funny, or at least fair game for a send-up, is not new and the man as nun is a recurring comic motif. We have already noted that in Rossini's 1828 opera *Le Comte d'Ory*, the dissolute count and his men gain entrance to the Countess Adele's castle by disguising themselves as nuns seeking shelter from a storm. Masquerading as the Mother Superior, Ory tries to insinuate himself with Adele in a duet which exploits the disguise in musical as well as dramatic terms. Later, when left alone, the male nuns express relish for their situation, discover the wine cellar and proceed to get drunk. A little more comic mileage is extracted as their riotous drinking chorus swiftly changes to a modest prayer when they are interrupted.

The basic, straightforward joke here is that of nuns doing things which nuns are not supposed to do – in this case get drunk. Nineteenth century romantic literature is peopled with nuns behaving similarly out of character – usually with some sexual objective in mind. In more recent years we have seen singing nuns, the nun as detective, the nun as killer and the nun as sex object – Sylvia Kristel dons the appropriate apparel in the seventh *Emmanuelle* film. The idea of a man dressed up as, or disguised as, a nun is a routine comic device in the cinema. During the last few years we have seen Burt Reynolds and Jack Weston as nuns, also Peter Cook and Dudley Moore, and in *The Magic Christian* Peter Sellers in a winged wimple and back gown running a disco and managing to look remarkably like Joan Crawford. In a 1989 movie which seems to owe a great deal to *Some Like It Hot*, Robbie Coltrane and Eric Idle are *Nuns on the Run* who take refuge in a convent.

In all these examples the joke is on the surface and like Rossini's, comparatively mild, working on the collision of opposites and of unlikely juxtapositions – such as the massively burly Robbie Coltrane in a substantial brassière and the veil framing Burt Reynold's famously aggressive moustache. Nobody seems to have taken offence at these impersonations, no protests were forthcoming from the guardians of morality and protectors of the church. But underneath these apparently harmless jokes does lie a fundamental criticism, one which needles a hypocritical church and its sexual intolerance.

The nun is a symbol of purity and virginity and therefore of innocence and unworldliness. A young woman who becomes a nun is said to 'take the veil' and therefore becomes, quite literally, a veiled woman, secret and apart, inviolate. To present a nun behaving out of character – being worldly, witty, practical, knowing and so on – is to create a special kind of excitement, bringing humanity to a cold and distant creature. To give her a sexual dimension is to add a more definitely titillating or even blasphemous spin. For to critics of the Catholic church – in fact to anyone unimpressed by organised religion of any kind – the nun is also a symbol of both wasted and repressed eroticism. Dragging away the veil, exposing the untouched flesh, is the ultimate violation. On one side of the coin the rape of a nun seems more shocking than the rape of a secular woman; on the obverse a nun who reveals a sexual appetite is infinitely more erotic than the normally libidinal woman. It is a consenting desecration of the virgin – which is, of course, why the nun is a recurring theme in pornography, an image of simmering sexuality.

It may seem that the sexual ambivalence of the nun (the conflicting statements of outer veil and hidden potential for the opposite) gives her something in common with the drag queen whose outward and visible form conceals an intriguing mystery. But the drag queen does not deal with the carnal realities of sex (I am speaking here of theatre, not transvestite prostitutes); the drag queen comments on sex, ridicules and satirises the social construction of sexual relationships; the drag queen takes us on a delirious guided tour of the bizarre antics that women – and by implication, men – seem forced to get up to simply to survive in a sexually polarised world.

The drag queen as nun can only be a minor comic figure who works, like the pantomime dame, on the humour of contrast and of inappropriate behaviour. And that is how she is presented in the context of undisturbing family entertainment. But the nun can be seen as an emblem of other aspects of institutionalised religion – sexual repression and denial, the nurturing of guilt, of self-hatred, of the necessity for repentance which may be followed by forgiveness – but only under strict conditions of penance and sacrifice. The nun now becomes a different kind of figure, baleful and threatening, a destroyer of spontaneity, harbinger of misery. And it is from this corner of the convent that a new kind of drag queen emerged in the early 1970s – the exuberantly vengeful nun, spreading anarchy and chaos, gleefully overturning the most cherished and ingrained restrictions of the church, challenging the sacred tenets of a strangling moral code. She whizzed along the streets of San Francisco on roller skates; she appeared in London zapping the Festival of Light. We will get to know her better in the next section when we take a look at radical drag.

Notes

1. Kris Kirk and Ed Heath, *Men in Frocks* (London: GMP, 1984), p 112.
2. Linda Grant, *Sexing the Millennium* (London: Harper Collins, 1993).

Chapter five

Amateurs

ALTHOUGH banished from the legitimate stage by the end of the seventeenth century the drag queen did not, we find, exactly vanish. It is arguable that the transvestite is always acting, playing a role, deceiving her companions and the famous drag queens of the seventeenth and eighteenth centuries on whom we have been spying certainly chose highly theatrical settings for their appearances. For D'Eon, de Choisy, D'Entragues and even the curious Edward Hyde were happiest when observed by throngs of admiring onlookers – at the opera, at state balls, at court ceremonies, in open carriages and the public streets. Maybe de Choisy actually did appear as an actress for a while, and D'Eon gave his fencing exhibitions in theatres, but it was their aristocratic playgrounds, frequent involvement in church rituals and acceptance at the courts of Europe that provided the arenas for their grand entrances and sweeping exits. It is hard to believe that wealthy, well-connected aristocratic clerics and diplomats were the only drag queens of these years (or vice versa). We may wonder how those blessed with less wonderful life-styles, who had no access to lavish gowns, jewels and patches and no leisure to spend hours on elaborate hair and beauty sessions with giggling young women managed to express their needs. There would be the age-old outlets of course – country fairs and festivals of Twelfth Night, May Day and *Walpurgisnacht* when men were given permission to get into skirts and parade as witches or other grotesque creatures, to dance in the revels, to parody the manners of the local lady of the manor. For the young homosexual street prostitution in the big cities might be an option, or dropping in for an occasional evening at a Molly

House and its later equivalents. But the drag queen insists on theatre, and the stage, amateur or semi-professional, provided for many the ideal solution.

During the nineteenth century theatrical activity in England was very different from that we know today. With virtually no opportunities for formal training and therefore no demand for it, and with no Equity to protect professional standards, anyone with a spark of talent or just enthusiasm could barrel their way onto the boards. A National Theatre was a dream for the future and the idea of state subsidy incomprehensible. And apart from self-devised entertainments at home, live theatre was the only place where people could go for entertainment or to be taken out of themselves for a brief hour or two. Consequently theatre was extremely popular. London had its great actors performing in spectacular productions and actor-managers constantly toured the provinces (even the smallest towns had their own theatre) offering material of varying quality. Less organised companies of players had no problem in getting dates. Alongside all this was the rapidly growing network of music salons which would quickly develop into the music hall – a more palatable evening out for the working-class than yet another *Hamlet*. Another important branch of theatre was the amateur stage, particularly productions put on by wealthy, upper-class families which would have the double advantage of allowing sons and daughters to dress up and show off, and to raise money for local charities.

The standard of the plays performed was much lower than that which today's theatregoers expect with (apart from Shakespeare) little reverence for the dramatic literature of the previous centuries. Outside the metropolitan centres where a more sophisticated theatre-goer could be catered for, the dreams and expectations of a regional audience were easily satisfied – and why not, there were no comparisons available and direct emotions usually achieve a direct response. Playbills and contemporary reports offer titles of plays once immediately popular but now long forgotten and certainly deservedly so – crude melodramas, sentimental romances, one-act comedies and simple-minded farces probably not that far away from the fare that television feeds its mid-evening couch potatoes today.

It was into this uncertain, exciting, arduous and alluring theatrescape that the drag queen slowly began to make her reappearance. In an article in *The Sketch*, published in June 1904, an anonymous writer observes 'the custom of not allowing women to appear (on the stage) still dies hard in certain places, and the time is quite within the memory of men still far-removed from middle-age when, in some of the Colonies, popular opinion first allowed woman to take her rightful place in the drama. The modern author,' he continues, 'does not by any means ignore the service of men as women, though it must be admitted that, when he puts a man in petticoats, it is invariably for a humorous purpose and not for the serious conduct of a scene.'

If we assume, as I think we might, that Colonial standards of behaviour lagged somewhat behind those of sophisticated London, the inference is clear. By the middle of the century audiences were quite used to seeing men play women on the stage now and then and probably, at that time, playing them seriously (that is, real disguise). Later, however, when men played women it was now for the purpose of broad comedy with the audience knowing the 'woman' was really a man and appreciating the joke (false disguise). One example was a play called *The Strange Adventures of Miss Brown* in which Fred Kerr masqueraded as a girl – after the moustache he wore in the first scenes had been shaved off. A more enduring exercise in this genre is Brandon Thomas's classic farce *Charley's Aunt*.

It is interesting to note that it was during the middle years of the nineteenth century that the word 'drag' was coined to describe the petticoats worn by men playing female parts. Eric Partridge in his *Dictionary of Slang and Unconventional English* dates the word to 1887 but, of course, words – especially slang words – are in currency for a number of years before they become accepted. Look how long it took the British press to use the words gay and camp without inverted commas! Once an activity has been given a name or label then that activity becomes separate from any other it might be related to. Hence acting in drag was now perceived as a special category of acting rather than simply just acting. Which suggests that though the drag queen was returning to her rightful place in the theatre itself, she was now different from her colleagues, occupying a special category. Usually this would mean that the actor who wore drag would perform in comedy, as the dame figure whose career we will explore in the next section.

But there were beautiful young men around for whom the dame was just a future possibility. Their here and now meant the impersonation of beautiful young women and in the loosely structured, anything goes theatre of those times, especially in the regions, they frequently found a suitable niche. Most of these impersonators are forgotten now, their memory surviving only as slightly puzzling names on old theatre bills ('The part of Lady Hester will be played by Mr Henry Adamson'), or as passing references in letters and occasional newspaper reviews. There are two, however, of whom we do know a little though not through the enduring quality of their acting but from a court case which fascinated and scandalised the late Victorians and even drew a leader from *The Times*. They were Ernest Boulton and Frederick William Park. They were both known to be gay and are discussed in *The Sins of the Cities of the Plain*, a survey of homosexuality in London published in 1881.

Ten years earlier in April 1870 Boulton and Park had been arrested and charged, not with homosexuality or any of its variants in law, but with conspiracy to commit a felony. One evening the young men, with attentive male escorts, were leaving the Strand Theatre after a show when a detective approached them and asked them to accompany him to Bow Street. One of the escorts immediately ducked and ran, but the other remained with them. In a report of their appearance in the Magistrates' Court, *The Times* indulged their fashion-conscious readers with a detailed report:

'When placed in the dock Boulton wore a cherry-coloured silk evening dress trimmed with white lace; his arms were bare and he had on bracelets. He wore a wig and plaited chignon. Park's costume consisted of a dark green satin dress, low necked, trimmed with black lace, of which material he also had a shawl round his shoulders. His hair was flaxen and in curls. He had on a pair of white kid gloves.' Boulton, the report continued, was wearing 'petticoats and stays and a white skirt. He wore ladies' white boots. The bosom was padded to make it appear very full. Park wore blue silk and complete female dress. He wore earrings.'

The defendants were eventually tried in the Court of Queen's Bench before the Lord Chief Justice of England, Sir Alexander Cockburn, and a special jury. Clearly, the establishment was much exercised by this incident and it soon emerged that other men, quite well known ones, were also involved. These included Lord Arthur Pelham Clinton, William Somerville, Martin Luther Cummin and C F Thomas. Lord Arthur, however, died between the two hearings (in June 1870) at the age of thirty, of scarlet fever aggravated by anxiety over the case. The trial lasted six days and at the end the defendants were acquitted because there was no evidence of any crime they might have been conspiring to commit. *The Times* was relieved as 'a verdict for the Crown would have been felt at home, and received abroad, as a reflexion on our national morals, yet which, for that very reason, could not be hushed up after popular rumour had once invested it with so grave a complexion'. After their acquittal Boulton and Park left the country and resumed their old lifestyle in Lisbon.

It is through the evidence presented with such detail during the trial that we learn something of the careers of these two young drag queens. Both were from the middle-class. Boulton was twenty-two and the son of a London stockbroker; Park was the same age and his father was a Master of Superior Courts. They were known to their friends, and to each other, as Stella and Fanny.

It was asserted that the theatre was their consuming interest. Young men who had taken Fanny and Stella out under the impression (they said) that they were fast women, gave evidence that their conversation was usually full of theatre gossip and similar matters and they found it 'lively and agreeable'. Boulton's mother was a witness for the defence and she told the court that her son had enjoyed dressing up as a girl since he was six years old and one of his delights was to dress up as a parlour maid at home when he had often deceived his own relations. He was, she said, constantly occupied with private theatricals, either at home or with friends, and that he always played female parts. She also knew that he acted with Lord Arthur Clinton in a variety of places – the Egyptian Hall at Chelmsford was mentioned, also Brentwood, Scarborough and Southend. 'His success was something wonderful,' she added, 'and bouquets were thrown on the stage.'

Another witness, an actor and musician who had arranged Boulton's acting partnership with Park, said that they had toured Essex with great success and he produced in court a playbill which advertised: 'Mr Boulton will appear in his wonderful impersonations of the female character which have gained for him a great reputation in London and the provinces.' He read out a selection of favourable reviews from local papers and added that sometimes Boulton had up to fourteen bouquets at one performance, and that both young men were frequently invited to supper at country houses after the show and, if requested, went along in their stage clothes. They posed for local photographers who produced postcards of them which were in great demand. One programme put on at the Spa Rooms in Scarborough in 1868 included *A Morning Call* in which Boulton played Mrs Chillington, and *Love and Rain* in which he played Lady Jane Desmond, a Young Widow.

The defence was emphasising the theatrical, and therefore respectable, nature of the men's cross-dressing, which now gives us some incidental information about the theatre of that time. But there was another aspect of their activities which had to come under scrutiny, which was why they were wearing drag off-stage. It emerged that when the detective accosted them outside the Strand Theatre, it was not a sudden decision. Stella and Fanny apparently made frequent public sallies in drag and were familiar in the West End. The manager of the Alhambra Theatre in Leicester Square said he had known them for about three years and described their public behaviour: 'They walked about the house in an unbecoming manner. The faces of the defendants were painted. Their dresses were very low and they were powdered on the neck and shoulders. A lot of men got around them. I ordered them out at once.' Later he described them at another performance when they were sitting in a box. 'They were hanging over, lighting cigarettes from the gas jets below the box. All the people in the auditorium were looking up at them; they were making stupid noises chirruping to each other with their lips; they were chucking each other under the chin and playing at frivolous games. A third person was with them ... they were turned out and the price of the box returned to them.'

The big variety and music hall theatres of London's West End were at that time popular cruising grounds for young men and women on the town, the corridors behind the stalls, the bars and foyers providing admirable opportunities for strolling, inspecting the goods, flirting and eventually scoring. The Alhambra's manager seems to have been more offended by the exhibitionist style of Stella and Fanny's picking-up technique than by the fact that they were men in drag. When the police raided the lodgings that Boulton and Park shared they discovered some sixteen dresses, very glamorous and daring, in satin, lace and corded silk. 'There were a dozen petticoats, ten cloaks and jackets, half a dozen bodices, several bonnets and hats, twenty chignons, and a host of curling-irons, gloves, boxes of violet powder and bloom of roses etc.' It seems that a passing curiosity about these two was that, even when in their ordinary male attire, they were frequently taken for women.

If the defence emphasised the duo's theatrical credentials, the prosecution sorted through the moral ones, exposing liaisons they had made with other men. John Stafford Fiske, the American Consul at Leith, had written letters to 'my darling Ernie'. He had heard that Boulton was living in drag. 'What a wonderful child it is! I have three minds to come to London and see your magnificence with my own eyes.' And a young solicitor in Edinburgh had written: 'Even in town I would not go to the Derby with you in drag. I am sorry of you going about in drag so much. I know the moustache has no chance while this kind of thing goes on.' Perhaps although infatuated with Boulton he still preferred his lovers a touch more butch. But the possible homosexual nature of these relationships was not fully exposed in court and eventually the prosecution was stuck for want of a crime and, apart from their going about in public dressed as women – which amounted to no more than a misdemeanour – there was nothing that could be proved against them.

In his summing up, Park's counsel invoked theatre history and practice. 'In former times (female) characters were always performed by boys; yet it was a remarkable fact that in the immoral reign of Charles II, when this was frequent, no immorality appeared to have attached to the practice. These young men (Boulton and Park) had performed female characters in many towns, openly and publicly, for charities, to the knowledge of the whole community and they were actually invited to parties after the performance and

desired to retain their female costume. The practice of men performing female characters prevailed at that moment upon the stage,
even with the sanction of the Lord Chamberlain. These things were
done; and, if so, why should guilt be inferred against these young
men because they did it?'

The jury agreed and the verdict was greeted with applause
and shouts from the public gallery. Stella fainted, but Fanny remained quite calm. By this time both had begun to grow their
beards again.

Had detectives and theatre managers not been subject to fits
of moral panic the fame of Stella and Fanny would have been
restricted to a few faded playbills tucked away in some forgotten
drawer in Scarborough or Brentwood. It is a pity that their photographs do not seem to have survived: they were apparently quite
charming but one collection was confiscated by the police and
others destroyed, along with other evidence, by friends. Stella and
Fanny were votaries of the secular drag queen, the exuberant exhibitionist anarchic figure who overturns the rule-book of polite
society, mocks its manners and parodies its modest social strategies.
They were young and clearly glamorous, assertively camp and
responsive to the gaze of a delighted or bewildered audience. They
look back to the off-stage antics of those Elizabethan and Restoration male actresses Dickie Robinson and Edward Kynaston and
forward to the exuberant glamour of today's young, strutting drag
queens.

Another rather more modest but nevertheless interesting
drag act emerges from the dusty newspaper files of the last decade
of the nineteenth century. This young man turns up in Ireland; he
had no ambitions towards the professional stage but kept himself
very busy with local amateur and charity dramatic work. Nor was
he as extrovert as Stella and Fanny and no scandal of any kind is
attached to him in any context. He seems to have given up his
female impersonations in his mid-twenties, and thereafter devoted
himself to the agreeable life of local squire.

Raymond de Montmorency Lecky Browne-Lecky of Flintimara, Warrenpoint, Co Down, and later of Ecclesville, Fintona, Co
Tyrone, Northern Ireland, was born in 1881. His enthusiasm for
acting developed when he was a youth and he soon discovered that

he had a notable talent for playing female roles. His mother encouraged him and his audiences from the upper-class or landed gentry enjoyed watching him and were, we are told, continually urging him to add yet another female character to his ever-extending collection of vignettes.

At first his fame was local, but he needed no pushing to appear further afield and caught the attention of the theatre critic of the *Irish Figaro* who was amazed. 'When I heard he was to play Lady Audley,' he wrote in 1899, 'I went expecting a burlesque of Miss Braddon's story. Nothing of the sort! High tragedy if you please, and Mr Browne-Lecky thrilling us all as the fascinating heroine, arrayed in all the armoury of jewels, exquisite toilettes and beauty, drawing us not with a single hair but with a wealth of soft, airy curls. Bewildered, I felt inclined to exclaim as Lady Macbeth did scornfully to her craven spouse, "Are you a man ?"'

The local press was less effusive (maybe they had seen it all too often) but still full of praise. 'Mr Browne-Lecky ... acquitted himself in the most perfect manner,' or 'Mr R de M Browne-Lecky played the heroine, wearing beautiful dresses, and made up most perfectly as a woman – and a very handsome woman, too, allow me to say.' After a charity performance at the Abbey Theatre in Dublin, the local critic, after some sharp comments on the inadvisability of amateurs tackling farce, remarks: 'Though I have a strong objection to the impersonation of females by men, even in pantomime or farce, his work it must be admitted was not unnatural or unconvincing.'

The works he tended to appear in were, consonant with the taste of the period, trifling but bearing that in mind his range seems to have been quite wide embracing monologues, fast farce, light comedy and melodrama. His most powerful, and most admired role was certainly that of Lady Audley in *Lady Audley's Secret*, an adaptation of Mary Elizabeth Braddon's melodramatic novel written in 1862 and tremendously popular for many years. The eponymous heroine is a pretty blonde bigamist who deserts her child, murders her first husband and has similar plans for her second – clearly the kind of role that any self-respecting drag queen would die for. But Raymond was not too proud to appear as a housemaid or lodging house slavey. Other roles he played have names that suggest the kind of plays popular at the time – Mrs Gushington Nervesby and Mrs Prettipet, for example.

Raymond's mother was a formidable character, a kind of Lady Bountiful with attitude. 'Mrs Browne-Lecky is known and loved as an absolutely unconventional woman,' one enthusiastic reporter informed her readers. 'Assured of her own position and always in the first flight socially, she takes no pains to emulate the proclivities of the smart set and being always out of doors and among young horses, she affects a tailor-made style of dress. With an amused look on her face she turned to a friend next to her at a recent afternoon At Home and said, "I believe I am the only woman in the room with a collar on!" To her the filmy lace throat bands stiffened up with safety pins did not constitute "collars".' And the *Ladies' Field* felt it was off-beat enough to note that at the local horse show 'she wore a plain linen stand-up collar and looked thoroughly well in it'. There was also a daughter, Patricia, who seems to have taken a seat somewhat behind her trenchant mother and fragrant brother. She also did some acting and singing but her engagement notice pointed out that 'in this particular her ability has always been rather overshadowed by that of her brother who goes in very enthusiastically for Thespian pursuits'.

And Raymond's enthusiasm was apparent in every detail of his appearance. Photographs show a tall, well-built young man with a heavy oval face, a full mouth and large eyes that look dark and somewhat sad. He seems rarely to have smiled at the camera but rather gazed at it directly, head slightly tilted. For his stage appearances he made up and dressed with extreme care and acquired a considerable wardrobe of drag. The periodical *Irish Society* revealed that a 'Mrs Slyne of Grafton Street makes his dresses and hats' and he must have been an excellent advertisement for this lady's skills. His clothes were interesting enough to warrant detailed description in the press. The *Ladies' Field* reported that 'as Lady Audley, Mr Browne-Lecky queened it bravely, at first in pale blue satin, covered with black Brussels lace and a toque of pink roses with white ostrich tips, and later in black satin with beautiful passementerie, and a wonderful array of diamonds'. The jewels he wore were a family treasure, a remarkable and famous collection. Presumably Mrs Browne-Lecky with her plain linen collars and sporty clothes had little inclination to wear them, but Raymond used them as often as possible.

Browne-Lecky continued his interest in drama and music throughout his life, but his drag appearances seem to have stopped around the time of his mother's death when he was about thirty years old. In 1911 he and his father moved from Flintimara to Ecclesville which had been his mother's home and which was haunted by a ghost whose silk skirts could be heard rustling on the stairs. During the First World War, he adopted his mother's role and organised entertainments for war charities and later he added a private theatre to Ecclesville where he put on plays and concerts. Always outstandingly – if sometimes eccentrically – dressed, he continued as local squire and benefactor until his death in 1961 at the age of eighty. The contents of Ecclesville were sold in an important two-day sale which (in 1962) realised more than £23,000. A gold and diamond ring reputed to have been the engagement ring of the girl Raymond did not marry went for £390.

Amateur dramatics on Browne-Lecky's rather elevated level, in which young men habitually played at least some of the female roles, were commonplace during these years and not considered odd as they most certainly would be today. In his *Plain Tales from the Hills* (1888) Rudyard Kipling includes a story called 'His Wedded Wife' which demonstrates that such activity was not unusual. A young lieutenant tricks a brother officer by dressing up as a woman and pretending to be his wife. When the ruse is revealed the brother officers are delighted with the joke and the lieutenant explains: 'I used to act at home with my sisters.' The narrator is less amused. 'Personally I think it was in bad taste; besides being dangerous. There is no sort of use in playing with fire, even for fun.'

What Mrs Browne-Lecky thought of her talented son we have no idea, but presumably she did more than merely tolerate his activities and perhaps even encouraged him to spend money on designer clothes, patronise private dress-makers and have the run of the family jewels on the principle of 'if you're going to do it you might as well do it properly in accordance with our social status'. Ernest Boulton's mother also seems to have taken a positive view of her son's pleasure in masquerading as a convincing young woman; she defended him in court stoutly enough. We have also seen how the mothers of both de Choisy and D'Entragues brought their sons up as little girls. Mothers tend to take a lot of stick whenever anyone feels a need to 'explain' cross-dressing. In this context the one famous transvestite who seems to have found his own answer was Edward Hyde, the Governor of New York and New Jersey in 1702 who, challenged when opening the Assembly in drag, declared: 'You are very stupid not to see the propriety of it. In this place and particularly on this occasion I represent a woman and ought in all respects to represent her as faithfully as I can.' He was actually a cousin of Queen Anne and bore some physical resemblance to her. Other transvestites, however, simply put the blame on mother.

It is outside the scope of this account to try and find reasons to explain the transvestite urge, but it is relevant to point out that the need to make clear distinctions between the gender of children virtually from birth (blue for a boy) is comparatively recent. Until they were five or six, both boys and girls were commonly dressed in similar clothes, garments which today we would describe as 'feminine'. Nor was this confined to the upper classes. I have a photograph of my father taken when he was about two years old, in 1912. He sits in a studio on plumped up cushions, little feet in buttoned shoes poking stiffly from beneath a frock trimmed with lace, a few stray curls escaping from his stringed bonnet. Another photograph, taken some ten years later, shows a scruffy street urchin wielding a cricket bat in his back yard. Dressing babies in the same clothes was probably a boon to the working-class as it would not be necessary to buy new ones each time another child appeared. Gender distinction, the separation of the males, came a few years later around the age of five with the first hair cut, shirts with collars, short trousers with braces and sturdy shoes.

This commonly accepted perception of the girlishness of little boys and the boyishness of little girls helps to explain why the title role in J M Barrie's play *Peter Pan* (1904) was designed for an actress and has, with one exception, been played by women ever since. The 'boy who never grew up' would retain this childhood androgyny, recognised by an audience who sees that a grown woman with her smooth skin and general hairlessness has more in common with children than has a grown man. To cast a mature male actor in the role as the Royal Shakespeare Company did in 1982 gives Peter an adult, knowing edge unsympathetic to the play. Nor should Peter be played by a woman in the thigh-slapping style of pantomime's Principal Boy, for much the same reasons.

Today we insist on early labelling. A mother dressing her son in frocks now would probably cause a local scandal and inspire the descent of social workers. This need to label, to separate, to make distinctions, to make sure there is no mistake, began in the late nineteenth century notably in medicine and what were then felt to be related areas. The word 'homosexual' was coined in 1869 and became current in England in 1890, thus creating a new, discrete category of behaviour which has created confusion and anxiety ever since. It wasn't until 1910 that Havelock Ellis made the first proper distinction between homosexuality and transvestism. The period we call the *fin de siècle* produced a new urge to distinguish between men and women, between their roles and their function in society. Some commentators have detected a similar need today, a hundred years later, with women making strong demands and men, in reaction, thrown into doubt and confusion.

Against this background, the drag queen becomes a symbol of sexual uncertainty and in many ways an agent of release from it. She slips fluently between the assertiveness of women and the passivity of men, creating a kind of balance which can make both men and women feel more secure. Perhaps mothers fostered the femininity they perceived in their sons beyond its social acceptability as a reminder that the male-dominated world in which they lived was essentially fragile. Mrs Browne-Lecky's own taste for tailored, masculine clothes might, perhaps, be seen as her contribution to the balance of this equation.

Certainly there was a great increase in the visibility of drag during the later years of the nineteenth century, also an evident interest in its fetishistic aspects. The literary historian Peter Farrer has unearthed and published selections of short stories, vignettes and letters to Victorian newspapers and magazines all relating to cross-dressing. Some of these are light comedies in a *Charley's Aunt* vein – young man dresses up as a girl to win a ladies' golf tournament kind of thing. But in some the sexual allure of female underwear is very clear. An excellent example is a brief story called 'The

Strange History of a Lace Petticoat', which was published in a magazine called *Modern Society* in 1892. It describes the theft of a provocative dancer's transparent petticoat and how it secretly passes from male to male, each of whom draws pleasure from handling the lace and silk. 'He fingered the dainty garment caressingly, and as he caught a whiff of its faint, insidious perfume, he conceived a wild desire to become the owner of it. . . .'

Little wonder then that it was during these years that the drag queen made her triumphant return to centre stage. Occasionally, when youthful, she might offer real impersonations of real women but now she is mainly working in collusion with an audience that recognises the man beneath the skirts, but does not (yet) wish to remove the final veil. Now the drag queen really spreads her skirts and begins to reclaim her many personae, half-hidden over the years but which she would now begin to develop and exploit through the coming century: the comical dame, the glamour girl, the social satirist, the sexual tease; the reminder that sexual anarchy lies only just below the surface and can rise at any time to challenge what appears to be an increasingly ordered society, and that biological realities can be concealed and transformed by the illusions – sometimes elegant and graceful, sometimes coarse and unsubtle, but always mysterious – of the theatre.

Part III

The Rise and Rise of the Drag Queen

Chapter one

Enter Pursued by Laughter

THE female impersonator had become a comic figure, a creature of burlesque and parody at the end of the seventeenth century. Her appearances on the stage during the next 150 or so years were occasional but by the middle years of Victoria's reign rehabilitation was under way and she strode into the twentieth century with a broad grin, arms akimbo, wearing a weird assortment of clothes that parodied high fashion, a bird's nest of a wig and a wildly overstated make-up. She was likely to skid on a banana skin revealing striped or frilly bloomers and her humour was robust and earthily domestic as she took the audience into her confidence and shared with them the trials of married life. She had become the pantomime dame; widely popular, inhabited by all the leading comedians of the day and serious theatre critics gave her serious appraisal.

The stalwart figure of the dame was to dominate perceptions of female impersonation for many years and in her traditional form she still makes her appearance in pantomime, going through her time-honoured comedy routines – the bread-making slapstick in the kitchen, coping with the haunted bedroom, dressing to the nines for the walk-down at the grand finale. During the last twenty years or so annual Christmas pantomimes have, sadly, become the exception rather than the rule and these once prime outlets for the dame are now limited. But you can't keep a good dame down; skilfully she has been busy metamorphosing herself into dozens of variations on the basic model. If the nineteenth century created a female impersonator who was an almost cartoon-like figure of low comedy, the twentieth century's contribution has been to add glamour and today's dame is as likely to shimmer and glitter just as much as her sisters the drag queens but always with that essential added edge of caricature.

Where the dame came from, and why she achieved such a height of popularity at the turn of the century, are questions worth a little exploration. Elderly or middle-aged women seem always to have been figures of fun to the English. I suggested in the chapter on early drama that the character of Noah's wife in the Chester cycle of Mystery Plays could be seen as an early model for future dame figures. She is a shrewish, bossy gossip, antagonistic to her husband, derisive of his boat-building activities – almost the stereotype of all the nagging wives and intrusive mothers-in-law pilloried by stand-up comics at pier-ends and in working men's clubs. However, there is no real dramatic continuity for this particular persona – the elderly woman as comic figure doesn't seem to have occurred to the Elizabethan playwrights. However, in different forms and on different social levels, she does reappear with the Restoration when she was played, of course, by real actresses. Lady Wishfort in *The Way of the World* claiming that her face looks like 'an old peeled wall' is an outstanding example and later came Mrs Hardcastle, Mrs Malaprop and a whole parade of scandalmongering harpies in the social comedies of Sheridan and Goldsmith. The greatest dame in drama is probably Oscar Wilde's Lady Bracknell – a role which unsurprisingly perhaps has attracted a number of male interpreters – but W S Gilbert also created quite a few in the Savoy Operas.[1]

These operettas reveal Gilbert as being soppily sentimental over pretty young girls but extraordinarily cruel to the older, usually unmarried woman who is a leading figure in each work. 'She may very well pass for forty-three in the dusk with the light behind her' cues in the general tone as early as *Trial by Jury* (1875). That is a well-turned, funny line but Gilbert's distaste seems to grow stronger until Lady Jane in *Patience* (1881) and Katisha in *The Mikado* (1885) are put into humiliating situations and given lyrics which need all the help they can get from Sullivan's soothing melodies.

This perception of Gilbert as misogynist is not the result of some new, feminist interpretation. As long ago as 1951, the writer W A Darlington felt the need to defend Gilbert on this matter, claiming that the writer's feelings towards his stock spinster characters was 'the exasperation of a father towards an unattractive daughter who will not accept the fact that she is unmarriageable, but goes on setting her cap at men and making a fool of herself.' Setting aside the evident fact that Darlington's 'excuse' today sounds just as sexist as Gilbert's original sin, there was probably some truth there. The nuclear family had not yet evolved and middle-class extended families still tended to live under the same roof and there would indeed be unmarried daughters – not to mention sisters, cousins and aunts – around absorbing time, money, attention. The Savoy Operas provided safe entertainment for the middle-class, for families who believed the theatre in general was immoral and dangerous. No doubt many exhausted fathers got a vicarious thrill from seeing their own family problem lampooned so unmercifully on the stage. And they may have found some consolation, and some soothing away of their guilt, when at the end of each opera the 'elderly ugly daughter' achieves a conveniently jolly marriage.

But this is one of the secret powers of the dame, she is the vicarious agent of lethal dreams. Appalling and humiliating things happen to her which her audience (perhaps shamefully) would like to see happen to a real woman – but it's alright, really because we know that they are only happening to a man. That teasing duality, like Sullivan's music, provides a distancing effect. The stand-up comic raging on about his wife and his mother-in-law has no such resources, no way of detaching himself from his material; it is his clear involvement that makes his diatribes so ugly. The dame is kinder – to us, to herself and to her targets. Once more we are reminded that while the drag queen inevitably focusses on women, all the forces that created that particular woman are also under attack. She knows that elderly, ugly daughters don't achieve that status all by themselves; they need a living context which tells them their value, which decides they are ugly and assures them that they are too old for marriage at forty. Which was what late Victorian society, and its much vaunted values, was about. The status of women has changed so much since then, as has society's attitude, that the pantomime dame today has no significance in this area and so she often appears as little more than a one-dimensional joke.

Apart from offering a covert comment on society, and engaging in knockabout routines, the dame could also turn on the pathos and instantly engage her audience's sympathy and affection. Of a leading mid-century drag artist James Rogers, the theatre commentator Clement Scott commented: 'The humour of Rogers was gentle and exquisitely pathetic.' Although extravagant clothes were an important feature of a dame's appearance in pantomime, the actual characters she played were often far from grand. Aladdin's mother the downtrodden Widow Twankey, Jack of the beanstalk's mother struggling with poverty and Mother Goose are all essentially working-class figures. And it was usually their intimate moments, confiding 'girlish' secrets to the audience that provided this opportunity for pathos. What were called 'slavey' types were popular creations outside pantomime – in variety, the music hall and vaudeville. These were definitely creations drawn from the lower classes – the maidservants, lodging house keepers, laundresses and flowersellers, all women struggling with the rough edge of life. We have no way of telling whether their touching monologues were designed to draw the laughter of disdain, or to alleviate an uncomfortable side of life with the humour of affection. All we do know is that the artists were greatly admired and certainly touched their audience's hearts. This quality of pathos and an innate gentleness possibly explains also why the dames were – and still are, when played by an actor of sensitivity – so popular with children who far from being terrified of the grotesque image seem able to look right through to the clown behind the skirts and then to the heart behind the mask.

But the essential clownish anachronism of a man in female clothes is the primary cause of laughter. How this works is neatly expressed in a non-theatrical context by Mrs Judith Loftus in Mark Twain's *Huckleberry Finn*. When Huck is dressed as a girl, Mrs Loftus spots the disguise and explains why: 'You do a girl tolerable poor, but you might fool men maybe. Bless you child … when you throw at a rat or anything, hitch yourself up on tiptoe and fetch your hand up over your head as awkward as you can and miss your rat about six or seven foot. Throw stiff-armed from the shoulder, like there was a pivot there for it to turn on, like a girl; not from the wrist and elbow with your arm out to one side, like a boy. And, mind you, when a girl tries to catch anything in her lap she throws her knees apart; she don't clap them together ...' Which is a nice enough analysis of those differing body languages that children pick up on very quickly.

It is sometimes questioned as to whether one can properly call the men who specialised in playing pantomime dames female impersonators. The reason for this is that none of them played women on a full-time basis, their drag acts were just one aspect of their comic talents. Dan Leno, regarded as the greatest of all the dames, often appeared in pantomimes playing one of the male comic roles, as Idle Jack for example or as Reggie, the boy babe in the wood when he was teamed with the massive – and equally admired – Herbert Campbell as Chrissie. Today we can admire some dame performances – Alastair Sim as the headmistress in *The Belles of St Trinians*, Les Dawson and Dick Emery's creations, Frederick Ashton and Robert Helpmann as the Ugly Sisters in Prokofiev's ballet of *Cinderella* – yet we would never describe these actors as female impersonators.

Certainly the first dames to appear in pantomime were actors expanding their range. The history of pantomime is long and complicated, containing elements of ancient Roman theatre and of the *commedia dell 'arte* but its genesis in England seems to have been the Harlequinades produced by John Rich between 1723 and 1760. These shows had elaborate scenery and special effects; they were popular but not associated with Christmas or with children. Over the years other forms of popular entertainment were plundered or grafted on; stories were taken from an eclectic range of sources including German fairy tales, slices of history and popular legends; elements were lifted from opera, ballet, music hall and musical comedy; all the available tricks and technical resources of theatre were employed to enhance the magic and spectacle. The theatre historians Raymond Mander and Joe Mitchenson comment: '(Pantomime) has moulded all these elements together over the past three hundred years into something which no-one but the English understand, or even want!' In the series of revues *Sweet and Low* produced in London during the 1940s, there was a sketch in which a Duchess (played by Henry Kendall, himself a noted dame) attempts to explain the mysteries of pantomime to a bemused G I played by Bonar Colleano: 'That's not a dame, that's the principal boy . . .'

Where and how this casting of cross-dressed principals began is as uncertain as many other aspects of this curious hybrid form of entertainment. Even though boys played girls on the stage up to 1660 and after that girls delighted in playing boys, there seems to be no unbroken line of continuous tradition. Perhaps the dame figure had her earliest incarnation when the male actresses of the Restoration were booted off the serious stage, and certainly burlesque involving men as comic women was familiar to eighteenth century audiences: we remember Charles Bannister dragged up as Polly Peachum for *The Beggar's Opera*, and another actor John Edwin had played Dame Turton (a low comedy creation), both at the Haymarket in 1780. These were not pantomimes, but burlesque which was a fairly adult and sometimes risqué form of amusement.

The first dame in what we would recognise as a pantomime was probably William Chatterley who appeared as Miss Abigle Antique in *The White Cat* in 1811 – notice that the character's name gives us a clue to her status, an early appearance of Gilbert's 'elderly ugly daughter' perhaps. In 1812 the great clown Grimaldi was Queen Rondabellona in another Harlequinade and in 1814 offered his Dame Cecily Suet in *Harlequin Whittington* at Covent Garden. These were not sudden, out-of-the-blue assumptions but represented the absorption of other theatrical customs into the developing pantomime which once there seem to have become formalised into a tradition. The same vagueness applies to the arrival of the Principal Boy. At the Adelphi Theatre in 1855 a show described as 'A Grand Coalition or Burlesque and Comic Pantomime' called *Jack and the Beanstalk; or Harlequin and Mother Goose at Home Again* presented Madame Celeste, a respected straight actress, as Harlequin giving her a claim to the title of first Principal Boy. A contemporary review commented that when actors and actresses, who are not pantomime players, take on roles such as Harlequin and Columbine then 'it will be readily conceived that not alone a mere material vehicle of whim has been provided, but that the whole is realised and animated by intellectual capacity of high histrionic rank.'

But usually the first Principal Boy is identified as Madame Vestris, one of the nineteenth century's most famous male impersonators. She was also, however, an astute theatre manager being the first woman to manage a London theatre when she opened the Olympic in 1831. In this capacity, Eliza Vestris had a hand in the evolution of the pantomime when she collaborated with James Planche (the librettist of Weber's *Oberon*) to create a series of burlesques. It was Planche who later explored the fairy stories of Perrault and came up with what are now familiar pantomime subjects – *Puss in Boots, The Sleeping Beauty* and *Beauty and the Beast* among them. These shows were much to the public taste and helped to displace the old Grimaldi type of harlequinade. Naturally enough, Madame Vestris played the hero in all Planche's creations and once more a tradition was created.

Meanwhile, a dame figure was emerging from another possibly less salubrious area of the entertainment industry, the music hall where she first appeared as a singer of popular songs, sometimes comic, sometimes pathetic. The embryo music hall was the all-male Song and Supper Clubs that flourished in the early years of the nineteenth century and which were an attempt to provide a more comfortable alternative for young men about town to the rougher and slightly more dangerous ordinary pubs and taverns. There was a host who acted as chairman who would keep order and invite his customers to get up and do a turn. Out of work singers and actors would keep their hand in by performing as well, some of them wearing women's clothes to add point to their numbers. Later Concert Rooms and what were to be called Tavern Music Halls were popping up all over the working-class areas of East and South London. They were no longer all-male and, though patronized by fashionable men and by men and women of questionable character (as one writer put it), these taverns were mostly orderly and provided agreeable evenings out. What is acknowledged to have been the first music hall proper was The Canterbury which opened in Lambeth in 1852 and enlarged in 1854. Entertainment was varied and of a high quality even extending to excerpts from ballet and opera. It was here that extracts from Gounod's *Faust* were first heard in England. A popular performer was E W Marshall who regularly assumed skirts for his songs.

Soon most male performers were including a drag number in their repertory, but they were never exclusively female impersonators. In a long and crowded programme an artist might be expected to make several appearances and a turn in skirts would simply add variety and display another aspect of his talent: he might be singing other songs in the characters of a shepherd, a costermonger or a sailor for example. The drag was one part of a wide comic vocabulary. The songs chosen were mainly comic and often made fun of the marital dilemmas of middle-aged women. There was no attempt at this time for the performers to present themselves as youthful or glamorous figures in drag: a grey wig, bonnet and shawl or a pinafore were the only props needed.

This, then, was the other background from which dames were emerging. But throughout the nineteenth century the singing pubs and music hall taverns were patronised essentially by the working-class and young men about town looking for adventure. They were certainly completely off limits to the middle classes, who would also shun the more splendid music theatres of the West End where they might run the risk of bumping into Fanny and Stella. At the most, they might patronise Mr Gilbert and Sir Arthur Sullivan's light operas at the Savoy Theatre. But the Christmas pantomime was a different thing: it was family entertainment, a legitimate treat for the children. And it was when pantomime extended itself to include elements from the music halls that the dames were seen and enjoyed by a much larger section of the public. Variety itself did not achieve full social acceptance until the first Royal Command Variety Performance in 1912.

The man who thought up the neat idea of bringing stars of the music halls into pantomime was Augustus Harris who, at the age of twenty-eight, took over the management of the Theatre Royal, Drury Lane. The first production under his regime was *Mother Goose* in 1880 – and he started as he meant to go on. The line-up included Kate Santley, a star of light opera, as the Prince and Arthur Roberts from the music halls delivering topical songs. There was a chorus of lovely young ladies, two ballets and a grand transformation scene. The following year it was *Robinson Crusoe* with Fannie Leslie in the title role and Arthur Roberts again, this time playing Mrs Crusoe. The pirates were a chorus of attractive young women and once more there were ballets and a spectacular transformation scene.

Harris, known to his friends as Gus and to others as Druriolanus, had built on the work done by Madame Vestris and Planche, adding in his own ideas and thus set what has ever since been thought of as the 'traditional' English pantomime. The male impersonators slapped their thighs as Principal Boys and the dame comedians went on the rampage for a whole evening. There was always space for the speciality turns which had made them successful in the first place, but the need to sustain a whole evening in one character naturally led to a considerable extension of their range and several of the leading comics of the day are remembered specifically for their dame impersonations at the expense of other characterisations they perfected. Appearance in one of Druriolanus's pantomimes set the seal on an artist's career; it was considered the height of achievement partly because of the 'high class' audience and partly because it represented an acknowledgement of the artist's abilities. Wilkie Bard, a famous dame, once announced that while he was extremely proud of being in demand at Drury Lane audiences should remember that he started his career singing in pubs. The assertion seems to suggest that other artists preferred to forget or cover up their humble beginnings.

Druriolanus piled success on success during the next sixteen years until his death in 1896, turning his spotlight Christmas after Christmas onto the greatest popular stars of the day. But not everyone was happy about the direction pantomime had taken. One outspoken critic was the theatre historian W Davenport Adams; the only good thing he could find to say was that at least the profits from a successful show at Christmas enabled a manager to produce 'legitimate' theatre for the rest of the year! He found the invasion of music hall artists onto the legitimate stage offensive because 'they have the effect of familiarising general audiences, and children especially, with a style and kind of singing, dancing and 'business' which however it may be relished by a certain class of the population, ought steadily be confined to its original habitat.' Several times he makes the point that the songs, dances, gags and dancing to be seen on the pantomime stage were unsuitable for children and should be seen as offensive by their parents. 'Over and over again must mothers have blushed at the exhibition of female anatomy to which the "highly respectable" pantomime has introduced their children.' The cross-dressing made him particularly uncomfortable. 'A man in woman's clothes cannot but be more or less vulgar, and a woman in male attire, of the burlesque and pantomime description cannot but appear indelicate to those who have not been hardened to such sights.' He concludes his attack: 'A genuine "boy prince" would, I think, be an attraction in productions of this sort, and I don't see why the mother of Aladdin should not be enacted by a lady of suitable capacity.'

Mr Adams was, perhaps, tending to miss the point of pantomime, but his attitudes to the clothes – not enough of them in one case, and the wrong sort in another, were reflected in yet another form of entertainment which was just beginning at this time. The first musical comedy *In Town* was produced at the Prince of Wales Theatre in 1892, and the star comedian was the highly popular Arthur Roberts – who had been Harris's Mrs Crusoe a decade earlier. He found the experience very different from what he had been used to in variety and pantomime, having to conform to a written plot which didn't allow for passages of improvisation, and recognising a fairly realistic setting. Although this was technically the first musical (as opposed to operetta) it didn't set the trend. That happened two years later when the great impresario George Edwardes found he had a copper-bottomed hit on his hands with *A Gaiety Girl*. In his determination to add contemporary realism to his shows, he rejected all the dress codes of pantomime and burlesque: women were not to wear trousers or tights, men would not wear skirts, the ladies and gentlemen of the chorus would be dressed with modest elegance in designer clothes from Bruton Street and Savile Row. In this respect musical comedy has followed these precedents through hundreds of long forgotten shows right up to the present day, which may be one reason why drag never really had a role in musicals.

By the end of the century the status of the dame comedians had risen considerably. They still played variety, music halls and pubs during the year but now had the chance of a much prized season in pantomime each Christmas. The changes in the form that Augustus Harris instituted at Drury Lane were quickly adopted by theatres in the big provincial towns. At Christmas 1900 for example, there were two pantomimes playing in the West End, twenty-four productions in the London suburbs and thirty-eight in the provinces. So there were many well-loved dames playing all over the country and a number of which were particularly regional favourites. But between 1880 and 1910 it was London who produced the major stars.

Note

1.   Recent male interpretations of Lady Bracknell include Billy James, Los Angeles *c.*1979; Quentin Crisp, New York, *c.*1980; Dame Hilda Bracket (Patrick Fyffe), London, 1987; and Paul Clayton in Paul Doust's *Lady Bracknell's Confinement*, 1989.

Chapter two

Dames by the Dozen

GROUCHO Marx once made a distinction between the amateur and professional senses of humour. The funniest thing in the world for the amateur, he suggested, would be a man dressed up as an old woman in a wheelchair rolling out of control down a steep slope and crashing into a wall. But to make a pro laugh, he said, it would have to be a real woman. This is the path the dame comedians trod – somewhere between Mr Punch actually killing his wife with a hammer and the cartoon cat who after being squashed flat by a boulder reassembles itself to fight again. For a few seconds the disaster seems real and the audience explodes with laughter, but the dame reconstitutes herself and the implicit cruelty is assuaged with reassurance.

And unquestionably the dames were essentially funny men; the laughter they were able to generate did not rely exclusively on skirts and an Adam's apple bobbing under a frilly bonnet; their work as great clowns extended to other personae as well. Men who are funny in themselves are rare today, men like Ken Dodd, Tommy Cooper, Les Dawson and Eric Morcambe. The drop in popularity of variety as an attraction for a mass theatre audience and the rise of television as the pre-eminent showcase are responsible. There are plenty of funny lines, but few funny men.

The most famous of the early pantomime dames and still regarded as the greatest was Dan Leno, clearly a comedian of superlative genius and whose dame characterisations were one aspect of his repertory: beefeater, shop walker, waiter and grocer were among the much-loved characters featured in his songs and sketches. But in the chequered history of pantomime, his is the only name that has ever been linked with that of the great Grimaldi himself. Leno was born in 1860, the son of a couple who played second-rate music halls. The stage name of his mother's second husband was Leno, which young Dan assumed. He began his career as a singer of Irish songs and when touring in Lancashire discovered clog dancing, entered competitions and after a six-day contest was proclaimed Champion Clog-dancer of the World. The swiftness of his foot-work and his India rubber legs, soon matched by a natural verbal invention and dexterity, were features of his future comic routines. His first pantomime engagement was as dame at the Surrey Theatre in 1888 where his huge success attracted the attention of Augustus Harris who secured him for the 1889 pantomime at Drury Lane where he played 'The Naughty Aunt' in a concoction based on *Babes in the Wood* and *Robin Hood*. He become a star at once and returned to Drury Lane regularly until 1903, the year before he died at the age of forty-three.

In an impression of Dan Leno, Clement Scott – the most powerful theatre critic of the day – wrote: 'In petticoats and as a representative of the lodging-house and slavey class, he would have beaten Jimmy Rogers at his own game. When we see Dan Leno as a woman and hear his delightful patter it never strikes us that here is a man imitating a woman. It is a woman who stands before us, the veritable Mrs Kelly, not a burlesque of the sex, but the actual thing. He catches every expression, every trick, every attitude, every inflexion of voice, and all is done without suspicion of vulgarity. In his grim earnestness consists his humour. The comedian who laughs at his own jokes soon becomes wearisome, but it is Dan Leno's astonished face when he looks at the laughing audience that gives him his power. In brief a most admirable, versatile, persuasive, volatile and intense comedian and artiste. Whenever he is on the stage, be it theatre or music hall, he literally holds the audience tight in his power. They cannot get away from him. He is monarch of all he surveys.'

Another commentator, Ernest Short, observed: 'The essence of Lenoesque humour was the speed with which absurdity was piled on absurdity, leaving time for nothing save laughter not too far removed from tears. When Dan was on the stage the laughter was not noisy.' By today's standards Leno's scripts when read coldly on the page make one wonder what all the fuss was about and one needs to bear in mind what those who actually saw him point out his speed of delivery, his range of inflexions and his ability to enthrall an audience with a swift glance or a raised eyebrow. This is an example from one of his confidences delivered as an ill-used widow:

'He's so kind – so different from my first husband. Oh, I've been married before, girls. Yes, I'm a twicer. My first husband was a Spaniard. When he was cross, oh, the way he used to look at me, with his black eyes and dark olive skin. Oh, girls, beware of olive-skinners.'

And here he is on Mrs Kelly, one of his invented characters to whom he gave a reality that audiences accepted with delight. 'You see, we had a row once, and it was all through Mrs Kelly. You know Mrs Kelly, of course – Mrs Kelly – Mrs Kelly? You know Mrs Kelly? You must know Mrs Kelly. Good life-a-mighty! Don't look so simple. She's a cousin of Mrs Nipletts, and her husband keeps the what-not shop at the – Oh, you must know Mrs Kelly. Everybody knows Mrs Kelly. . . .'

In between pantomimes, Leno toured continually, appearing in music hall all over the country with a workaholic intensity which led to a nervous breakdown (from which he recovered to continue his punishing routine). In 1901 he was commanded by King Edward VII to give a performance at Sandringham, and when he died his funeral procession was watched by more than three miles of mourners standing three deep.

The 'discovery' of the twenty-eight year old Dan Leno might be seen as one of Augustus Harris's greatest strokes of luck. But Druriolanus had a discerning eye for talent and for artists who would bring in the crowds. The dame in his second pantomime was Arthur Roberts, destined to have a long and successful career in all branches of popular musical theatre. In 1882 *Sinbad the Sailor* had featured the beautiful Vesta Tilley with her tiny waist and spangled tights as Captain Tra-la-la, but also Herbert Campbell as Mrs Crusoe.

Campbell was born in 1844 and started his career as part of a black-faced minstrel act, but by 1870 had become established on the music hall circuit as a comic singer and a dame comedian – one of the songs associated with him was called 'In My Fust 'Usband's Time', once more reflecting the audience's curious preoccupation with elderly widows. Campbell was to stay in pantomime at Drury Lane for twenty-three years. For a few years his regular partner was Harry Nicholls (with whom he would occasionally swap roles, as it were, Nicholls doing a memorable impersonation of Ellen Terry) but he found a perfect comic foil when Leno turned up and together they became a popular partnership. When they teamed up together it was Campbell who played the dame: he was a tall, well-built man and towered over the diminutive Dan. In *Dick Whittington* (1894) Campbell was Eliza the Cook, Leno was Idle Jack. For one routine Campbell chose to send up the 'new woman' in collar and tie, plus fours and spats intimidating with her cane a quivering Leno as a rattled (and rattling) guardsman. As the babes in the wood three years later, Campbell is the huge Chrissie in frilled party frock with a vast sash, while Leno is Reggie in a little boy's suit.

The contrast in size between the dame and her male targets has always been an important element. Reviewing a production of *Cinderella* at Liverpool in 1907, *The Stage* commented:

'Comical contrasts in stature have served in stage pieces for many years so that, although not a novelty, the diminutive husband with the satirical name Hercules, and the massive wife christened Tiny, obviously serve for great fun.'

Campbell and Leno worked on this contrast throughout their partnership; it even worked when Leno was playing dame. In *Bluebeard* (1901) the lofty Campbell in the title role glares down at the sixth slave he has just bought (a winsome Leno as 'sister Anne') and roars: 'There's some mistake, I never ordered a *remnant*!' Both men died in 1904, leaving a sad gap. Harry Randall took over as dame in 1904 and the following year Walter Passmore, a singer from the D'Oyly Carte Opera Company at the Savoy, played the Baroness in *Cinderella*. But managers would be needing replacements – and there were quite a number available. A new generation of dames was ready.

There was, for example, George Robey who eventually became known as 'The Prime Minister of Mirth'. He made his debut – as a trial turn at a matinee – at the Oxford Music Hall in Tottenham Court Road in 1891 and was an immediate hit. Within ten years he could afford his own personal staff to help him get through four shows (at different theatres) a night. His trademarks were a clergyman's coat and heavy, arched eyebrows which he could raise with magisterial effect. Robey's versatility was impressive and he was able to move easily between pantomime, variety and – later – spectacular revue. At the Alhambra in 1921 he led a ballet in which the ladies of the chorus were uniformed policemen down to the waist and fairies in tutus below that. He also impersonated Millais's picture 'Bubbles' – with a big clay pipe. Like all the great variety acts, Robey travelled all over the country so his dame appearances were not confined to London and each Christmas he would turn up in another regional city, Birmingham or Liverpool or Manchester. He died in 1954 the year he received a knighthood.

There was also Wilkie ('Billy') Bard who was so proud of his early career as a singer of coster songs in pubs. When established as a dame he would use the opportunity to introduce and popularize songs such as 'She sells seashells'. He died in 1944. Another really outstanding dame figure of these years was Malcolm Scott who, unlike most of his rivals, did not have a musical hall background but started his career as a straight actor. But he went onto the halls at the London Pavilion in 1903. Within three years he was established as a ranking dame. Also unlike his fellow dames Scott, for his solo acts in variety, specialised in comedy impersonations of famous women among whom he included Catherine Parr, Nell Gwynn, Boadicea and Salomé. Eventually his billing was 'The Woman Who Knows'.

A 1905 caption to a photograph of Scott (face impassive beneath a cloth cap) says: 'Malcolm Scott is one of the most perfect "ladies" on the pantomime stage. He has done many daring things: among them he has visited Hanley, he has worn sandals with evening dress and he has blushed with modesty for the thrilling things done at sea by Admiral Percy Scott, his brother.' Scott's appearance was not at all glamorous, but neither did he assume the caricatured, slightly grotesque look Dan Leno and the other dames had given to their widows and downtrodden 'slavey types'. In fact Scott seems to have been one of the earliest of the female impersonators proper, rather than – like the others – being an all-rounder for whom playing dame was a periodic assumption.

There were many other comedians who became dames during the first decade of this century, celebrated and much-loved at the time but whose names are forgotten now: Scott Barrie, Harry Conlin, Dan Crawley, Tom Conway – famous for his considerable girth – who worked as a double act with George French, John Humphrey and George Graves. The so-called traditions of the pantomime had been set. Many of the basic stories used for the shows did not contain a role suitable for a dame comedian, so characters were invented – such as the Cook in *Dick Whittington* and Widow Twankey – to become immediately institutionalized. Another increasingly popular dame character was that of the nurse who fitted easily into stories involving children such as babes in the wood, and Snow White usually had one as well. There was a general agreement that if, in *Cinderella*, the Baron was married then the Baroness would be the dame role. However, if he was a widower then the Ugly Sisters could be the drag parts. There seems to have been a feeling that a pantomime could only sustain one, or at the most two, dames. This particular piece of theatrical tact appears to have been abandoned in 1953 when the London Palladium's *Cinderella* offered Cyril Wells as the Baroness, plus Jon Pertwee and Tony Sympson as Buttercup and Dandelion (Julie Andrews had the title role).

The basic 'look' of the dame was also established. For most of her role, the dame wore the ordinary clothes of the working-class woman – a plain skirt, an apron or shawl, sturdy boots and her hair parted severely in the middle, drawn ruthlessly back behind the ears and decorated perhaps with a top-knot or stray ringlet. This look pre-dated Dan Leno: his mentor from the Surrey Theatre George Conquest Jnr used the same appearance when playing dame. 'The spectacle of George Conquest's portly figure attired in the garb of a respectable lower middle-class female with a high forehead resembling a pink bladder of lard was very laughter provoking,' wrote one critic. And this look scarcely changed for almost fifty years. Shaun Glenville can be seen in photographs dressed exactly like this for his performance as Mother Goose in 1924, and so can G S Melvin as Nurse Merryweather in *Babes in the Wood* twelve years later. In 1920 at the London Hippodrome, Nellie Wallace played dame – one of the first real women to do so – and she too dressed in the same style. Among the glitter of the trans-formation scenes, the ballets and romantic ballads, the dame was a constant reminder that pantomime (as evolved by Harris) had roots in working-class entertainment: she involved the audience directly with her confidences, delivered her 'personal' songs, engaged the attention of children and was the prime target for physically testing knockabout routines.

But the dame's wardrobe of drag contained other outfits too. Clothes for speciality moments (which probably had nothing to do with the story) of which a high point was the sending up of current fashions as when Herbert Campbell presented the 'New Woman' or when Dan Leno entered the Magic Pool as an elderly Mother Goose, worn with work, and emerged young and lovely in a very pretty dress which Zena Dare might have worn. But the frills and demure blouse, the fluffed out curly hair and flower-trimmed bonnet are totally subverted by Leno's bleakly dismayed ex-pression. In a production photograph it looks very much as if Mother Goose has been goosed. Then there was the drag for the big walk-down at the end when all the troubles are over, the babes found, Cinderella gets her prince and the goose lays its golden egg. This was always an over-the-top ensemble – huge crinoline, spar-kling and spangled, high powdered wig infested with birds and flowers, neck and arms hung with absurd jewellery: if a working-class woman of the period came into a fortune would she blow it on such a display of conspicuous consumption? Audiences it seems liked to think so and obviously enjoyed the sight of the underdog, the down-trodden dame coming out on top at last.

The dame could offer another image as well – that of the pretentious dowager, regal with fan, tiara, furs and a high collar of pearls in a reflexion of the style adopted by Princess Alexandra, the Princess of Wales, and adopted by the queens of high society young and old. Queen Victoria herself didn't seem to offer much of a role model for dames – maybe such a reference would have counted as treason, or at least roused the anger of the Lord Chamberlain; or maybe she was too dull or too sacred. It would be many years before Billy Wells, a popular dame of the post-war years, added a hilarious study of the Widow of Windsor to his repertory of characters.

So the dame's range of female personae was fairly wide,

ranging from charwoman to *grande dame* and incorporating elements of the clown, the stand-up comedian, the popular singer and
the benevolent uncle (or aunt). I have outlined these basic elements
in some detail because during the forty or so years when pantomime was supreme, a tradition of female impersonation evolved
and became codified which has informed the art – in all its aspects –
throughout the present century. There were a few exceptions to the
rule, as we shall see, but during those years the dame was the only
form of drag that the theatre-going public was aware of. Moreover
it was accepted, it was respectable, it was something almost every
comedian tried his hand at one time or another. But things would
change. New forms of entertainment were being created, there
would be a war, women's fashions would change radically – as
indeed would women, perceptions about class would alter and all
these would have their influence on the next generation of female
impersonators. But the dame figure has her roots in the late nineteenth century and continued – like pantomime itself – to acknowl-
edge them in ways which began to make the shows seem so often
archaic rather than traditional, no longer the flexible and malleable
vehicle of its origins but fixed, predictable, stuck in a groove. The
pantomimes lapsed into formula; standard scripts became the
norm, simply incorporating 'traditional' features such as the
haunted bedroom scene, the nursery and so on.

For these set pieces the dame was usually left to her own
devices and expected to provide the comic routines herself. In 1951
the distinguished actor, director and revue artist Henry Kendall was
asked to appear in *Old King Cole* opposite Vic Oliver in Manchester. He has described his surprise when he was first given his script:
'Tom Arnold was paying me a big salary, but it seemed out of all
proportion to the size of the part, but on closer inspection I found
there were pages and pages of blank paper headed "Scene 6" or
"Scene 7". Being a novice in this pantomime lark I hadn't realised
that I was supposed to supply the missing material! – and when I
did, I really panicked! All through my career, even in revue, my
parts and dialogue had always been written for me, and here I was,
with only ten days to rehearse in, expected to build up a "Dame"
part from practically nothing!'

He managed though. 'With the help of Bob Nesbitt and a

few old pantomime veterans who were playing small parts, I managed to evolve one or two reasonably comic scenes including the time-honoured "sack" gag, also the ditto "haunted bedroom" scene which included a "strip-tease".'

In the event Kendall's Queen Aggie in that pantomime was a triumph; he was expensively and elaborately gowned, he relished the expected knockabout antics and led the audience in a group of old time music hall songs. But there are, he pointed out, dangers for the actor who diversifies his talent in this way. 'Pantomime is all very well for variety artists who can fill in with summer shows and music-hall dates – and of course, television – but it's a mixed blessing for a straight actor. Very few managers will engage a star for a West End show if they know he has to leave the cast at Christmas to fulfil a pantomime engagement; and exactly that happened in my case. Not a part came my way after *Old King Cole*.'

Performers with the kind of background Kendall was referring to were increasingly rare in the 1950s. But even by the 1920s artists from the music halls were becoming rare birds, no longer around to deliver their own 'personal' songs and instead Principal Girls and Boys were reduced to plugging pop songs, which made pantomime a focus of great rivalry among music publishers each year. Satirizing current fashions continued, as did making fun of social crazes such as G S Melvin with his comic interpretation of the open-air cults of hiking and cycling, and Will Evans who in 1920 informed his audiences that 'All the girls are busy knitting jumpers' as indeed they were – and so were the men in the chorus. Female dames were tried (not very successfully) and by the late 1950s the Principal Boy had become a real man – a ballad singer (Edmund Hockridge, 1958), a television comic (Jimmy Tarbuck, 1968) a pop singer (Cliff Richard, 1964) or a straight actor (Edward Woodward, 1972). But nothing seemed able to save the pantomime. There seemed to be something of a revival in the 1960s with a succession of glamorous big-name productions at the London Palladium and the then top-ranking impersonator Danny La Rue in his own spectacular at the Saville in 1968. But by the early 1970s it was clearly becoming redundant as a form of mass entertainment and in 1992 *The Daily Telegraph* could only list twenty full-scale, professional pantomimes nation-wide.

But these five or so decades of pantomime did produce a splendid gallery of dames many of them written about by critics with almost the same awe with which they recorded Gielgud's Hamlet or Eva Turner's Turandot. The classiest commentators from Clement Scott to Harold Hobson were all vulnerable to these anarchic old women, just as much as the audiences were. But assessing the excellence of a dame must, inevitably, be a more subjective process than that of assessing a great Hamlet, say, or a great Tosca. In these examples there is a basic text from which the actor or singer works; experience and constant comparisons give the critic his tools for appraisal based on the artist's interpretation of those texts.

As we have seen, the dame has no such basic and constant text to rely on. The player's personality, powers of invention and improvisation, ability to provoke laughter in adults without alienating the children (and vice versa) and ability to create moments of intimacy as well as broad comedy are all important. The response of the audience itself is important, and a dame playing in Manchester or York will inevitably have a different approach, accent and terms of reference from one playing the West End of London or Oxford. So one individual's 'great dame' may not necessarily be another's. The comedian Nat Mills (whose double act with his wife Bobbie received top billing through the 1930s) was described by Vesta Tilley herself as 'the best Mother Goose since Dan Leno'. Today the music hall artist George Williams – himself an accomplished dame – says: 'My favourite dame was George Lacey. His Mother Goose has never been eclipsed. Wonderful!' George Williams remembers another dame whose name has virtually disappeared from the records, T D Newell whom he saw in 1924. 'He was a most wonderful and original dame. I remember him sitting on a beer box looking out of the window through lace curtains, and saying: "Her supposed to be a widow! I've seen the shadows on the blind. And why does the milkman give her all the cream and why does the gas man come out in a dream. ..."'

One of the dame's basic themes was still going strong – the nosey, gossipy woman, chattering about her neighbours, but with possibly rather more sexual innuendo than Dan Leno applied to his Mrs Kelly. And it is a theme that has remained, seen at its best among the comedians of the north of England and brought to perfection by the late Les Dawson who told journalist Patrick Newley: 'I'm just a working men's comic. I know my roots and I don't really like to stray out of them.'

George Lacey was discovered by the manager Francis Laidler who was always asking his agents to try and find him some funny women, but his dames were always men. Another dame was held in great affection was G S Melvin, the satirist of the open-air cult, who died in 1946. His range included revue and variety, when he launched some of his famous songs such as 'I'm Happy When I'm Hiking'. Generally he presented his dames in caricature style, creating an outrageous girl guide with spectacles, a kiss curl and flaming red nose. He also specialised in the 'Nurse' roles, which have also been a constant dame theme. George Williams does the Nurse Wintergreen who tends Snow White and Les Dawson's Nurse Glucose was always a great success with children. He would sometimes entertain them in his dressing room after a show, still in drag and in character, handing out sweets.

One of the greatest dames was Shaun Glenville the son of Mary Glenville Browne, manageress of the Abbey Theatre in Dublin, who appeared as an Irish balladeer at the Holborn Empire in 1907. He played in musical comedy and in straight plays in London and the regions and developed his particular talents for pantomime. He did not always play dame, but he always appeared together with his wife the beautiful Dorothy Ward, famous for her legs and consequently a greatly admired Principal Boy. Mrs Crusoe, Dame Trot and the Queen of Hearts were among Glenville's funniest and most affectionately remembered creations. Creating hilarity and mayhem around the country were George Graves, George Jackley, Wee Georgie Wood (who also specialised in the pathetic comedy parts such as Buttons and Wishee Washee) and the still well-remembered Norman Evans, whose 'Over the Garden Wall' act was yet another manifestation of the gossipy female persona.

By the 1960s the annual pantomime circuit was getting smaller and the year-round variety theatres were closing as the new wave of pop and rock singers were failing to replace the dancers, speciality acts and stand-up comedians who once provided audiences with their live entertainment. A career as dame in the established tradition was becoming impossible. Those who made an impression during those declining years were rarely full-time female impersonators but comic actors whose main work lay in other media – notably television and cinema. Perhaps the most popular was Arthur Askey whose character of 'Big-Hearted Martha' (a play on his usual billing as 'Big-Hearted Arthur') recurred in many pantomimes over the years. At the London Palladium in 1964 he was Widow Twankey in a chic kimono and a Vidal Sassoon style wig; he was back in 1968 as Mrs Crusoe in mini-skirt, fun fur and Dusty Springfield wig. Notable too were Terry Scott who, with his partner Hugh Lloyd, were a big success on television. They made ideal Ugly Sisters; Lloyd shy and retiring, Scott brassy and cruel. Scott's version of the 'traditional' strip-tease number is one of my own 'great dame' memories as, to suitably sleazy music Scott divested himself of layer after layer of increasingly ugly, violently coloured clothes. Other connoisseurs of the dame will remember Dickie Tubb, Albert Modley, Richard Hearne and Sonnie Hale as Daphne Dumpling in the 1955 *Dick Whittington*.

Among the crop of dames in 1992 were the apparently inexhaustible Danny La Rue, John Inman, Roger Kitter and Roy Barraclough (all familiar television actors) as well as older, well-established artists like Chubby Oates (with a fifty-four inch bust) and Jack Tripp. Up-and-coming dames included Chris Harris who presented a happily traditional Widow Twankey in Bristol, wearing clothes that looked back to Dan Leno and who included well-worn slapstick routines involving putting up wallpaper and baking cakes. Alan Ford, another Widow Twankey, this time at Stratford East, offered something quite different, according to one commentator a 'bad-tempered widow-woman with cigarette smoke in her throat ... unkempt and unwashed.'

Pantomime may have been dying around the dame for several decades, but the dame was not left stranded with nowhere to go. It was necessary to diversify, to recreate herself in other forms and in other places. 1914 brought the Great War, but it also brought about changes in showbusiness and in women, that would provide both opportunity and armoury for a different kind of impersonator, one for whom glamour was a prime ingredient.

Chapter three

All Legs and Limelight

NATURALLY the dames were represented as middle-aged or even elderly characters – full of life and energy, perhaps, but still getting on in years. The men who played them were usually rather younger, at least at the beginning of their careers – Dan Leno was twenty-six when he got into drag for his first dame at the Surrey Theatre in 1886. And the men who eventually became famous dames made their names in the first instance as comedians, novelty dancers or balladeers who included perhaps one drag spot to vary their routines. Absent from theatrical records are reports of young men playing young women, men who made a career of female impersonation from the beginning.

But of course they existed. We have already met Fanny and Stella who between their glamorous excursions into London's nightlife, took their acting quite seriously. And we have no reason to believe they were unique. In his unusual and interesting novel *The Antique Collector*, Glyn Hughes offers a convincing portrait of a drag artist who played the rough pubs and music halls of the trans-Pennine tracts from Halifax to Blackpool before and after the turn of the century. Although the work is, of course, fiction it is thoroughly researched and smells of authenticity. Again, we have no reason to imagine that such characters were unusual. They were, however, denied the main stages of the commercial theatre and had to be content with obscure dates in the regions. It might have been quite simply that being young and not yet very experienced these fledgeling drag queens were just not up to the standards that an increasingly demanding metropolitan audience wanted.

A more likely explanation, however, is that there was no place in current theatre for young men impersonating pretty young women. Female impersonation was associated firmly with comedy. For serious plays, even trivial ones, there were plenty of young actresses around. There was also the question of what a late Victorian audience perceived as glamour and how they reacted to it. There were, of course, legions of 'famous beauties' around and women from high society were just as likely to be given such a title as any actress or music hall artiste. Such purely physical attractions were not enough, in themselves, to justify impersonation; women who were impersonated tended to be satirized not so much for their looks but for their other activities. In fact, if a man did impersonate a famously attractive woman he would be much more likely to make fun of the looks themselves rather than try and offer a copy of it like so many drag queens do today.

For example, in 1903 a pretty young woman called Camille Clifford made a memorable debut in a show called *The Prince of Pilsen*. She had a deliciously up-tilted nose and wore a gown which displayed her shoulders, emphasised her bosom and clung to her hips giving her the soon to become classic 'hour glass' figure. She had a particularly alluring walk which some described as 'a glide'. She became an instant model for high glamour and was known as The Gibson Girl. Her style was widely copied by aspirant young women and the image appeared on postcards, calendars and posters. The female impersonator Malcolm Scott ('The Woman Who Knows') quickly included her in his repertory of celebrated women, exaggerating the figure and topping it off with a typical 'dame' wig with its centre parting and hair scraped back. Later drag queens would try to be even prettier than Camille.

Another woman who created a rather different kind of sensation in the first decade of the century was the Canadian dancer Maud Allan, an experimental dancer who tried to interpret Chopin and Mendelssohn with a few feet of scarf and bare feet thus creating a tiresome trend as eager young women tried to copy her style for amateur entertainments. Allan's *Vision of Salomé* in which she danced the whole story displaying a wide, bare midriff and hung about with large pearls was considered scandalous and she was accused (you guessed) of inciting public immorality. Another target for satire and the challenge was taken up by, among others, the versatile Harry Gabriel Pelissier who – a very bulky man – bounded about the stage with a long green scarf and flourishing a daffodil. These two examples suggest how the impersonation of even attractive young women was influenced by the dame tradition. There is also the feeling that too close an impersonation of the desirable woman by a man might touch the nerve of the Victorian's sexual anxiety. It was safer to see young women as one-dimensional, innocent maidens and older women as forbidding dragons: Yum-Yum and Katisha, Cecily Cardew and Lady Bracknell. The reverberations of the Oscar Wilde case had created the new fear of homosexuality and erotic transvestism was little more than an underground whisper.

But change was on its way and, perhaps unexpectedly, Harry Gabriel Pelissier was one if its agents. During the first years of the present century, light entertainment in England was beginning to develop in new directions. The music hall and pantomime traditions continued, offering opportunities for the dame impersonator. The musical was now on its way, though as we have seen, managers disliked elements from burlesque in their shows and the 'low comedy' spots in the hits like *The Arcadians* or *The Chocolate Soldier* were in the hands of bright young soubrettes and their male partners. Revues – intimate and spectacular, which would eventually include drag spots – were being developed. Another form of entertainment which had began to flourish by the end of the century was the concert party. Typically this would be a small troupe of multi-talented variety artists touring the country and giving shows. Sometimes the groups would consist of women and men, sometimes just men. Being small companies, with no scenic resources and minimal instrumental accompaniment, they tended to be confined to the suburbs of larger cities, but the 'pierrot troupes', as they came to be known, soon became a regular fixture at various seaside towns which were now reaching their peak of popularity as resorts for family holidays.

Pelissier's Follies was one of the first of these little companies and the energetic actor-manager achieved success in London (and a Royal Command to Sandringham) before his early death at the age of thirty-nine. Typical too was Fred Karno's *Mumm-*

ingbirds which consisted of five young men, of which the leading player was Sydney Chaplin and another member was Stan Laurel. When the opportunity came to send the party to America, Karno included Sydney Chaplin's young half-brother Charlie with them and no doubt Charlie Chaplin's early experience with the troupe helped him with the drag scenes in his 1915 film *A Woman* in which he dresses as a woman to avoid pursuers. When he first puts on the clothes he is still wearing the famous little moustache, which puts him the comic-grotesque dame category. When he shaves he becomes a very pretty and convincing girl and we have an early example of the dame tradition meeting the newly developing interest in glamour impersonation.

The minstrel and pierrot shows continued, with lessening success until the Second World War and for years many people's most vivid seaside memories include the concert party in a tent on the beach or at the end of the pier. One of the most famous was *The Quaintesques*, an all-male show which, under the guidance of Billy Manders, ran for many years in North Wales. These shows gave young men their first chance to appear as pretty young women; they also promoted the mimicry or impersonation of well-known, usually theatrical, personalities as a legitimate turn on the variety bill. Often it was the girls in the company who would impersonate women, but in all-male troupes the men also had a go. A new form of drag entertainment was being born.

Though revue is associated largely with the 1920s and 1930s as a result of the varying influences of Max Reinhardt, Florenz Ziegfeld, Albert de Courville and Charles Cochrane, attempts towards the form had been made much earlier. In 1905, for example, George Grossmith and Henry Gratton devised a show called *Rogues and Vagabonds*. One number was about three chorus girls. Two were played by Kitty Hanson and Elsie Clare but the third was always Gratton himself. He would wear different drag each night, appearing sometimes as a bright young thing on the town, sometimes as the conventional dame figure, sometimes as a Principal Boy in the spangles and tights. Hanson and Clare spent each evening in a mild sort of agony, never knowing how Gratton would appear and whether its effect would put them quite off their stride. Another particularly gifted actor who was to enjoy a long career in various kinds of musical show was the immensely popular Nelson 'Bunch' Keys who once remarked: 'I have a fly paper mind. Things stick to it.' In the revue *Buzz-Buzz* (1915) he offered an impersonation of the musical comedy star Jose Collins who was having a huge personal success in *The Maid of the Mountains* (which, incidentally, includes the song 'A Bachelor Gay Am I', once a popular housewives' choice). In the following years revue would continue to offer opportunities for a drag spot.

The First World War produced a significant increase in female impersonators. This was marked in America by the newspaper *Variety* which in 1923 observed that the numerical strength of impersonators was heavily swollen after the war when recruits from the ranks of many service acts entered vaudeville and remained there. Another factor was that after the Great War (as after the second) many servicemen found themselves without a job. One solution was for those men who had already participated in concert parties and touring shows devised to entertain their fellows-in-arms to get together again and entertain the civilians. In some cases a young soldier might have discovered that he had a talent to amuse while serving and decided to try and make a career in showbusiness irrespective of other considerations. All of which accounts for both the survival and revival of the concert party in the 1920s.

One correspondent described to me the memory of a show she saw at Paignton in Devon when she was a schoolgirl in 1926. The entertainment was an all-male concert party formed from ex-servicemen who could not get work. 'The effect was most grotesque but one performer, though as tall and loose-limbed as the rest, looked and sounded uncannily feminine. "She" sang – or rather said, to music, in a very light voice "I've a wife and a kid ... oh, I would ... if I could ... but I can't ... but he did" and brought the house down!' The comic emphasis was now some way from the innocent monologues of Dan Leno and the new breed of drag queens were starting to make capital out of their equivocal status; a 'woman' confiding about her experiences with men now becomes an almost transparent cover for homosexual flirtation.

The concert party she saw might well have been the most celebrated of all, *Splinters* which consisted entirely of ex-servicemen and in France was known as *Les Rouges et les Noirs*. The show – described on its billing as a 'revusical vaudeville' came to the London Coliseum in 1920 and featured Hal Jones as 'Splinter'. The leading lady was Reg Stone and in the first London production the ladies of the chorus were named as Mr Vivian Taylor, Mr Jack Richards, Mr Ernest Green, Mr Jimmy Slater, Mr Teddie Martin and Mr Jack Hives.

Splinters was produced by Eliot Makeham (who was also in the men's chorus) and played the Queen's Theatre in Shaftesbury Avenue and to capacity houses in all the major centres for almost two decades. It went into several editions, had its own slogan ('Start saying Splinters, then see it!'), made three films and provided a spring board for many of the most successful impersonators working in the years between the wars. Many of them were still working in the 1960s, including Jimmy Slater, Chris Sheen, Billy Carrol and Douglas Harris. The company continued to exist for two decades but by the late 1930s was clearly past its sell-by date. An early photograph suggests that the ladies of the chorus, with short skirts and bobbed hair, were young, pretty, slim and to the untrained eye typical of chorus girls everywhere. Another snap, taken in 1936, shows the ladies growing older – clearly six stalwart chaps in drag.

Today we would probably find *Splinters* nothing more than mildly amusing. But, like the other concert parties, it was instrumental in helping to create the kind of glamour drag that would burst out in the similarly founded shows that appeared after the Second World War. It seems that initially the World War I shows took the attitude that putting a man in a frock was in itself funny and the effect, as noted above, was 'most grotesque' in the dame tradition. However audiences were soon showing greater interest in the more glamorous-looking girls, amazed and delighted by the illusion. Presumably the fact that the men were ex-servicemen and were therefore somehow 'forced' into drag to earn a living helped to excuse audiences from looking more closely at any other possible significance of the boys in drag.

Line-ups of lithe, leggy chorus-girls did not pop up from nowhere. They reflected in miniature changes which had been happening in the way women themselves dressed and the way women were being newly perceived. Late Victorian and Edwardian clothes managed to both emphasise and deny the female body. Shape to the upper half was given by a corset – or 'bustier' – which extended from breast to mid-thigh producing a smooth, pigeon-like effect. Padding of the lower half had reached a peak of exaggeration with the bustle, but even though that was becoming more reduced in size a woman still had a prominent, smooth and cushiony backside. Neither fore nor aft was there any embarrassing reminder that a woman might have two buttocks and two breasts, small, distinct and separate. And her legs remained a mystery, too. There was every reason why a female impersonator would avoid any reference to the sexual woman and why the dame, operating from the safe area of what was taken to be non-sexual middle-age, dominated the art for so many years. There was one artist who enjoyed a period of popularity in London at the turn of the century and who could be categorised as working in the glamorous style. This was the Swedish female impersonator who was billed as '?Lind?' – with two question marks. His speciality was impersonating the Spanish dancers which were favourites on variety programmes, but a studio photograph shows a stately woman with the pigeon-shaped bosom and the sweep of a possible bustle behind. His main gesture to glamour seems to have been the exposure of his smooth, round shoulders; but he also looks much younger than the dame figures and is undeniably attractive.

By 1920 the change in the way women looked was quite remarkable. Although fashion historians like to chart this process on a detailed year by year basis, the two significant changes were that skirts became shorter and women cropped their hair. Both were a result of women's demands to be more active, to participate easily in sports, to be independent, which meant dispensing with restricting skirts, layers of petticoats and with hair that needed a great deal of attention. The invention of the brassière made the elaborate corsetry of previous years redundant for younger women. The range of images available to women was suddenly much wider: they were being suffragettes and flappers, driving cars and taking jobs, moving more significantly about the world. By 1919 the cinema was beginning to exert its influence too. Close-up photography under the unyielding Californian sun meant movie actors had to be young, beautiful and with flawless complexions. The cinema was also busy presenting a new gallery of sexual images (for men as well as women) to captive audiences across the western world. It was, as Jack Lemmon remarks in *Some Like It Hot*, 'a whole new sex'.

A glimpse of the whole process of this transitional period can be seen in the career of one young drag queen, a fifteen-year-old Welshboy who adopted the stage name of Peggy Deauville – a name that carried its modish ring through five decades. He began his career as an impersonator when he was fourteen and audiences responded to his versatility, which included acrobatic dancing and a penetrating singing voice. During the Great War, many sections of the serving forces were able to make their own entertainment, but groups of performers were also sent out from this country to divert the harassed troops (as in succeeding wars) and Peggy Deauville was one of them. He went to France in 1914 and remained there throughout the war. Initially he was placed on what was called the HQ rota, which meant being posted to different places as a solo turn. But after three years he was assigned to a concert party called *The Duds* and then to *The Bohemians* which ended up in Paris. Peggy stayed on there for four years playing, among other theatres, the Folies Bergères. 'The concert parties I joined,' he told me, 'were really professional and only the best of performances were accepted by the staff officers in charge of the entertainments.'

Apart from singing, dancing and playing in comedy sketches, Peggy specialised in giving impressions of famous women which, as we have seen, was becoming a favourite item in concert parties and revue. He portrayed Edith Cavell, Gaby Delys and Jane Renoir (whom he closely resembled). Photographs show a tall, slender youth with big eyes and a wide mouth which is sometimes provocative, sometimes offering a cheeky grin. In France he enjoyed travelling in drag and is so photographed in some magazine war reports wearing the conventional Pierrot costume with frilled collar and black pom-pom buttons but with the addition of high-heeled shoes and black net stockings and surrounded by a squadron of amused and admiring soldiers. 'As I was very slim in those days so corsetry was not necessary,' he recalled.

He placed great emphasis on always being fashionably dressed and the crucial changes in fashion are reflected. During the war years he wore clinging drapes and hobble skirts, fringes, shoes with straps crossed around the ankle, a bandeau across his forehead and a waist-length plait of hair. A few years later he presents the typical flat-chested flapper in harem trousers, a long necklace of knotted beads and cropped hair. Peggy Deauville worked consistently over the years, and toured in Europe again during the Second World War. In old age he would still do the occasional turn for functions at his local branch of the British Legion.

Concert parties – whether composed of ex-servicemen or not – provided the ideal training ground for the new form of glamour drag. But the dames continued to emerge from their ranks as well, most notably Clarkson Rose who was born in 1890. After graduating from singing in pubs to chorus work he spent a few years acting in the straight theatre but in 1921 created his own concert party which he called *Twinkle* in which he continued to involve himself until his death in 1968. It was a popular, greatly-loved show and made world-wide tours, but Clarkson Rose's greatest fame was as one of this country's leading dames. In fact he could be found as dame somewhere every Christmas for fifty years and one newspaper dubbed him First Dame of the British Empire. He brought a rare and devastating hauteur to the role. Whether he was Mrs Crusoe, Widow Twankey or an Ugly Sister, the eyebrows raised in aristocratic query and the superior turn of the mouth were consistent trade marks.

Another great dame who introduced a note of upper-class superiority into the surrounding mayhem was Douglas Byng. He began his career in a concert party called *The Periodicals* at Hastings in 1914 but he was to develop into a unique and extraordinary figure on the drag scene. He first played pantomime in Bournemouth during the First World War, but as the prince's friend. Dames came later but although he mastered the expected knockabout comedy routines he was, he says, 'always a snob about my dame characters. I refuse to be a cook or a nursemaid, and insist on being Alderman Fitzwarren's housekeeper, or governess to the Babes in the Wood'. Byng was the grandest of dames especially when able to dress and behave as a regal duchess or other powdered and bejewelled dowager and appeared in more than twenty-five pantomimes.

Constantly in demand as a dame though he was, Byng's

talents extended beyond that particular arena and he achieved even greater fame in revue and cabaret. His opportunity came when he got a job as a dancer and understudy to Ernest Thesiger in Nöel Coward's 1925 revue *On With the Dance*. This was one of C B Cochran's spectacular revues and had a glittering cast which included Alice Delysia who sang 'Poor Little Rich Girl'. The comedian Archie Bascombe was scheduled to join the show for its London opening and meanwhile Byng played one of his roles for the try-outs in Manchester and Liverpool. In the event Bascombe was unable to be in the show and Byng retained the part. This was a hilarious, low comedy sketch called *Oranges and Lemons* in which two slightly *passé* women, sharing a room in a boarding house disrobe for bed. Byng played Grace who is 'rather set for maturity' and dressed in slightly matronly clothes. Ernest Thesiger was Violet, the same age but more skittishly dressed in a fringed tea-gown. Their sparring develops into up-front bitchiness with Violet presenting herself as an experienced woman of the world, Grace responding with middle-class censoriousness.

> Grace: (looking under her bed before getting into it).
> I always do this in case of cat burglars.
> Violet: How droll of you. I'm never nervous of that sort of thing.
> Grace: Indeed!
> Violet: I expect it comes of being so cosmopolitan.
> Midnight visitors hold no terrors for me.
> Grace: I should be more inclined to conceal that fact than boast of it. Good night!

When, later, two men stumble into the darkened room and try to get into the beds it is, of course, Violet who panics and Grace who offers a cooing welcome.

Byng's star rose swiftly and he appeared in many revues for C B Cochrane and André Charlot. His speciality was performing character songs which he wrote himself. They were sophisticated and often slightly suggestive: he was a master of the innuendo. His 'I'm a Tree' became a national favourite and other hits included 'Doris the Goddess of Wind' and 'Old Father Thames'. These eccentric numbers were alternated with sketches and songs in drag: Boadicea and Nell Gywnn were impersonated and he dressed appropriately for songs like 'La Belle Chichi', 'The Pest of Budapest' and — much later — 'Blackout Bella'. Soon he was on the cabaret circuit, playing the smartest clubs in London, Paris and New York, part of the very smart international set associated with the café society of those years. Byng's memoirs are ankle-deep in the dropped names of long-forgotten social lions.

Sophisticated, camp, a caricature of glamour, Byng was unique in bridging the gap between pantomime — which was essentially a working-class entertainment — and the sophisticated amusements of the upper-classes. The two forms inevitably fed off each other with Byng's dames having that extra sharpness and style needed for revue and cabaret work. In cabaret he would sometimes not use full drag at all: a length of material, an elaborate collar, a flower ... would say it all. Byng was also an elegant actor, especially in drawing-room comedies and could still be induced to do a turn for special occasions right up his death in 1987.

Even in his younger days, Byng never tried to present himself as a conventionally glamorous woman, the edge of caricature was always present. Other neophytes from the concert parties, especially *Splinters* did. Those with personal ambitions realised it was unwise to remain with an all-male show for very long and attempted to carve careers for themselves as individual acts. One problem was that once an entertainer had played in drag, then such was the nature of the theatre, that they were unlikely to secure non-drag work on the professional stage. This often led to periods of hardship with impersonators having to take part-time jobs to make ends meet. They also realised (as another generation of drag queens was to realise three decades later) that glamour in itself is not quite enough, so began to exercise their talents for comedy and for the ever-popular act of impersonating showbusiness personalities. Notable was Jimmy Slater who did a fan dance in the briefest of bras and g-strings and whose extensive wardrobe included dresses given to him by Sophie Tucker. Douglas Harris from the 1924 cast of *Splinters* teamed up with the Australian impersonator Kenne Lucas and another partnership was that of Ford and Sheen who made a feature of their glamorous appearance and were one of the few drag acts to appear in a film (*Skimpy in the Navy* with a young Max Bygraves, 1949). Bartlett and Ross was another act which survived on glamour, as elegant in the gently draped frocks of the 1930s as they were in the tighter, body-hugging evening dresses of the 1950s.

All these acts, sooner or later, capitulated to the years and concentrated on comedy and pantomime. Double acts were able to create contrasting characters, making them ideal Ugly Sisters. Terry Bartlett, for example, offered a really ugly Ugly Sister while Colin Ross upstaged him in perfect make-up and elegant gowns. Their repertory included a ballet routine on points, a mother and daughter act and a mermaid sketch. Their partnership came to an end when Colin Ross died and in the 1960s Terry Bartlett partnered a new young impersonator, Chris Shaw, for a few years.

These established acts were ready and available to join the second generation of all-male revues that sprang up again after the Second World War. The first of these was called *We Were in the Forces* and opened (while the war was still on) at Warrington in March 1944. As before, the initial promotions suggested that the performers were ex-servicemen recreating for the civilian public the shows they had concocted to amuse themselves while serving. The success of the original show took everyone by surprise; the public flocked and filled the theatres and the promoters made a great deal of money. There was nothing to suggest, in those dark days, that the public had any appetite for drag shows on this scale. Perhaps audiences attended out of a sense of loyalty to the soldiers, or perhaps just because those days were dark, the gaudy colours and brash attack, the exaggerated clothes and sense of anarchic fun were attraction enough. Managers, seeing they were onto a good thing, set up more and more revues for touring the nation's theatres. Their titles emphasised the shows' origins – *Soldiers in Skirts*, *Forces Showboat* and *Forces in Petticoats*.

At the top of the bills were the old stagers, Bartlett and Ross, Ford and Sheen and Douglas Harris whose send-up of Carmen Miranda was a highlight of the shows in which he appeared. These seasoned artists provided the professional expertise (and sometimes the gags) from which the younger members would benefit. Chris Sheen, for example, was able to give a young chorus boy his first speaking role in *Misleading Ladies*, an impersonator with promise called Danny Carroll later known as La Rue. The older men's style of drag definitely tended towards the dame tradition where the basic joke is that here is an ordinary bloke in a frock. The chorus boys presented a rather different image, their emphasis was on glamour at all costs. It became a tradition for each show to end with a mannequin parade, usually down a white staircase, offering a display of spectacular frocks that most of the women in their audiences couldn't hope to possess – and probably wouldn't have the occasion to wear if they did! Here the drag effect was more ambiguous; these were men who were giving nothing away, who were deliberately trying to create the illusion of being real girls. It is difficult to guess what the audiences made of it all. These men were clearly effeminate and therefore presumably homosexual (after all, a 'real' man in drag lets you know he's a man in some way). But in those years homosexuality was one of the most taboo of subjects, known about but never mentioned; queers were effeminate perverts, a social evil. So one wonders how packed houses all over the country could sit back and relish the spectacle before them. Maybe the fact that it was theatre made it safe – possible to observe and be amazed but without the danger of personal involvement or the threat of association.

During the late 1940s the shows proliferated until four or five were touring at the same time typically giving twice-nightly shows six days a week – which represents a sizable audience. At the same time the number of authentic ex-servicemen in the companies steadily lessened but the titles were retained. But eventually managements realised they could no longer claim that the shows had any genuine link with war-time experience and the titles became *Showboat Express* or *Misleading Ladies*. They were now up-front drag shows: 'You cannot afford to miss – the show without a miss' was a typical line used on posters. The continuing popularity of the revues meant that a constant intake of new performers was needed, and the only people who were willing and eager to strut their stuff in drag were camp young effeminate lads who felt they had nothing to lose and everything to gain. 'You don't have to be gay to do drag – but it does help,' observed Kris Kirk and the fact that the shows were now almost entirely populated with wonderfully proud, up-front queens was obvious to even the most protected soul. As a result the entertainments, which had already lost their appeal to patriotism, now lost their claim to be 'family entertainment' (which is probably why my mother refused to allow me to see one, thus denying me a valuable formative experience so early in life).

The shows finally died out in the mid-1950s and life was not easy for the boys who had hoped to make a career from drag which had become an anathema throughout showbusiness. Only a very small number of pubs and clubs would hire a drag act. The older, more experienced acts, managed to survive. Alan Avid and Gary Webb enjoyed some success on the cabaret circuit before Avid retired to form his own business. Gary Webb made a come-back as a solo turn (using the name Lee Stevens) in the late 1960s, appearing at, among other places, London's prestigious Blue Angel nightclub. Eric Lloyd (billed as The Forces Sweetheart) became a theatrical costumier and Trevor Morton went on to emerge as an outstanding dame. Billy Wells had been a star of *Forces Showboat* after a career which had begun in a concert party at Margate in 1928, and had included membership of Ralph Reader's *Gang Show* – another useful grounding for female impersonators. His range included the already noted impression of Queen Victoria as well as ballerinas and even little girls. He continued as a sought-after dame and ran an Old Time Music Hall company in the Channel Islands. Others took menial, non-showbusiness jobs, or tried their luck abroad. Paris, with its celebrated travesti clubs was a main attraction.

A number of factors contributed to the demise of these extraordinary, flamboyant drag shows. Some were purely practical – the novelty had worn off, the shows themselves and their players were acquiring an unsavoury reputation, theatres were closing all over the country as the nation began to turn its eyes towards television. But there was another factor involved which was very influential, not just in helping to close these particular shows, but in driving flashy, glamour drag underground for almost ten years. During the early 1950s perhaps the biggest purge of homosexuals that had ever happened in England began and lasted for several years. Prosecutions for private acts rocketed (cases included well-known people such as Tory Junior Minister Ian Harvey and the actor Sir John Gielgud), there was a series of highly-publicised trials (notably what became known as 'the Montagu Case'), government panic after the defection of homosexuals Burgess and Maclean. The popular press got in on the act, of course, fuelling the flames of fear and suspicion with articles on such topics as 'How to Spot a Homo' (sports jackets and suede shoes were a dead giveaway!). An article in the *Sunday Pictorial* called 'Evil Men' observed, among other things, 'Homosexuality is rife in the theatrical profession ... they have mincing ways ... call each other girls' names openly ... wear women's clothes.'

The police had always taken a close interest when drag shows visited their local theatre, and the artists had to be very careful, and with the repressive climate getting overheated these most up-front and obvious of templates for the popular press's image of what these 'evil pansies' looked like found themselves rejected inside as well as outside their own profession. Wanted ads in *The Stage* increasingly stipulated 'No Drag'. Fifteen years later, similarly victimised drag queens would rebel and begin the movement for active gay liberation. But this was Great Britain in 1954; law reform lay in the future, and even if the great purges led to the Wolfenden Report and on to modest decriminalization. Low profiles were the order of the day.

Chapter four

Glamour Girls and Terrifying Termagants

FOR a few years the drag queen kept her profile low. Glamour girls dispersed from the all-male revues found ordinary jobs, perhaps finding opportunities to revive their recent glory at private functions or with occasional pub work. The older, more experienced, drag acts had pantomime to fall back on but little else during the year. But as the 1960s wore on there were small, scattered signs of revival. At the time these little manifestations seemed more a response to the anything goes spirit of the time rather than the slow build-up to something more significant.

Today it is fashionable to trash the 1960s, to use the phrase 'Swinging London' (the invention of an opportunistic American journalist on *Time* magazine) as a weapon with which to attack almost everything that happened during those years on either side of the Atlantic (including the lessening of censorship, particularly of literature, the wide circulation of the contraceptive pill which allowed women sexual choice and sexual experimentation without risk of pregnancy, and the lessening of the constraints imposed upon homosexuality, characterised by the passing into law of the Sexual Offences Act in 1967 which partly decriminalised sexual activity between consenting male adults in England and Wales and a rise in militancy in the United States which two years later, in 1969, focused on riots at the Stonewall Inn in New York City which protested the continual harrassment by the NYPD of the gay men and drag queens who frequented the bar).

What is too often forgotten is that in the mid-1960s there really was a new vibrancy in the air, a tremendous outburst of creativity on all levels of entertainment. More importantly, entertainment was, for the first time crossing those difficult boundaries of class, culture, age and sex. Swinging London embraced the Beatles as well as Fonteyn and Nureyev; it took David Hockney on board alongside Mary Quant; there were Solti, Sutherland and a young Pavarotti at Covent Garden and then afterwards at the newly-invented discos, Samantha's on Regent Street and The Scotch of St James's were there in which to bop the night away. Because men were growing their hair longer and women were emulating the skinny bodies and Vidal Sassoon cropped hair of the models promoted by the new wave of photographers, something dubbed 'unisex' arrived to shock and entice. As far as drag went, however, this was a red herring: men never actually dressed as women nor women as men, but the concept did open up tentative discussion about the fascism of frocks and the tyranny of trousers.

Important too, was the final definition of a completely new consumer market – the teenager. A decade earlier young people were still going straight from school into the straightjacket of a job, turning almost overnight from children into harrassed young workers – apart, that is, from those who continued their education. But now teenagers were a coherent group, with money to spend and demands to make in music, fashion and entertainment. Once again clothes and style became a signifier as 'rockers', 'Teddy boys' and 'mods' asserted their allegiancies through what they wore. Few younger people found it difficult to get a job and rented accommodation was comparatively easy to acquire. Overall, there was a sense of relaxation, of loosening up, of rebellion against conformity, of a need to change. As usual, reactionary right-wing voices spluttered in horror and saw the fall of the Roman Empire mirrored in every mini-skirt and Beatle mop.

It was in the context of this bustling and stimulating background that drag began to reappear and take up a definite, if at first small, place in the life of a now multi-cultured, multi-layered city. Homosexuality had become much more openly debated since the publication of the Wolfenden Report in 1957 and during the following years London's gay scene was, inevitably, becoming more active and, to a certain extent, more open. A few of the older, established gay clubs with an old school tie aroma continued their virtually passing-for-straight existence, but the younger gay crowd had more confidence, like their non-gay brothers they wanted their own style, their own music and their own outlets. A new range of gay clubs sprang up, each slightly different in feeling, catering for varying tastes. Although the famous 'permissive society' as expressed in the social activities and entertainments of the mid-to-late 1960s certainly excluded any openly gay participation, London was not exactly a gay desert. Dancing was forbidden in the clubs and there was usually no entertainment apart from a juke box. Drag as working-class pub entertainment was to be found in the East End and south of the river where it was bubbling along nicely amusing a predominantly heterosexual audience, families, local heroes and their birds. At the Artists and Battledress Club (always fondly known as 'the A & B') in an alleyway off Wardour Street in Soho, owner Stan Cowley wore an expressive range of hats which, in part, reflected the discreet notion that this was a room in which the gentlemen members, theatrical and from the armed forces, could mingle. It was a homosexual version of the Garrick Club, founded by the eighteenth century actor-manager so that actors, members of the legal profession and gentlemen could mix with equality.

And in the heart of the West End, there was one drag performer whose career was peaking to national fame. This was Danny La Rue. Setting aside the famous pantomime dames of the early years of the century, it was very rare for a drag performer to become a household name. Perhaps the only previous example was that of Arthur Lucan, who, with his wife, Kitty McShane, presented Old Mother Riley and her daughter Kitty.

Lucan, who was born in Boston, Lincolnshire, created the character of an irascible Irishwoman who was constantly getting into ridiculous situations and constantly worried by the doings of her naughty daughter. Despite his own misgivings, his impersonation (and accent) were accepted without comment in Ireland. Lucan and McShane achieved remarkable popularity; they toured the halls constantly, were frequent broadcasters and, like other proletarian stars of the period such as Gracie Fields, George Formby and Will Hay, were cinema favourites. Between 1937 and 1952 they made more than a dozen films, sometimes two a year, of dismal quality, each putting Old Mother Riley in some sort of farcical scrape. 'The films were very cheaply made and the padding is difficult to sit through, but Lucan at his best is a superb comedian,' Leslie Halliwell wrote in *The Filmgoer's Companion*. The last one was called *Mother Riley Meets the Vampire*. Arthur Lucan died in 1954 and characteristics of his acts were taken over by his understudy Roy Rolland who presented Old Mother Kelly. The relationship between Lucan and Kitty McShane has also inspired at least two plays.

Old Mother Riley was in the grand tradition of the English dame figure; the act appealed to children and adults, and Lucan was also able to create moments of touching pathos as in a sketch called 'The Matchseller.' Lucan never appeared on stage in men's clothes and the stage door was always surrounded by people curious to see what Old Mother Riley really looked like. He collapsed and died on stage at the Tivoli Theatre, Hull, May 17th 1954.

'There is a strange and chilling parallel between my act and that of Arthur Lucan,' Danny La Rue wrote in his autobiography, *From Drags to Riches*. 'I project the glamorous showbiz image, while he portrayed this old lady, Mother Riley. But under the skin they were sisters. I depend upon the use of masquerade and we both achieved fame from an image that was not our own.'[1] This is a simplistic view.

Lucan was a success for thirty years because he created a comic character; although a gross caricature, easily recognisable as a stereotype of the working-class woman. La Rue has never created a character – except for Danny La Rue – and has admitted that he thinks of himself as basically a comedian. 'I never even think of myself as a man or as a woman when I'm in drag. I'm just an actor playing a woman. My gowns are the tools of my trade, just as costume changes are to Laurence Olivier. My act is playing a woman, knowing that everybody knows it's a fella. That's the point of the joke. If I played a woman's role from beginning to end, where would Danny La Rue have got to?'[2] This latter remark may account for the complete failure in 1984 of *Hello, Dolly!* in which La Rue played the matchmaking Dolly Levi.

However, the central flaw to the production was that one character, Danny La Rue, was playing another, Dolly Levi, and the battle for supremacy between these two over-blown creations – allied to La Rue's inability to create a character – totally destroyed the internal dynamics of the show. Broadway musical heroines have traditionally been played by larger-than-life women (*Hello, Dolly!* had been written for Ethel Merman, although first played by Carol Channing) who have themselves proved role models for drag queens and inspiration for drag acts and it is ironic, but somehow appropriate, that when a drag performer took on a role that had by then become identified with drag queens, the confusion it caused broke the back of the show. Interestingly, La Rue's understudy was not another drag act, but singer and actress Carol Kaye.

It is also worth noting here that when *Hello, Dolly!* composer and lyricist eventually wrote a musical with a genuine drag queen at dead centre, *La Cage Aux Folles*, it proved one of the more expensive London flops of 1986. Adapted by Harvey Fierstein from the play and internationally successful film by Jean Poiret (which spawned two sequels), *La Cage* had been an enormous Broadway and touring hit, Frank Sinatra had been tipped to star in the movie and the show has subsequently proved an immensely popular staple with British amateur operatic and musical societies (maybe because it allows so many male members of a company to slip into a frock). One of the main complaints about the brief West End run was that Albin, the drag cabaret star 'wife' to club owner Georges, was simply another version of Dolly Levi or the eponymous Mame and that *La Cage* was basically a show about family life. Even though the show's best song, 'I am what I am' became something of a gay anthem, it would have been just as effective if Albin had actually been not a drag queen but a housewife with a secret life singing her defiance.

To a certain extent, Broadway's audiences for a musical are rather more sophisticated than their London counterparts: the former could see that *La Cage* was an essentially *heterosexual* show, the latter stayed away in droves from the London Palladium, home of 'family entertainment', because they misinterpreted the musical as being about drag and about queers. Anathema. In the light of this, it is hardly surprising that Danny La Rue has successfully undertaken the role of Albin in amateur productions of *La Cage* in such places as Jersey in the early 1990s because he was fulfilling his function as a family entertainer in a slightly risqué family show in which traditional family values are fully endorsed. He was rather less successful when he took on the role of Captain Terri Dennis in a tour of Peter Nichols' autobiographical play *Privates on Parade*.

First staged by the Royal Shakespeare Company in 1977 and released as a film in 1983, *Privates on Parade* drew upon Nichols' experiences with the Combined Services Entertainments, successor to the wartime ENSA, in Malay in the late 1940s during that country's struggles for independence from the British. Captain Terri is based upon Barri Chatt 'a dancer and drag-artiste who'd lately arrived from England with his female partner ... his off-stage gear was so androgynous that his costumes in the show looked almost butch ... His hair was dyed peroxide yellow, his eyebrows were plucked and pencilled in and all his other body hair shaved to a baby's smoothness. He wore what he called 'the full slap' (new word) which could be either day or night. After dark the cupid's bow lipstick was more emphatic, the eyeliner a darker blue. Silk scarves flopped at his neck, sandals displayed his painted toe-nails, at the pool his trunks were provocatively laced down the side.'[3] Captain Terri's homosexuality is perfectly evident, he is the archetypal queen of that period who knew that it paid to advertise with an *outré* appearance and a conversational line which attempted sophisticated wit whilst usually rising no higher than calling men by women's names ('Jessica Christ,' Captain Terri exclaims at one point; 'Oh that Bernardette Shaw! What a chatterbox!' he declares at another).

Captain Terri can provoke laughter, equally he can provoke a kind of terror: 'Mister Dennis, I think it's only fair to warn you I'm not a homosexual,' Steve, the naive new recruit to the company protests. 'Don't worry, love, it won't show from the front,' Captain Terri ripostes — making the point that in *his* eyes to be homosexual is far superior to being heterosexual.[4]

And Dennis is a tease, but he is also seductive — conjuring images of the world's most glamorous women, Marlene Dietrich, Carmen Miranda (Dennis King provided some wonderful pastiche songs), for battle and jungle weary and women hungry troops. This was not the kind of role La Rue's audience expected nor wanted to see him playing – ironically, as his own career had its roots in similar shows, similar performances.

Born Daniel Patrick Carroll in Cork in 1927, Danny La Rue 'first played female impersonation roles'[5] in naval concerts parties and plays towards the end of the Second World War. All-male revues had been popular throughout the war and continued to tour Britain well into the 1950s (Paul Buckland's 1959 novel *Chorus of Witches* gives a fascinating impression of what life on and most particularly off-stage for these performers was like). After dabbling with straight theatre, La Rue found himself touring in all-male revues such as *Misleading Ladies* and *Forces in Petticoats*. But by 1952 he was working in smart cabaret clubs such as Churchill's and Winston's and within a decade had opened his own club – Danny La Rue's – in Hanover Square.

Here sophisticated cabaret, built around La Rue and co-starring the diminutive comic Ronnie Corbett, Barbara Windsor, Toni Palmer and Amanda Barrie, an opulent setting and excellent fare quickly established the venue as one of the major attractions in the by-now 'Swinging' capital. La Rue, who had played his first pantomime as far back as 1953, had worked consistently, endlessly trekking the length and breadth of the British Isles, ceaselessly polishing an act that poised to conquer a considerable portion of the globe. It wasn't until the 1960s that La Rue really hit the big time, but for the dozen years between 1966 and 1978 he was an almost permanent fixture in the West End.

Beginning with the musical *Come Spy With Me* (co-starring Barbara Windsor), Danny La Rue appeared in a series of six spectacular shows, each of which was tailor-made for him. *Come Spy With Me* was followed by *Queen Passionella and the Sleeping Beauty*, 1968; *Danny La Rue at the Palace* (Barbara Windsor was again co-star) in 1970; *The Danny La Rue Show*, 1973 (both of the latter ran for two years); *The Exciting Adventures of Queen Daniella*, 1975; and *Aladdin* in 1978. In 1976 Danny La Rue had appeared in Canada, later gaining a following in Australia and New Zealand. He continued to tour Britain, appeared in several Royal Variety Performances and received such awards as the Variety Club of Great Britain's 'Showbusiness Personality of the Year' in 1969. He counted amongst his admirers royalty and celebrities such as Noël Coward ('Danny La Rue is the most professional, the most witty ... and the most utterly charming man in the business'[6]), Judy Garland and Rudolf Nureyev. Comedian Bob Hope declared him to be 'the most glamorous woman in the world'.[7]

The 1960s were a transitional bridge between the age of austerity which followed six years of world war and the new Jerusalem which most people believed loomed just beyond the horizon. Increasing affluence and a culture moving steadily towards domination by youth, made the 1960s an ideal backdrop for an entertainer like Danny La Rue – whose act was the epitome of glamour in a glamour-starved country and a final gasp of British music hall and variety. Although he had come out of a drag tradition, his act became increasingly heterosexualised as he moved further and further into the spotlight of popular approbation. There was never any hint that Danny La Rue enjoyed wearing a frock ('My act is playing a woman, knowing that everybody knows it's a fella') and in some respects he looked more masculine when in his gloriously exaggerated female costumes than when he was in mufti. He was a comedian who did not very good impersonations highly dependent upon larger-than-life component parts, a passable singer who had appropriated the music hall song 'On Mother Kelly's doorstep' as his theme tune and ultimately time moved on leaving him stranded with a diminishing audience and little claim on the West End or the *arrivistes* who took over smart society. The writing was already on the wall as early as 1973, when his single feature film was released.

Supported by such sterling performers as Alfred Marks, Lance Percival, Lally Bowers and Frances de la Tour, La Rue starred in *Our Miss Fred*, an ineffectual comedy which harked back to the British film industry's obsession with World War II and which presented the star as an actor who escapes from occupied France disguised as a woman. 'A carefully nurtured vehicle for Britain's top female impersonator somehow doesn't come off,' Leslie Halliwell wrote in his *Film Guide*, 'celluloid both constrains his range and reveals his inadequacies.'[8] Because he was – and remains – an entertainer rather than an actor, because he is best with the large gesture and the knowing wink, La Rue proved simply too big for the corset of the cinema screen. And as the 1970s progressed, drag itself began to change as the more sophisticated acts were built around subtle characterisation and incisive wit which to some degree sent up the people who made up La Rue's audiences. But although Danny La Rue's last West End success was in 1978 (*Hello, Dolly!* in 1984 was an unmitigated disaster), he hasn't hung up his bra or wigs.

'Danny La Rue is one of those curious performers in British showbusiness that have become complete institutions – no matter what they do,' Patrick Newley wrote in a review of a recent appearance by La Rue. 'Max Miller, Gracie Fields, Vera Lynn, Morecambe and Wise – they are all revered by the public ... At one time Danny La Rue was the king of the West End. If you stood outside the Palace Theatre you could see his name in neon lights and crowds and crowds of middle-aged ladies queuing up to see his record breaking show *Danny La Rue at the Palace*. Now we see him at the Brick Lane Theatre in London's East End for a two week run – but as always with La Rue it is completely sold out. The man has pulling power, hasn't lost the gift of the gab and of course the frocks are still amazing.'[9]

The 1990s have been spent touring in shows which are a reminder of Danny La Rue's music hall roots and which reflect his love for this particular approach to performing. *The Good Old Days* (1993) was billed as an evening of 'nostalgia from the Roaring 20s to the Fabulous 50s' and it sold out wherever it went. 'Dougie Chapman Associates congratulate Danny La Rue on 52 "Sell Out" Shows' an advertisement in *The Stage*[10] proclaimed. La Rue may no longer be the king of the West End, but there's no doubt to his adoring but increasingly elderly audience he's a king untimely deposed and on a royal progress from one civic venue to another.

Drag was virtually the only entertainment on offer in those of the growing number of gay venues which did provide entertainment in the 1960s and 1970s. The acts ranged from the appallingly amateur to the almost professional – but there were few who could depend upon their performances as a means of support. There was also virtually no cross-over between those acts who played the East End and South London pubs (more-or-less catering to a gay crowd) and the acts who had pretensions to be genuinely theatrical (with the implication that such acts were quite divorced from anything evidently homosexual). There were those, however, who maintained a delicate balancing act – working by day, performing by night in venues where they were quite likely to attract mixed audiences and even a modicum of press attention.

Rogers and Starr were one of the more successful drag acts of that time, but because there were few opportunities for them in the mainstream and no real gay cabaret circuit such as exists now then existed, they were performers part-time and display artists by profession. Theirs was a sophisticated and glamorous act which was greatly strengthened by their writing most of their own material, point songs and production numbers. They were in demand for private functions as well as club and restaurant dates and by 1970 could be found operating at both ends of the spectrum – in revue at Hampstead Theatre Club and in cabaret at a gala promoted by *Jeremy*, one of the earliest of the up-front gay magazines.

'*Fagged Out* ... came as a witty and lively change from the sameness of Danny La Rue and the slightly tasteless cavortings of *Birds of a Feather*,' I wrote at the time, making a passing reference to a spectacular but short-lived drag show Paul Raymond had mounted at the Royalty Theatre which spared no expense but appeared to be both a cash-in on the popularity of Danny La Rue and an attempt to introduce London audiences to the kind of *travesti* show which had long been popular in mainland Europe, Paris, in particular. 'Rogers and Starr are the kind of drag artists who possess real theatrical magic,' I continued. 'They can captivate an audience as soon as they set foot on stage.'[11] I particularly remember a lyric from that show – witty but deliciously risqué:

> They're changing guard at Buckingham Palace,
> Christopher Robin's gone down on Alice ...

It was presumably the engagement at Hampstead Theatre Club which led to Rogers and Starr being booked as support to Max Bygraves in variety at the Victoria Palace and a subsequent West End appearance in a revue inappropriately called *Hullabaloo* in which the star was the gay but deeply closeted comedian Jimmy

Edwards. *Hullabaloo* proved a disaster and, perhaps, that the West End didn't need more than one drag act at a time. Rogers and Starr split, one heading for Canada, the other for Australia, neither to be heard of again.

It was at about this time that a most anarchic but amusing play about gender confusion briefly appeared in the West End. David Percival's *Girlfriend* had a cast of four (headed by Margaret Leighton and Michael Horden) and was about the confusion that arises when Laurie, son of the house, brings home, Jo (played by Michael Des Barres, later to find a modicum of fame as an androgynous rock star), his entirely ambiguous lover. Jo's gender is never defined and the levels of ambiguity are enhanced by one's own perceptions dependent upon one's own sexuality: Is Jo a girl? If so, *Girlfriend* is about a heterosexual relationship. Is Jo a boy? If so the play is about a homosexual relationship. That the character was played both on stage and in the subsequent film (*Girl Stroke Boy*) by an actor (Des Barres, Peter Straker) suggests the film was about a relationship between two men. But here was a writer extending the idea of unisex (androgony by a more fashionable name) to its logical conclusion. The final message, 'just love, it doesn't matter who', was admirable.

The Canadian Jean Fredericks was another female impersonator with a cross-over audience, but this was because although he worked in drag his act was genuinely musical and could as easily be bracketed with Anna Russell, Victor Borge, Florence Foster Jenkins or La Gran Scena. Tall and plump and possessed of a well-trained counter-tenor voice, Fredericks could produce a ringing soprano, full-toned and accurate, with no strained falsetto. He did not try for glamour in drag, but looked like a vast and formidable *Lieder* singer of indeterminate age. Although he performed in clubs and pubs and hosted drag balls at Porchester Hall in West London, Fredericks also worked in traditional recital conditions at such places as Chelsea Town Hall and the Chenil Galleries, also in Chelsea.

He had a solemn pianist and swept onto the stage, beginning in all seriousness with operatic arias and drawing room ballads. For a while the uninitiated would be fooled into thinking they were attending a genuine operatic recital. But comedy would creep in as

Fredericks began to ape the platform manner of German sopranos or subtly send up the sentimental lyrics of a Victorian ballad. Proceedings then became steadily more frenetic as Fredericks employed various props — using a Union Jack as a drape for a patriotic song or donning a Viking helmet for a Valkyrie call or throwing jewels at the audience during the appropriate aria from Gounod's *Faust*. Fredericks was also a trombonist, and for some unaccountable reason that instrument also seemed to inspire humour.

Jean Fredericks was a good example of a creative drag artist who built up an act beyond a merely amusing appearance. But, as was so often the case with the more imaginative acts, his outlets were restricted, not least because it had a limited appeal because a certain degree of musical knowledge was needed if it was to be fully enjoyed. However, musical expertise has evidently increased, witness the success of the British duo Hinge and Bracket and the American La Gran Scena Opera Company.

The natural progression from Jean Fredericks's drag recitals was obviously an entirely *travesti* opera company. This is exactly what New Yorker Ira Siff founded in 1980. I interviewed Siff in 1994, prior to a return season at London's Bloomsbury Theatre.

What had provoked him to create an opera company?

'Since you use the word provoke, I'll tell you the truth. The provocation was the state of opera singing in 1980, when I formed La Gran Scena, which was in dire need of a shot in the arm in New York, of something more lively and committed than the bland stuff that was being churned out at the time. On the serious artistic side, I wanted to do something that was a *travesti*, but was also very much in the vein of my friend Charles Ludlam, who was doing the Ridiculous Theatre Company and who had done *Camille*. It was something which walked the line between a spoof and a *travesti*, and was at the same time a tribute to all-stops out dramatic acting, and the committed stage presence of tremendous opera stars and film stars that we don't seem to have any more.

On the lighter side, I had been a tenor and a cabaret performer, and I wanted to find a way to use opera, which is what I had been involved in emotionally since I was fifteen, and by this time I was thirty-five and I wanted to use opera in my performing that was both comedic and dramatic. When I realised that that delusion of grandeur involved full scenes with other people, I held auditions and launched an opera company as opposed to continuing to do one-man shows.

The idea of a company made up from men in frocks came first, but it took about five years for the nerve to follow the thought, because at that time I was very 'dragophobic', and I didn't like a lot of the drag performing I'd seen. But when I saw Ludlam, it became clear to me that you could use the drag to heighten the drama and the comedy, and if you looked funny it could be a plus, not a minus. I became more comfortable with the notion, but it was interesting that I didn't actually get into the dress until the dress rehearsal for the company's debut, and until then I'd never been in the dress, and I was never in the make-up until the photocall, which was a few days before that. It was quite a surprise. It's a very important element of the company, but looking like, acting like, walking like 'women', is *not* an important element at all. In fact it's something I discourage, because I think that it often comes off misogynistic, and is an affront to the way women really are.'

'La Gran Scena's parodies – too mild a word? Hatchet jobs would be nearer the mark – work at many levels, from the basic drag joke (the company is all male, but sings mostly at the original pitch), to some really sophisticated gags, like the wayward Lucia inserting *Ah, non giunge* into her Mad Scene cadenza,' Rodney Milnes, that most exacting of critics wrote in *Opera*. 'The whole show represents New York humour at its zaniest and, far from being just a camp giggle, is executed with total professionalism. The best joke of all is that they are all good singers, and you have to be if you are going to send up such sacred monsters as Dames J*an and K*ri, or Sc*tto and C*b*lle, up sky high ...'[12]

So although there is a great deal of humour in La Gran Scena's performance, essentially the music is taken completely

seriously – much in the same way as in the dance in the *travesti*
New York company Ballets Trockadero de Monte Carlo. It's
homage rather than pastiche, to great divas such as Callas and
Sutherland?

> 'Absolutely. In the same way as the Trocks, its a homage to
> that sort of performer, without getting that specific. Because
> it's not a drag queen doing Joan Sutherland instead of doing
> Bette Davis. But there are passing references, and glimpses
> and moments of recognition, but I must say they're fewer
> and further between as the company gets older and the era
> of those divas gets further away. The characters we've
> created seem to be getting more vivid and the passing refer-
> ences more fleeting, because current divas don't inspire those
> passing references ...'

Like Jean Fredericks (more so?), La Gran Scena would appear to be
a specialist act. Who is it aimed at? Opera buffs? Opera *queens*?
Drag enthusiasts? And would the company work for an audience
who knew nothing whatsoever about opera?

> 'I know that it does, although it takes them a few minutes to
> get into it. We've played a number of unpronounceable little
> towns in Holland over the last few years, in three tours to
> over fifty cities, and aside from Amsterdam, Rotterdam,
> Utrecht and Maastricht, they were very provincial little
> places. Farm towns. The audiences during our opening
> number – 'The ride of the Valkyries' – look a bit bewildered,
> but as the evening goes on they get more into it and by the
> end they're always screaming and cheering and up on their
> feet. It would be a lie to say it's *more* fun than to play
> Amsterdam, but it's as *much* fun, in a different way, to win
> them over and get them involved. I try, through the nar-
> ration in the show, to help a person who comes in and
> doesn't know anything ... Sometimes audiences don't rea-
> lise that it is a *travesti* company ...'

Does Siff think that drag on stage manifests itself differently in

Europe than in the United States? Charles Pierce describes himself as a 'male actress' (he has worked gay venues across America as well as legitimate theatres in both New York and London but reached his largest audience when he appeared in the film of Harvey Fierstein's *Torch Song Trilogy*), Divine *was* an actress and a disco diva, Ballets Trockadero de Monte Carlo *are* dancers, La Gran Scena *is* a company of divas who could well appear at opera houses – whereas British drag veers away from company towards something which is music hall or burlesque?

> 'Maybe what has made the American drag queen more defensive is the level of some of the drag in the United States, and, frankly, I didn't grow up with it, as a lot of it is mostly in the South West, Texas. But it's on the kind of level that inspires one to say: "That's not me, I am ..." and then name something else. I think it's now more politically correct in the gay community to embrace drag as one's calling. But the gay community used to be so dragophobic; I remember at a Gay Pride march in the late 1970s – with a friend of mine who is a long deceased drag queen, who at that time showed up in a beautiful purple frock – and I remember some angry queen coming over and saying "This is a Gay Pride march and we're homosexuals, not fags." I thought it was the most ridiculous thing in the world, but I realised that I had felt that way too, although I didn't feel that way about particular people I was fond of, but I had that general view too.
>
> And I think of now, of course, in my neighbourhood in Manhattan, East Village and Wigstock, it's become a very fashionable thing to do drag. Boys go out and do it. And I think that's funny. It's just the way the pendulum swings.'

Has Siff found responses to La Gran Scena differ from country to country? Are some more responsive to the company as an opera company? Are others more responsive to the company as a drag troupe?

> 'I would say in Germany we are responded to as 'art' and in Berlin and Hamburg the voices are taken terribly seriously. I

find all of us falling to the temptation to fall into vocal stunts
– holding notes a long time, extra embellishments or a *pianissimo* unjustifiably held to fifteen seconds. Getting into the
vocal antics. In New York and London they're more into the
opera lore, the verbal jokes that go into the narration, and
enjoying and demonstrating that they 'get' the references to
the *libretti* of the operas, and the visual puns that we're
doing on the librettos. In New York and London they seem
to be opera queens who know their recordings and their
texts. In the South American and Spanish countries they're
up for anything, and they go wild from the moment it starts
and they get it on all levels. It's wonderful because the Latin
countries seem to be open to it on all levels. I think the more
repressed a society, the more repressed it goes at something
that breaks those barriers down.'

Siff is also emphatic about what happens to Madame Vera Galupe-
Barszh once a performance is finished:

> 'She gets dry cleaned and put away. It's something I discourage, and it's very hard when you have a company living out
> a psycho-sexual fantasy – or just a fantasy in the case of
> some of our members who play male singers, or who are not
> gay, or not playing divas, who may not be acting out a
> psycho-sexual fantasy – but it's particularly difficult for
> anyone who has that diva living inside them and gets this
> opportunity to do it, and then hears all that bravoing, to
> detach himself from it. But it's a requirement that I make of
> myself and everyone in the company that the diva stuff is left
> for the stage. It's really very important because we must get
> real. We're a small fringe ensemble working on a shoe-string
> without enough funding to survive, like everyone else. No
> matter what you get back, that's all we are. And the rest is
> for the stage.'[13]

La Gran Scena has achieved longevity – fourteen years – and international acclaim – they are written about in the mainstream press

and reviewed by music and opera critics. Whether this is an indication of a greater acceptance of drag amongst serious music lovers or whether it indicates a continuing awareness of the place *travesti* has always held within the confines of music theatre promoting a more willing acceptance is open to doubt. Possibly because both opera and dance are essentially unnatural forms of expression (people do not usually communicate by singing to each other or dancing at each other), the use of drag in either form may simply be viewed as adding another level of ambiguity, a further level of artistic expression.

Besides the American *travesti* dance company the Ballets Trockadero de Monte Carlo, drag has an honourable place in conventional dance companies – Sir Frederick Ashton and Sir Robert Helpmann famously danced the Ugly Sisters in Ashton's own *Cinderella* for the Royal Ballet in the 1960s and the role of the evil fairy in *The Sleeping Beauty* can be a drag role. Drag is very much a component part of Lindsay Kemp's company and aspects of *travesti* have been utilised by the adventurous choreographer and dancer Michael Clark.

There is at least one other act which is rooted in musical pastiche which has transcended club origins to become a British institution which celebrated twenty-one years in showbusiness in 1993 by mounting a nationwide tour which remained on the road for over a year. Dr Evadne Hinge and Dame Hilda Bracket, alter egos of George Logan and Patrick Fyffe, made early appearances at gay clubs such as The Escort in Pimlico, London SW1 ('Dancing, Music, Cabaret' promised) and Earls Court's The Masquerade. A highly original act based around the conceit that the Dr and the Dame are elderly spinsters, the backbone of the small Suffolk community of Stackton Tressle, who share a home, fond memories, a love of music, but cannot control their slightly waspish tongues and therefore binker and banter in the intervals between the musical numbers.

Hinge and Bracket are amongst the foremost British drag artists to have established themselves in the past twenty-five years. Yet they cannot honestly be called a drag *act* – they were at the forefront of a new development in drag which was based in creation of completely convincing characters. Danny La Rue was the apogee of the comic in a frock: Dr Evadne Hinge and Dame Hilda Bracket, like Australia's Dame Edna Everage, the South African Mrs Evita Bezuidenhout (Pieter-Dirk Uys) or the American Divine (Glen Milstead), were lovingly observed characters who had their own personal histories and who have steadily developed over the years in much the same way as characters in a fictional sequence such as Armistead Maupin's *Tales of the City* evolved over six books. To compound the illusion, both Dame Hilda and Dame Edna have published autobiographies: *One Little Maid* and *My Gorgeous Life*.

Dr Evadne and Dame Hilda are quintessentially English, eccentrics from the same school as Margaret Rutherford or Athene Seyler, Martita Hunt or, more recently, Liz Smith or Dora Bryan. The act itself appears gentle – interpretations of numbers by composers such as Ivor Novello or Gilbert and Sullivan. But the repartee is witty and sparkling and both the Dr and the Dame are masters of timing. Their act works on two levels: there are those who are perfectly aware that these two slightly daffy elderly women are in fact two youngish men in drag and there are those who are not quite sure and probably think they are enjoying a deliciously nostalgic musical evening performed by two elderly women who behave in a manner that is a little more *outré* than is usual.

By 1980, Hinge and Bracket had played five West End seasons, made six long-playing records, undertaken two tours of Australia and, like Danny La Rue and Dame Edna Everage, became favourites with members of the British royal family. That they also became immensely popular on radio – including three years as Radio 2's *Dear Ladies* – shows how seriously their impersonations were taken.

But most drag performers have a desire to go further and like La Rue's attempt at straight musical theatre with *Hello, Dolly!*, Hinge and Bracket attempted that dangerous transition. However, attempting Oscar Wilde's *The Importance of Being Earnest* as a play within a play in which Dr Evadne became Miss Prism and Dame Hilda Lady Bracknell was simply too confusing for audiences. For much the same reasons as La Rue's *Hello, Dolly!* failed, *The Importance of Being Earnest* flopped. 'One need not be a purist to find the comedy less than satisfying,' Robert Shelton complained at the time. 'Hinge and Bracket's trumps lie in the rather marvellous way they let their creations take over and become eccentric caricatures. The confines of someone else's play, including Wilde, only bring their bubbling nonsense down to earth with a bit of a thud.'[14]

A more successful venture was Dame Hilda's appearance as Katisha in Regency Opera's production of Gilbert and Sullivan's *The Mikado*. But the role of Katisha, the elderly woman who is in love with heir-apparent Nanki-Poo and the reason for his fleeing his father's domains, is much more suitable for a drag performer attempting to legitimise his act. Katisha is an important role, a real battle-axe with three songs ('Oh fool, that fleest my hallowed joys', 'From every kind of man' and 'Hearts do not break') but doesn't have to contend with the enormous responsibility of Wilde's most famous character nor carry an entire show as does Dolly Levi in *Hello, Dolly!* Unlike La Rue, Fyffe and Logan always remain firmly in character. They never metaphorically nudge the audience, wink, deepen their voices nor bellow: 'Don't worry, we're really fellas!' Thus the illusion is maintained, audiences know exactly where they are and Dame Hilda playing Katisha is an appropriate and witty conceit – one slightly batty elderly spinster playing another.

The levels of course are positively Shakespearean, just as they have been when the young Welsh drag act Ceri Dupree has done an impersonation of a Danny La Rue impersonation (a man impersonating a man impersonating a female celebrity) or of Dame Edna Everage (a man impersonating a man impersonating a woman who has her own reality). Dupree, whose impersonations include Mae West, Marlene Dietrich and Bette Davis, has appeared in cabaret, notably at Madam Jo-Jo, the most famous *travesti* revue club in London (when he was 'doing' Dorothy Squires, the real thing was in the audience: 'She stood up at her table and joined in when I was singing "My way". She loved it.'[15]); toured extensively, playing everything from clubs and pubs to surviving music halls and brought a full show, *A Star is Torn*, into the West End for a brief run.

Although Dupree belongs in the tradition of La Rue, he has also invented a character, a bored Welsh housewife called Brenda Llewellyn trapped in the awful hair and frocks of the 1970s, and longing for a glamorous showbusiness career. A couple of gins help her to recreate the people she would like to have been.

But it's affectionate. 'I don't want to offend anybody,' Dupree says. 'I want to be funny, but not cruel. I would never do Dietrich in a wheelchair, for example, or use bad language just for a cheap laugh. A gentle piss take is what I aim at. Obviously with people like Joan Collins, Elizabeth Taylor and Zsa Zsa Gabor you play on them being bits of tarts, the men and the diamonds and all that. But it's very gentle.'[16]

Dupree is a female impersonator whose impressions are of larger-than-life women who, within the confines of his act, can be made even larger by a process of exaggeration. The American impersonator Jim Bailey also bases his act upon those larger-than-life women who are usually considered 'gay icons' – even though not all gay men 'adore' Judy Garland or Barbra Streisand, the two mainstays of his highly successful act. Bailey doesn't consider himself a female impersonator or a drag act, he describes himself as an illusionist and his impersonations are both physical and vocal and come from close study and detailed interpretation of his chosen subjects. Bailey has appeared on Broadway and at the London Palladium, he has made television specials, taken 'straight' roles and performed at a Royal Variety Performance. Like Hinge and Bracket, Bailey can create his illusions without even being seen – they have their radio shows, he has his records, which work because the vocal impersonations, particularly of Garland, are so accurate. Accepting Jim Bailey at his own estimation of himself creates no problems, he is a male performer who just happens to work best when he is playing women. This is showbusiness glamour *par excellence*.

Dame Edna Everage, the most widely known of the characters created by the Australian actor and writer Barry Humphries, would most emphatically describe herself as glamorous, but that abundance of confidence is an important aspect of her self-deluding character. It is no surprise that this most predatory of characters should have achieved her greatest success in the 1980s, the decade in which the concept of Me became over-riding.

Dame Edna, who started life in a 1956 revue sketch as Mrs Edna Everage from Moonee Ponds, a suburb of Melbourne, intending to let rooms to participants in that year's Olympic Games, is frankly terrifying, a termagant who manipulates her audience into a position of submission by the sheer terror she instils in them from the very moment she first appears on stage. And although Dame Edna has also become a television celebrity – utilising a variety of formats in an attempt to recreate the tension of the stage shows – she remains most effective when holding a packed theatre enthralled as she verbally abuses individuals in the audience, to the delight of those ignored who, never-the-less, shiver in terrified anticipation that they, too, might become a victim.

It is clear from Barry Humphries's autobiography *More Please* that his characterisation of Dame Edna is in part based upon his mother, a woman who appears to have been remote and snobbish, a Melbourne harridan to both be rebelled against and revenged upon. It is also evident that his frustrated relationship with his mother has profoundly influenced his personal life, manifesting itself in what seems to be an inability to cope successfully with close relationships which, in turn, has driven him throughout his life to seek attention by playing up and performing. In his extended essay *Dame Edna Everage and the Rise of Western Civilisation*, John Lahr intimates that Barry Humphries can only really be himself when he is on stage in front of an audience who have paid money to give him their undivided attention and adoration. That Dame Edna's sometimes manic performances can over-run by as much as an hour indicates a need that borders on the desperate.

Humphries arrived in London at the beginning of the 1960s. He appeared in two Lionel Bart musicals, *Oliver* and *Blitz*, wrote the words for the long-running *Private Eye* strip cartoon *The Adventures of Barry Mackenzie*, about a none-too-bright Australian on the loose in London, and ventured into cabaret at the Soho club The Establishment owned by *Private Eye* entrepreneur, comedian Peter Cook. Like Danny La Rue's Mayfair club, The Establishment became something of an emblem of 'Swinging London', home of satire, representing libertarianism and a bastion against censorship and values by then viewed as outmoded.

Edna Everage was not an instant success. A woman of extreme vulgarity who thinks of herself as the epitome of style and taste, Edna was and has remained a bully, imposing her extraordinary views by a strength of will that tolerates no contradictions. Breath-takingly vain and an egoist of daunting proportions, Dame Edna considers herself a paragon: caring about and considerate of others, on a mission to spread a little love and laughter around the world.

Usually tried out on Australian audiences before they reach Britain, Barry Humphries' shows generally include one or more characters than Edna. After the redoubtable Dame, his most famous creation is Sir Les Patterson, Australian Cultural Attaché who, like Edna, has been elevated in line with their character's increasing popularity. Sometimes a third character will provide an interlude between the outrageous bawdy of Sir Les and the venomous wit of Dame Edna.

Running in London between 1987 and 1988 and returning in 1989, *Back With a Vengeance!* was no exception to this general rule. No doubt *Look At Me When I'm Talking to You!*, due in London in 1995, will follow the usual formula. But as Barry Humphries himself said in another context: 'If it's not broken, don't mend it.'[17]

'There's an old tart down here can hardly believe her ears,' splutters Sir Les Patterson, adjusting his substantial crotch and soaking the first six rows of the stalls with a string of saliva and waves of whiskey. 'It's a priceless gift – being able to laugh at the misfortunes of others,' shrieks the increasingly venomous Dame Edna Everage, fixing the audience with a stare that can best be described as akin to that used by a snake hypnotising a rabbit.

The same front rows of the stalls recoil in terrified – but eager – anticipation. Which of them is about to be subjected to public humiliation by the recently widowed Australian housewife and megastar? Some attempt to shrink into or slide under their seats; few are bold or foolhardy enough to make themselves noticeable and it's more than likely that anyone volunteering themselves for ritual humiliation would be rejected on the grounds they were show-offs wanting to steal some of the Dame's thunder.

When Barry Humphries (in whatever guise) is on stage, danger has returned to the theatre. Here is an evening which is as near to traditional music hall as we are likely to get today and one which depends as much upon the willingness of the audience to become sacrificial victims as it does upon Humphries' skills as an inquisitor.

When Edna Everage debuted in New York in 1977, I took a group of friends to an evening performance early in the all-too short run. Chatting to a mostly uncomprehending New York audience, Dame Edna sweetly enquired if there was anyone in the audience from Britain. Those of us in the know kept quiet. My American friends, however, noisily indicated that I fitted the bill:

> 'And what's your name?' Dame Edna asked.
> 'Peter.'
> 'Peter. Peter,' she said, savouring the name as if it were rare and exotic. 'That's nice.'

The show moved on. But I knew the routine. My name – along with those of other unfortunates singled out from the audience – had been noted and remembered. I would be called into play when it was appropriate.

That was sooner than even I expected. Late-comers were creeping down the aisle and into the row of seats immediately behind the row in which I was sitting. Late-comers are a regular butt of the Dame's ire:

> 'Hello, late-comers,' Edna cried, freezing the young couple in their tracks. 'Where are you from?'
> 'New Jersey,' the male half of the couple mumbled.
> '*New Jersey!*' Dame Edna was incredulous. 'New Jersey? Say 'Hello' to Peter. He's in front of you. He's from London, England and he *got here on time.*'

Throughout the course of the evening we were returned to – usually just when we thought it was safe to sit a little higher in our seat. We were the reason for the laughter of others and it was not a comfortable experience.

Sir Les – as brassy and boldly drawn as a Donald McGill postcard – had opened *Housewife! Superstar!* as he opened *Back With a Vengeance!* – with a confidential chat about the then up-and-coming celebrations for the Australian bicentennial. He'd been trying to drum up interest amongst the Poms in events which his fellow countrymen were already finding boring. But his tone is bawdy, the emphasis blue. 'I know what you ladies are looking at,' he leers out to an audience already lost to laughter. 'You're looking at my pianist.' The thick Australian accent turns this last word into 'penis'. Sir Les is a comic grotesque – with attitudes that are appalling and behaviour which must cause anyone with even the meanest streak of *machismo* in them to wish it immediately eradicated.

Sandy Stone, long dead but returned as a ghost to his suburban Melbourne home opens the second half with a lengthy monologue in which we are invited to laugh at his prejudices (most of them racial) we may too easily recognise as our own. From his 'Art Decko' armchair, Sandy fulminates about Australia's cross-culturalism and grasping daughters-in-law. More drily humorous than either Sir Les or Dame Edna, Sandy Stone allows a pause before the great climatic onslaught of Dame Edna. As he is dressed in dressing-gown and slippers, he also makes for a quicker costume change than would Sir Les.

Dame Edna Everage is *not* a drag act (no more than are Hinge and Bracket). What Barry Humphries has so successfully contrived with the Moonee Ponds housewife is an almost totally believable character who has such vitality that she has become a personality in her own right – recognised and accepted as Dame Edna by a vast audience who wouldn't want to know about The Black Cap or the Vauxhall Tavern or any of the other pubs where drag acts regularly entertain large audiences of gay men. In some respects Dame Edna does not belong with men in frocks but with such contemporary phenomenons as Joan Collins who – in her own way – is yet another kind of drag act. Dame Edna's success stems from her certain knowledge that we share with her a love of laughing at the misfortunes of others and her ability to provide (as she so acutely admits) 'healing through laughter'. Hers is a sometimes cruel wit which provokes laughter as a release from fear of victimisation and because of our acceptance of our own cruelty. The second, Edna, half of any given show is by far the funnier, not least because it is so cathartic. By the end of what can sometimes be a very long evening, the audience will have been forced through an emotional wringer which combines equal measures of terror and laughter. The climax comes with Dame Edna tossing arm-loads of gladiola into the audience who – in a rite that echoes Dionysus – hold the flowers symbolically erect, waving them in time to whatever number the Dame has created for that particular show. A highly educated and articulate man, Humphries is clearly aware of the links between the Classical world and the kind of theatre he creates.

Barry Humphries' audience is enormous – he doesn't have to worry about his gay fans, because his fans transcend class and sexuality. Dame Edna Everage is possibly the most popular and the most successful drag act in the world today. But as the millenium approaches, there is no sign of an abatement of interest in any kind of drag – certainly in Britain there are more drag acts performing than ever before and drag itself is increasingly in evidence in all areas of the arts. Jean Genet's *The Maids*, specifically written to be played by men, is regularly interpreted as the author intended; within the past few years there have been productions ranging from *Hamlet* to *Lady Windermere's Fan* which have effectively utilized men in roles usually associated with women and even television programmes such as the Australian soap *A Country Practice*, based around an outback hospital, have used transvestite characters.[18] 'I suppose you think I'm queer ...' Larry/Anita (Kym Lynch) blurted when his secret was discovered. 'I have most of the urges of a normal man.' Evidently transvestism in the performing arts is more acceptable than ever, in real life the same misconceptions hold sway. PR

Notes

1.   Quoted in Danny La Rue (with Howard Elson), *From Drags to Riches: My Autobiography* (London: Viking, 1987), p 38.

2.   Danny La Rue interview with Vincent Firth in *Film Review*, quoted in Peter Underwood, *Danny La Rue: Life's a Drag* (London: Leslie Frewin, 1974), p 9.

3.   Peter Nichols, *Feeling You're Behind* (London: Weidenfeld & Nicolson, 1984), p 105. *The Kenneth Williams Diaries* (London: HarperCollins, 1993) also include discussion of this theatrical troupe and the various performers associated with it.

4.   Peter Nichols, *Privates on Parade* (in *Plays: One*, London: Methuen, 1987), p 314.

5. Danny La Rue, programme biography *Come Spy With Me*, Whitehall Theatre, 1966.
6. Quoted on the cover of Danny La Rue, *From Drags to Riches*, cited above.
7. Quoted on the cover of Danny La Rue, *From Drags to Riches*, cited above.
8. Leslie Halliwell, *Film Guide*, 3rd edition (London: Paladin, 1979).
9. Patrick Newley, 'Brick Lane Music Hall: Danny La Rue', (London: *The Stage*, November 25th 1993).
10. Advertisement, (London: *The Stage*, February 24th 1994).
11. Peter Burton, 'Rogers and Starr', (London: *The Stage*, April 16th 1960.
12. Rodney Milne 'La Gran Scena' (London: *Opera*, April 1989).
13. Peter Burton, 'Travesti not travesty' (London: *Gay Times*, April 1994); interview with Ira Siff, February 15th 1994.
14. Robert Shelton, 'After this, King Lear in drag?' (Brighton: *Evening Argus*, September 15th 1987).
15. Roger Baker, 'Ceri Dupree: When goddesses walked ...' (London: *Gay Times*, September 1993).
16. Ibid.
17. Iain Johnstone, 'Split Personalities' (London: *Sunday Times*, February 20th 1994).
18. Miles Anderson and Gerard Murphy played Claire and Solange in *The Maids* (half of a double-bill with *Deathwatch*) for the Royal Shakespeare Company in 1987; Martin McKellan played Gertrude in *Hamlet* in a production from Theatre Clwyd which opened in 1991 and Dublin's Rough Magic Theatre Company brought a production of *Lady Windermere's Fan* to London in 1994 in which director Lynne Parker created a society of drag divas, dominated by Sean Kearns as the Duchess of Berwick. The device is perfectly legitimate and can be highly effective with a writer like Wilde whose plays revolve around disguise and social masks.

Chapter five

Hollywood and Bust

THE cinema is little more than a hundred years old, yet any history of the cinema must of necessity be a history of drag on film. There can be few actors who have not at some time in their career donned the apparel of the opposite gender.

Drag has most often been used to provoke hilarity and from the earliest days of silent film to big budget movies like *Tootsie* and *Mrs Doubtfire* comedians such as Wallace Beery, Fatty Arbuckle, Charlie Chaplin (*A Woman*), Ben Turpin, Stan Laurel and Oliver Hardy (themselves impersonated by Susanah York and Beryl Reid in *The Killing of Sister George*), Buster Keaton, Eddie Cantor, Harold Lloyd, Jimmy Durante, The Marx Brothers, Joe E Brown (who later in his career played a millionaire who falls in love with a man impersonating a woman in Billy Wilder's classic *Some Like It Hot*), W C Fields, Will Hay, Bob Hope, Jerry Lewis, Peter Sellers (notably as Gloriana, Grand Duchess of Fenwick in *The Mouse That Roared*), Danny Kaye, Norman Wisdom and Woody Allen donned dresses.

Actors who have donned frocks include Cary Grant (famously in *I Was a Male War Bride*), William Powell and Sir Alec Guinness (he was Lady Agatha d'Ascoyne in *Kind Hearts and Coronets* and his character in the film of Graham Greene's *The Comedians* had at one point to disguise himself as an Haitian laundress; however, perhaps his most notable drag role was as 'Mrs Artminster', a criminal on the run who has donned female disguise so as to avoid apprehension in Simon Gray's stage play *Wise Child*. Only the most laconic of references is made to these acts of professional transvestism in Guinness's carefully modulated autobiography *Blessings in Disguise*).[1] Alastair Sim was superb as both Miss Millicent Fitton, Headmistress of Ronald Searle's notorious school for girls, St Trinian's and her brother, the shady Clarence, in *The Belles of St Trinian's*, *Blue Murder at St Trinian's*, *The Pure Hell of St Trinian's* and *The Great St Trinian's Train Robbery*. Like Guinness's Lady Agatha, Sims' Millicent Fitton was a splendid instance of an actor undertaking a female role in all seriousness and producing a perfectly believable and richly comic creation. Kenneth Williams and Charles Hawtry offered a comic double act as policemen disguised as women in the course of duty – and rather enjoying the experience – in *Carry on Constable*. Nuns are a common comic thread uniting Peter Cook and Dudley Moore (*Bedazzled*), Burt Reynolds and Jack Weston (*Fuzz*) and Robbie Coltrane and Eric Idle (*Nuns on the Run*). Coltrane also donned a capacious frock to play 'Annabelle', the transvestite hostess of the Fruit Machine Club in *The Fruit Machine*.

Elsewhere we have seen James Fox in a dress, Lionel Barrymore superbly sinister as a criminal released from Devil's Island who returns to Paris disguised as an old woman to exact revenge on those who put him there in *The Devil Doll*, Rod Steiger, Helmut Berger doing Marlene Dietrich playing Lola-Lola in *The Blue Angel* in Visconti's *The Damned*, Brian Deacon, a soldier who has gone absent without leave and hides out on a farm run by Glenda Jackson disguised as a woman in *Triple Echo*, Jeff Bridges, Roman Polanski, Melvyn Douglas, James Cagney, Jean-Paul Belmondo, George Sanders, Horst Bucholz, Burt Lancaster, Ray Walston, Marlon Brando who in the western *The Missouri Breaks* plays a lawman who dons women's clothes in an attempt to get to outlaw Jack Nicholson.

There have been far fewer actresses who have donned male attire, though a selected list is impressive and would include Mary Pickford, Gloria Swanson, Mabel Normand, Marion Davies, Beatrice Lillie, Cicely Courtneidge, Gracie Fields, Miriam Hopkins, Judy Garland, Judy Holliday, Jeanne Moreau (*Jules et Jim*, *Viva, Maria*), Veronica Lake, Louise Brook, Marlene Dietrich, Katherine Hepburn, Annabella, Merle Oberon, Lilli Palmer, Diana Rigg, Greta Garbo, Josephine Baker, Julie Andrews (*Victor/Victoria*), Jessie Matthews (*First a Girl*), Mitzi Gaynor, Doris Day and Anne Heywood (playing a male-to-female transsexual in *I Want What I Want*).

But although there's been a great deal of drag on the silver screen, there have been few movies which have actually used drag as the central theme – these would include Katherine Hepburn in *Sylvia Scarlett*, Greta Garbo in *Queen Christina*, Jessie Matthews in *First a Girl* and Julie Andrews in *Victor/Victoria*, Tony Curtis and Jack Lemmon in *Some Like It Hot* (which became the stage musical *Sugar*, later *Some Like It Hot*), Dustin Hoffman in *Tootsie*, Michael Caine in *Dressed to Kill*, Michel Serrault in *La Cage Aux Folles* and the two less successful sequels, William Hurt in *Kiss of the Spider Woman* (based upon Manuel Puig's polemical novel, which became a stage play, a film winning an Oscar for Hurt and, finally, a London and Broadway musical by Kander and Ebb) and Robin Williams in *Mrs Doubtfire*.

On the whole women who've donned male attire on film have fared considerably less well than have those men who've donned frocks. *Sylvia Scarlett* (1936) and *Yentl* (1983) are perhaps the most distinguished disasters in this field.

In *Sylvia Scarlett*, Katherine Hepburn in the title role plays the daughter of an English embezzler who has to flee to France to escape the British police. Sylvia disguises herself as a boy ('Katherine Hepburn is better looking as a boy than as a woman,' *Time*'s critic wrote at the time). Father and daughter take up with Jimmy, a cockney con-man played by Cary Grant. Meanwhile, Sylvia, still in drag, falls in love with an artist (Brian Aherne) who isn't exactly overwhelmed when he transforms himself back into a she. RKO shelved the film for several months after disastrous previews which had prompted Hepburn and director George Cukor to offer RKO another film for free if they scrapped *Sylvia Scarlett* completely.

'Viewed today, *Sylvia Scarlett* can be seen as amazingly ahead of its time, and Kate's androgyne a remarkable portrait of a sensitive, vital, straightforward woman facing her own sexuality in an engaging and often enlightening manner,' Anne Edwards wrote in her biography of the star.[2]

Yentl, based on a short story by the Yiddish writer Isaac Bashevis Singer, starred and was co-written and co-produced by

Barbra Streisand and in it she played a young Jewish woman whose desire for education can only be fulfilled if she passes herself off as a man. Streisand's involvement at every level of the film suggested a degree of hubris, and her performance, whilst ambitious, was not convincing. That *Yentl* was neither entirely a dramatic film nor entirely a musical didn't help and audiences stayed away in droves. Whilst *Sylvia Scarlett* had become something of a cult movie by the mid-1960s, *Yentl* has all but disappeared and is no longer even available on video.

Both Marlene Dietrich and Greta Garbo had successes in roles in which they wore men's clothes. Dietrich donned a black tuxedo in her first America film, *Morocco* (1930), a white one in *Blonde Venus* (1932) and a naval uniform in *Seven Sinners* (1940). But Dietrich, like Garbo, was sexually ambiguous on screen *and* off and it was these two women who popularised women's wearing of trousers. Garbo is virtually androgynous in the title role in *Queen Christina* (1933). Perhaps Garbo's greatest screen role, Queen Christina, a seventeenth century Swedish monarch with a penchant for wearing male attire and almost certainly a lesbian, allowed the star to fully exploit her own ambiguity. Interestingly, Garbo's appearance in this film is echoed by Tim Curry as Frank-N-Furter in *The Rocky Horror Picture Show* (1975), based upon the stage hit *The Rocky Horror Show* which made bodices, stockings and suspenders almost *de rigueur* amongst heterosexual men and which has recently celebrated its twenty-first birthday.

One of the more bizarre transvestite performances came from Mercedes McCambridge as one of a gang of thugs who rape Janet Leigh in Orson Welles's *Touch of Evil* (1958). The actress is uncredited, but easily recognisable.

Adapted from Reinhold Schunzel's play *Viktor und Viktoria*, which also served as the basis for 1982's Julie Andrews-starring *Victor/Victoria*, *First a Girl*, dating from 1935, was actually banned in the State of Maryland because the transvestite scenes were too much for the local censor. Jessie Matthews, who should have become a huge international star, plays an aspirant showgirl who is convinced by an ailing drag queen (Sonnie Hale) to stand in for him at a London music hall. Snapped up by an international impressario, Victor/Victoria creates a sensation because she appears as a man playing a woman. Griffith Jones plays the socialite who is strangely attracted but slightly repelled by this 'boy' who makes a marvellous 'girl'. Filmed in black-and-white, with spectacular dance routines, songs and costumes, *First a Girl* was remarkably explicit with its homosexual sub-text and must have shocked the more conventional audiences of sixty years ago.

Although the opening sequences of *First a Girl* are set in London, the action quickly moves to Paris – presumably because a transvestite floor show was just the kind of exotic entertainment British socialites would travel to the continent to experience. Blake Edwards, producer, writer and director of *Victor/Victoria* dispenses entirely with the British setting, locating the whole film in Paris and with Julie Andrews playing Victoria Grant, a refugee from The Bath Touring Opera Company, stranded and starving in Paris. To ensure that the film has international appeal, Robert Preston plays Toddy, the aging queen who coaches Victoria as she transmutes into the fabulous Victor and James Garner is brought into play as the love interest, no longer a British m'lord, now an American gangster with a bodyguard who turns out to be gay. The entire movie is located within a gay *milieu* and although some viewers may consider the use of the word 'gay' is anachronistic, it isn't. When it came into wide circulation in the late 1960s it had already been used in its contemporary context for several decades. In his *Dictionary of the British and American Underworld*, Eric Partridge defines a 'gay cat' as 'a homosexual boy' tracing his source to Noel Erskine's *Glossary of Prison Slang*, published in America in 1933.

I have tracked the word as meaning 'homosexual' as far back as 1929 in Noël Coward's lyric for 'Green Carnation' from the operetta *Bitter Sweet*. A quartet of young men sing:

> Faded boys, jaded boys, come what may
> Art is our inspiration
> And as we are the reason for the Nineties being gay
> We all wear a green carnation.

Such blooms were worn by Oscar Wilde and his circle of male friends as a way of proclaiming their homosexuality to other initiates. If Coward could use the word 'gay' to designate homosexual in 1929, it was almost certainly in circulation in sophisticated circles for some years before that. Words usually have had to have been in use for some time before they first appear in print and then are defined in dictionaries of one kind or another.

By so firmly placing *Victor/Victoria* within a homosexual context, Blake Edwards is reinforcing the popular view that homosexual men and lesbians are really their opposite gender constrained within the wrong body. The gay men in the film are essentially effete (Toddy) whilst the lesbians used as setting dressing are butch and straight from a nightclub photograph by Brassai.

Although the linchpin to the plots of both *First a Girl* and *Victor/Victoria*, neither film is really about cross-dressing but rather about cross-dressing as disguise. Both Jessie Matthews in *First a Girl* and Julie Andrews in *Victor/Victoria* dress as men because it is expedient – it will advance their showbusiness careers; the cross-dressing of Sonnie Hale in the former and Robert Preston in the latter is to avert prosecution for the fraud perpetrated by Victoria who has been passing herself off as a man impersonating a woman and to create releasing laughter as the implicit homosexual threat of the false male becoming involved with the real male is removed and the homosexual threat of the actual homosexual, Hale and Preston, is removed because they don dresses and become clowns.

The cross-dressing of the women in both films has been used to create tension, specifically *sexual* tension (straight men are shown attracted to a woman they believe to be a gay man impersonating a woman); the cross-dressing of the men is used to diffuse that same sexual tension. The gender confusion is compounded both by Toddy, who convinces Victoria that people will accept the illusion she is presenting because 'People believe what they see' and by Garner who, having reached a moment of erotic recognition and before going into a passionate clinch with Andrews declares 'I don't care if you are a man.' This last utterance neatly echoes Joe E Brown's famous reflection at the end of *Some Like It Hot* after he has been told by 'Daphne' (Jack Lemmon), the woman he loves, that she is really a he. 'Well ... Nobody's perfect.'

It's worth observing that *Victor/Victoria* is replete with references to *Some Like It Hot*, so much so that the perceptive viewer is left wondering whether or not Blake Edwards intended his film as a homage to Billy Wilder's. Even Lesley Ann Warren, who plays James Garner's mistress Norma, appears to be doing an impersonation of Marilyn Monroe, thereby applying an additional level of ambiguity to the film as in effect she is a woman impersonating a woman.

Released in 1959, Billy Wilder's *Some Like It Hot* tells the story of two impoverished musicians, double bass player Denis (Jack Lemmon) and saxophonist Joe (Tony Curtis) who have the misfortune to witness the St Valentine's Day Massacre in a garage in Chicago in 1929 and make their escape disguised as Daphne and Josephine in an all-girl band which features singer Sugar Kane (Marilyn Monroe). Curtis falls for Monroe and once the band has reached Miami takes on a third role, that of a slightly dotty millionaire whose vocalisation is borrowed from Cary Grant.

'In *Some Like It Hot*, I was really doing three characters under the cover of one,' Tony Curtis wrote in his autobiography. 'There was Joe, the musician; vain, shallow, only interested in going from job to job. There was that woman Josephine: aloof, arrogant, well educated, frightened of men. There was that rich, indolent, bored millionaire who happens to talk like Cary Grant for some reason. Each of them had a little seed from my own life, or lives.'[3]

Until *Tootsie* (1982) and *Mrs Doubtfire* (1993), *Some Like It Hot* was probably the most successful commercial movie to be sustained throughout by the use of drag. But unlike *First a Girl* or *Victor/Victoria* drag was not a metaphor for homosexuality – it is a film very much about heterosexual men in disguise to preserve their lives who find themselves in heterosexual heaven: surrounded by beautiful women who they can observe but not touch. So essentially heterosexual is the film that it gets only passing mention in Vito Russo's comprehensive *The Celluloid Closet: Homosexuality in the Movies*, when Russo comments that some critics found Jack Lemmon's performance in *Some Like It Hot* repellent because he 'seemed to be enjoying his role too much.'[4]

'Billy brought in a female impersonator to work with Jack and me and teach us things like how to hold our hands,' Curtis continues. 'If we held them up, our muscles showed. If we held them palm down, the muscles disappeared. When we walked in heels, we threw our weight forward and our bottoms under. We had our legs and chests shaved, eyebrows plucked, extensive make-up tests with lipstick and eyelashes and a variety of wigs with different cuts and colours. Our hips were padded underneath the dresses. We had a voice coach to help us pitch our voices higher.'[5]

Some Like It Hot is a brilliantly funny movie which combines a witty script (I A L Diamond and Billy Wilder), crisp direction (Wilder) and a clutch of highly polished performances (Curtis, Lemmon, Monroe, Joe E Brown). The audience is in on the central illusion from the very beginning and it is this fore-knowledge which creates the comedy. Laughter comes as a release from tension – observe the highly dramatic scene in which Curtis and Lemmon witness the St Valentine's Day Massacre, narrowly escaping from the killers to reappear in a rear view shot of the two of them, now in full drag, progressing down the platform at Chicago's station to entrain for Florida as members of an all-female band. Curtis is prim and purse-lipped, Lemmon is all adither and wobbling on his high heels. 'How do they walk in these things?' Lemmon asks. 'It must be something to do with the distribution of weight,' Curtis responds.

Yet regardless of the centrality of drag to the plot of *Some Like It Hot*, the film, like Hollywood's other major movies about men in frocks, *Tootsie* and *Mrs Doubtfire*, is not a movie *about* cross-dressing. *Some Like It Hot* is a high comedy about survival; *Tootsie* is a broad comedy about work; *Mrs Doubtfire* is a sentimental comedy about family life. Ultimately, these, and other movies which use drag are neither about cross-dressing nor about women, they are movies about men which reinforce male values all the way down the line.

In *Tootsie*, Dustin Hoffman stars as Michael Dorsey, a dedicated actor possessed of a reputation for being difficult which makes it impossible for him to get work. Deciding that if he can't find employment as a man, he'll try to get work as a woman and, disguising himself as Dorothy Michaels, auditions for and lands a leading role in a television soap. As Dorothy Michaels, Michael Dorsey utilises fully the character defects which, when he was working as a man, kept him out-of-work. He changes lines, he doesn't do what the director wants and he's generally feisty. This being a Hollywood movie, Dorothy Michaels quickly becomes a household name across America.

Just as in *Some Like It Hot* and *Victor/Victoria*, the donning of the attire of the opposite gender causes sexual confusion on-screen and hilarity in the audience who shriek when Dorothy falls for co-star Jessica Lange who thinks the older woman has barely suppressed lesbian tendencies and shriek again when Jessica Lange's screen father, Charles During, in turn falls in love with Dorothy.

Larry Gelbart and Murray Schisgal's screenplay is a wolf in sheep's clothing – ostensibly a movie about the way men treat (abuse) women (Dorothy Michaels finds herself the butt of anti-feminism, prejudice and sexism), the film is ultimately about the way Dorothy Michaels succeeds because she is a man and uses a man's tricks and wiles to win as *a* woman as well as winning *the* woman. It seems more than likely that Hoffman brought much baggage of his own to the role – including the knowledge that he's considered an intensely difficult actor himself and the fact that he's not cast from the heroic mould from which we expect movie *stars* to come. Ultimately, *Tootsie* is a rather shallow entertainment with intellectual pretensions above its station about how it takes a man to be a really successful woman. Russo is vitriolic: 'Hollywood is where a timid rehash of *Some Like It Hot* called *Tootsie* can successfully pretend to have something to say about sex roles.'[6]

In the equally successful (profitable) *Mrs Doubtfire*, separated from *Tootsie* by a decade, the actor and comedian Robin Williams donned a frock and a wig and a pound-and-a-half of make-up to become housekeeper to the wife who is divorcing him so that he can get closer to their kids. It can be no coincidence that the male role Williams plays is of an underemployed actor whose talents are mostly applied to voice-overs in advertisements.

It's worth noting here that a remarkable number of films which utilise *travesti* work within some kind of showbusiness framework: Jessie Matthews in *First a Girl* and Julie Andrews in *Victor/Victoria* are cabaret entertainers; Tony Curtis and Jack Lemmon in *Some Like It Hot* are musicians; both *Farewell, My Concubine* (1993) and *M Butterfly* (1994) use Chinese opera; Dustin Hoffman in *Tootsie* and Robin Williams in *Mrs Doubtfire* are actors; Merle Oberon as George Sand in *A Song to Remember* (1945) is a novelist; Marlene Dietrich in *Blonde Venus* is a nightclub entertainer and Garbo in *Queen Christina* is a head of state (a position that perfectly combines *show* and *business*). Entertainers know about dissembling, disguise, *deceit*.[7]

Mrs Doubtfire is a remorselessly heterosexist film which couldn't offend even the 'Family Values' and 'Back to Basics' brigade. There is even irony in the sequence in which Williams' gay brother (Harvey Fierstein) and his lover help Williams find the *persona* he will become once in drag before settling for the capacious bosom and matronly charms of Mrs Doubtfire because, in my opinion, Fierstein, who has worked in drag and is a gay man, has written more about family relationships (albeit 'Pretend family relationships') than he has about homosexual relationships. 'After this, though, it's back, with a vehement vengeance, to family values,' Andy Medhurst postulated in an article about drag on screen and, specifically, *Mrs Doubtfire*:

> In many ways, *Mrs Doubtfire* is *Tootsie* plus children. If the earlier film was about Dustin Hoffman proving that only a man could be a better woman, then *Mrs Doubtfire* wants to argue that to be the perfect father you have to take over the mother's role too – father knows best, even or especially when he's wearing a dress. It's an intersection of the man-in-drag comedy with the sentimentalised New Man fatherhood film (*Three Men and a Baby*, *Parenthood*). Men (and their families) benefit from finding their 'feminine side' – not on the face of it a bad message, but the film can only advocate this by simultaneously vilifying the mother (a palpably harassed Sally Field) for finding her 'masculine side' – wanting her career, not appreciating the joys of housework.'[8]

There have been more films in which drag plays an important part in the past decade than ever before. But does this mean that drag has become more acceptable? Does it imply that traditional views of masculinity are changing? Does the explosion of drag into popular culture intimate that we now live in a world where difference is at least tolerated, if not fully accepted?

To my mind, the answers to most of these questions is pretty negative. Most films which use drag as a plot component, use it as a comic device: a man in a frock is still seen as inherently comic (a woman in a suit is more usually seen as threatening). There are considerably fewer movies in which drag is used to chilling effect – as in *The Devil Doll* or *Dressed to Kill*. Nor do I think that an increased incidence of drag in movies implies that traditional views of masculinity are changing because almost invariably films about men (or women) cross-dressing are about individuals forced by circumstances to cross-dress and triumphing against their circumstances because they are really men. And if men's traditional roles are actually being reinforced by films in which they dress as women (*Tootsie*, *Mrs Doubtfire*), this implies that there's no change so far as tolerance or acceptance of difference is concerned.   PB

Notes

1. Alec Guinness, *Blessings in Disguise* (London: Hamish Hamilton, 1985). 'During *Kind Hearts and Coronets* I was required to make a balloon ascent dressed as Lady Agatha D'Ascoigne*, in Edwardian clothes,' pp 199–200. *Guinness mis-spells the name, it should be D Ascoyne.

2. Anne Edwards, *Katherine Hepburn: A Biography* (London: Hodder & Stoughton, 1985), p 117.

3. Tony Curtis and Barry Paris, *Tony Curtis: The Autobiography* (London: Wm Heinemann, 1994), p 154.

4. Vito Russo, *The Celluloid Closet: Homosexuality in the Movies*, revised edition (New York: Harper & Row, 1987), p 7.

5. Curtis and Parry, cited above.

6. Russo, cited above, p 323.

7. The most spectacular nightclub in Manhattan in the 1970s to be frequented by transvestites was G G Barnum's Gilded Grape where the only way to differentiate between men in frocks and women was because the men looked the more feminine.

8. Andy Medhurst, 'The frock of the new', (London: *The Observer*, January 23rd 1994).

Chapter six

Frock Tactics

THERE is a curious band of fellows in the town who call themselves 'Mollies' who are so totally destitute of all masculine attributes that they prefer to behave as women. They adopt all the small vanities natural to the feminine sex to such an extent that they try to speak, walk, chatter, shriek, scold as women do, aping them as well in other respects. In a certain tavern in the city they hold parties and regular gatherings. As soon as they arrive they begin to behave exactly as women do, carrying on light gossip as is the custom in a merry company of real women. Later on, one of their brothers, or 'sisters' (in their feminine jargon) would be dressed in a woman's nightgown with a silken nightcap, and thus representing a woman, bear a 'child' (a dummy being to hand for this purpose) which is afterwards baptised, while another man in a large hat plays the part of a country midwife, a third that of the nurse, the rest of them acting as unseemly guests at a christening. Each had to discourse at length about and with great impropriety of the pleasures of a 'husband' and children, and praise the virtues of the former and the wonderful talents of the latter. Some others, in the role of 'widows', lamented the deplorable loss of their 'husbands'. Thus each imitated the petty feminine faults of women gossiping over coffee, in order to disguise their natural feelings (as men) towards the fair sex, and to encourage unnatural lusts.[1]

What a performance! Ned Ward's description of a London molly-house in 1709 is one of the earliest accounts of what in the modern vernacular could be called 'a drag act in a gay pub'. Ward made two mistakes that still haunt discussions about the connection between male homosexuality and drag. The customers' elaborate satire was not mocking women, but the mores and rituals of the dominant culture. And homosexual effeminacy is less about wanting to be a woman, and more about refusing to be a man.

For gay men as much as for straights, drag is now thought of as being as much of a gay preserve as sodomy or camp. Something that gay men do that straights don't. Male homosexuality has often been seemingly inextricably linked with drag – for male homosexuality has usually been seen as a kind of drag of the flesh, of 'women being trapped in men's bodies.' But celebrity drag artists would furiously deny that there was anything 'gay' about their act – often because they themselves were in the closet. The pretence was maintained that it was all situational drag. Something they had to do, rather than wanted to. Female impersonation was just a job. It was the perverts who got pleasure out of it. This chapter looks at how gay men reclaimed drag from the theatrical closet, and made drag come to mean, not just women's clothes but gay men's clothes, and how pop has played with this new meaning.

After the Second World War all-male drag revues were a popular attraction in British theatres. Shows such as *Forces Showboat* and *Soldiers in Skirts* had developed out of the situational drag of the troops own entertainment revues, where servicemen had played both the female and male parts. By 1950 when the shows were reaching a peak of popularity queens had, for the most part, usurped the ex-servicemen in their casts.[2] The queens drastically changed the look of the shows – traditionally female impersonators had played unattractive, usually mother-in-law types. But the queens didn't want to look funny or grotesque, they wanted to look beautiful.[3]

By the mid 1950s the shows were losing their appeal – due to a lethal combination of theatre closures, the rise of television, and loss of novelty. Moreover as the homosexual became an increasingly visible spectre during this decade – the *Kinsey Report* had been published in 1948, the *Wolfenden Report* came in 1957 – all those queens camping it up no longer seemed quite so much like wholesome family entertainment. The shows closed and the drag queens moved on. Danny La Rue made it big, some went to work in pubs and clubs, but most packed their frocks away.

There were still only a handful of 'queer pubs' in the country in the 1950s, but drag acts were a popular attraction in some working-class straight pubs. Some of these such as Stockwell's Vauxhall Tavern and Camden's Black Cap began attracting gay men in growing numbers to their shows, and by the late 1960s had slowly metamorphosed into gay pubs.

As the gay scene grew dramatically during the 1970s, owners found drag acts a popular and cheap form of entertainment. Much of their appeal was not in how the drag queens looked, but in what they could say. In drag a gay man had permission to talk and sing about other men – about loving them, hating them and shagging them. Two gay drag act archetypes emerged. There were those, like Mrs Shufflewick before them, who created a character, and there were those who mimed along to records by gay men's favoured female singers: Judy Garland, Shirley Bassey or Marilyn Monroe.

The women that the 'character actors' (often benignly grotesque) and the 'mime artists' (often glamorous) were impersonating were larger than life and sassy. If they were comic, they were comic heroines, celebratory and camp. Drag was a way of inverting the effeminate stigma attached to being gay and wearing it as a badge of pride. But though the drag artists rarely took themselves seriously, as Christopher Isherwood explained, 'You can't camp about something you don't take seriously. You're not making fun of it; you're making fun out of it. You're expressing what's basically serious to you in terms of fun and artifice and elegance.'[4] The mime artists paid homage to the female stars with which gay men identified. This began in part through the absence of out male icons, but the character actors became the first gay created stars – the adored matriarchs of our 'pretended families', often establishing an incredible rapport with their audience. Many gay men were fiercely loyal to drag acts – they were, after all, one of the few things that gay men could point to and call 'ours'.

Sadly some acts often fell into misogyny – as if they were ridiculing women in an attempt to explain or justify their interest in men. Many were hopelessly untalented. Of those that weren't only Hinge and Brackett managed to achieve mainstream success. Most stuck with the gay circuit.

Few drag acts would have admitted to having any political intent, for most of them frocking up was only a bit of fun. But come the heady days of the late 1960s politics had also become fun, and being gay had become increasingly political – it was drag queens who were among the fiercest fighters during New York's Stonewall Riots in 1969. Yet drag's relationship with gay politics was somewhat fraught. The politer kind of gay law reformer was trying to downplay any link between homosexuality, effeminacy and drag – to pretend that gay men were as dully normal as straight men. Informed by feminism, the more radical strand of gay politics often viewed drag as demeaning to women, and of course much of the pub drag was. The Gay Liberation Front, formed in London in 1970, for the most part took a more inclusive view. They weren't in favour of assimilation at any cost, nor of downplaying our differences, but desired a radical overhaul of sexual and gender codes, of which drag could play a part.

Drag was seen by many as politicising in itself. The American activist Larry Mitchell asserted that 'there is more to be learned from wearing a dress for a day, than there is from wearing a suit for life.'[5] Some wore frocks to GLF dances, and some even to GLF meetings. The GLF's Street Theatre Group believed that to wear drag on the underground or to the shops was an empowering act of confrontation. Gay men in women's bathing costumes picketed the trial of feminists charged with disrupting the Miss World Contest, and in September 1971 drag played a central part in the GLF's most notorious zap, Operation Rupert: lesbians and gay men dressed as nuns released mice into the audience of the Christian rally, the Festival of Light, before climbing onto the stage and dancing the cancan in front of Cliff Richard and Malcolm Muggeridge.

A new kind of drag had evolved: Radical Drag. Its practitioners, the Rad Fems, were wary of straightforward female impersonation. 'We began to realise that there were ways of using drag,' recalled GLF member Michael James, whose most famous creation was a half-man half-woman split right down the middle. 'It's a way of giving up the power of the male role. We were holding the mirror up to man, showing that we rejected what maleness stood for.'[6] The GLF began a Transvestite, Transsexual and Drag Queen Group: 'almost all women – people born male who live as women, or more commonly, dress as women, whenever they get the chance.'[7] They knew that there was a world of difference between how people reacted to men in frocks on a theatre stage, and how people reacted to them on the street. 'There are many questions we are just beginning to examine. Why is Danny La Rue a West End institution, when we get kicked out of our flats for wearing a skirt? Apparently it's alright if you're doing it for money, but perverted if you do it for personal satisfaction.'[8] Although they felt they themselves were engaged in a kind of performance, as 'radical drag was constant street theatre, to make ordinary people think about sex roles.'[9]

The Rad Fems developed a more playful, almost androgynous, attitude to both clothing and gender. 'We don't want to discard the male role just to take on the female one,'[10] proclaimed one manifesto. There were now two options open to a drag queen 'to pass or not to pass'.[11] To look like a woman, or to take the best from both worlds.

Some, most notably the American troupes Hot Peaches, the Fabulous Cockettes and the Cycle Sluts, took this street theatre into Off-Off-Broadway theatres during the 1970s. In Britain 'genderfuck' drag was championed by Bloolips who claimed to 'kick over the stereotypes by using stereotypes.'[12]

But pop music had been embracing 'genderfuck' and androgyny since the 1950s. Its history is littered with men who have challenged and changed what it means to be a man, and blurred the boundaries of gender. Think of Elvis Presley allowing himself to be a sex object, or Johnnie Ray bursting into tears on stage. Pop is a prophecy that keeps coming true – where behaviour that had once been marginal soon becomes mainstream. The Beatles were originally derided for having dangerously effeminate collar length hair, but soon became 'those lovable mop tops'. Young people's refusal to conform to their parents' gender codes pushed the generation gap ever wider. The outrage it invariably caused was welcomed, and androgyny became a form of rebellion.[13] British youth cults, from teds, through mods and hippies, to today's rave scene, have all been castigated for the 'effeminacy' of their male followers' dress, and from mods onwards, because you 'can't tell the boys from the girls'.

Little Richard was the first star to bring self-conscious camp into rock and roll. But Richard's brand of androgyny was used to suggest not danger, but safety: 'We were breaking through the racial barrier,' he told his biographer Charles White. 'The white kids had to hide my records cos they daren't let their parents know they had them in the house. We decided that my image should be crazy and way out so that adults would think I was harmless. I'd appear in one show dressed as the Queen of England and in the next as the Pope.'[14] For a black male star such as Little Richard it was the lesser of two evils to signify homosexuality through dress and demeanour than to be thought heterosexual. He achieved cross over success by emasculating himself, and turning himself into a figure of fun, not of fear: the self-styled 'Bronze Liberace.'

Unlike in Britain, drag has never been part of mainstream American culture. Yet many black male singers from Little Richard and his contemporary Esquerita, to Prince and Michael Jackson have chosen to utilise a drag of the voice, the falsetto, as well as adopting an androgynous look. And the most popular black television star during the early 1970s was Flip Wilson, a male comedian whose best loved creation was Geraldine Jones. Whether Geraldine was meant to be a sassy black girl or a gay black man in drag was open to interpretation.

The Rolling Stones were the first rock act to use drag to suggest not being harmless but harmful. The granny drag they all wore on the sleeve of, and in the promotional film for, their 1966 single 'Have you seen your mother baby?' caused considerably more outrage in the States than it did in their home country. Mick Jagger tried to reassure horrified American reporters that 'The English don't need much convincing to dress up as a woman.'[15] At the televised Hyde Park memorial concert for Brian Jones in 1969 Jagger wore a white smock designed by Mr Fish, the archetypal 'Swinging Sixties designer to the stars'.[16] Fish explained that this was not a dress, but a 'unisex' look based on the tunics of those terribly manly Greek soldiers. Jagger was a past master at doing one thing and saying another himself. He minced across the stage, and would affect a heavily camp demeanour, but in his songs would reassure the audience how thoroughly heterosexual he was. Just as Mr Fish's little number may have looked like a dress, but was 'really' a soldier's uniform, so Jagger may have looked like a queen, but he was 'really' straight. His effeminacy even seemed to increase his attraction to women. Through Jagger pop learned to use the allure of camp, androgyny and drag, but to avoid explicit admissions of homosexuality. Frocks were an ideal way to signal a knowledge of the forbidden territory of homosexuality – particularly for those who were only interested in its surfaces. And as long as the public could convince themselves it was only an act, it was usually acceptable.

Though the subject of homosexuality still remained taboo in pop, by the late 1960s drag had become a popular subject for song.[17] Whereas popular music has usually centred on first person narratives, drag has given it some of its most famous characters. The Who were first with 'I'm a boy' in 1966, the story of Bill, a young man whose mother wanted another daughter and forces him into frocks, wigs and make-up. The next year Pink Floyd also made the British charts with 'Arnold Layne' whose cross-dressing was entirely of his own volition. 1968 gave us Van Morrison's majestic 'Madame George', as well as Desmond Jones in the Beatles' 'Ob la di o bla da' and then Sweet Loretta Martin in 'Get back'. Although 'Madame George' apart, all of these songs were humorous, all of the characters were sympathetic. Arnold Layne may have been a bit 'pervy' but Pink Floyd did not draw any connection between his cross-dressing and homosexuality.

Somewhat ironically, few listeners noticed that at least one of the 'Honky tonk women' in the Rolling Stones' 1969 single of that name, didn't appear to be a real woman. Mick Jagger didn't seem too concerned either. As ever it was left to the Kinks to make explicit what the Stones had only dared hint at, with 'Lola' a British number two in 1970. The song is, again, a humorous one, the joke being that its narrator has not realised what we, the listeners, all have – the 'woman' he has fallen in love with is a man. 'Lola' has a great pay off line: 'I'm not the world's most masculine man, but I know what I am and I'm glad I'm a man and so is Lola.' The narrator appears quite satisfied with the 'woman' he's just met in a bar – and if Lola ever got around to telling him he was a man, one can imagine him echoing the last line of *Some Like It Hot* – 'Well, nobody's perfect.'[18]

The blueprint for many of pop's drag queens was made in Andy Warhol's Factory. Jackie Curtis, Candy Darling and Holly Woodlawn were Warhol hangers-on that Andy put centrestage in his late 1960s films *Flesh, Trash* and *Women In Revolt* – where they improvised their amphetamine-fuelled fantasies. Warhol disputed that they were drag queens, 'because they really think they are girls.' Similarly though they looked grotesque, they all laboured under the misapprehension that they were glamorous. But because the movies celebrated a trash aesthetic, the very grotesqueness of the 'superstars' became glamorous. Lou Reed, of the Factory's house band the Velvet Underground, also eulogised 'lowlife', and sang about the demimonde of rent boys, prostitutes, drugs and hustling these drag queens inhabited. He was an anti-hippy, who wrote about how nasty the world was, rather than how nice it could be. His 'social realist' lyrics introduced into pop the previously taboo subjects of drag, drugs and homosexuality – all brought together on a song like 'Sister Ray' – and found an audience not just among those who recognised themselves therein, but with those who were thrilled by the songs' very Otherness. Lou Reed's 1972 *Transformer* solo album (with a photograph of Reed in drag on the back cover), contained both his infamous reminisce about Candy, Holly, Jackie and the rest of the Factory set, 'Walk on the wild side', as well as the songs 'Make up' and 'Goodnight ladies', which connected drag to both the nascent gay scene and gay liberation. The songs on 1976's *Coney Island Baby* were loosely concerned with Reed's highly publicised relationship with Rachel, a transvestite.

The first rock stars to regularly frock up themselves, did so with the excuse that they had created a character. In 1969 Alice Cooper was the pioneer of combining frocks and androgyny in his stage shows – a mix of bisex and violence that was quickly dubbed 'shock rock' by others. Alice's habit of cross-dressing was, like his on stage *pièce de résistance*, chopping toy babies in half, done to summon outrage from his audience and critics. He was quite successful. Audiences would regularly walk out in disgust, and at one show in Michigan a gang of bikers climbed up on stage and threatened to kill the band. Sadly by the time Alice Cooper broke through, though he continued with his onstage blood and gore theatrics, he had dropped the drag and bisexuality.

It was left to British acts to take them into the mainstream. Cross-dressing's passage into pop had undoubtedly been eased by the unisex look of the hippies. According to Grace Slick, 'When the guys started putting on make-up, it wasn't that much of a shift from the long hair and beads and purses and stuff that guys had been wearing in the sixties.'[19] Just as the hippies had swapped clothing and hair styles between genders, so glam rock fought to give male stars access to the previously female confine of glamour in dress. Marc Bolan, an ex-mod and an ex hippy, was the first to put a little glitter on his face. He then moved onto feather boas and womens' shoes, and rapidly found himself subject to rumours that he was planning a sex change operation.

It was his rival and friend, David Bowie, another ex-mod and ex-hippy, but moreover a huge Velvet Underground fan, who made glam all his own. As far back as 1964 the then David Jones was causing outrage and sexual confusion in equal parts purely by the length of his hair, telling a local newspaper at the time how, 'Dozens of times I've been politely told to clear out of the lounge bar at public houses. Everybody makes jokes about you on a bus, and if you go past navvies digging in the road, it's murder.'[20] But, like so many after him, the seventeen-year-old David also loved the attention. And if a pop star is to break through, he needs attention by the bucketload.

When his first manager, Kenn Pitt, had told David in 1969 to give an interview to the early gay magazine, *Jeremy*, Bowie had complied somewhat reluctantly. But by 1971 he had come to see the capital to be gained by flirting with homosexuality, or more specifically of 'ambisexuality'.[21] Bowie bought two dresses from Mr Fish: long flowing gowns, one salmon pink and the other pale green. As with Mick Jagger's tunic, Mr Fish maintained these were dresses for men, contemporary variations on those worn by medieval noblemen. Bowie wore them, along with a shoulder bag and eye shadow, on his first promotional tour of the States, and began claiming in interviews to have once been a 'shaven headed transvestite'. All this was groundbreaking – there was even a gang of drag queens who'd regularly attend his London concerts, hoisting their new hero upon their shoulders with jubilation as he sang his encores at a show at the Royal Festival Hall. David famously modeled the green dress on the front cover of his album *The Man who Sold the World*. Though his American record company demanded that the photo was replaced by an inoffensive cartoon, and a new sleeve was issued in Britain when the record was re-released in 1972.

In January 1972 Bowie took the unprecedented step of coming out in an interview with *Melody Maker*. Though Bowie claimed 'I am gay and always have been,' he also spoke of his love for his wife and child, and when the interviewer asked, 'Why aren't you wearing your girl's dress today?' David parroted Mr Fish's excuse, 'Oh dear, you must understand that it's not a woman's. It's a *man's* dress.'[22]

Just as his frock only looked like a woman's dress, Bowie had his own escape clause. When he said he was gay, or wore a frock, or sang a song like 'Width of a circle' or 'Queen bitch', he was only an actor playing a role.[23] He created a succession of characters: Ziggy Stardust, Aladdin Sane, the Thin White Duke, to do his dirty work for him. When the Velvet Underground or the Kinks had sung about drag or homosexuality they were both, in very different ways, concerned with songwriting as 'realism'. Bowie had the comfort of not being 'real', and was no more 'really' gay, than Tony Curtis and Jack Lemmon were 'really' cross-dressing jazz musicians. Or so he often liked us to believe.

By the time of Ziggy Stardust, Bowie was embracing a more androgynous look – wearing a technicolour leotard on his infamous first *Top of the Pops* appearance singing 'Starman.' He even airbrushed out his penis on the *Aladdin Sane* album sleeve, and wore a cheater as Newton in Nic Roeg's film *The Man Who Fell to Earth*. Surprisingly, in a culture where we are led to believe that for men to be attractive they should be as unlike women as possible, Bowie, like Jagger before him, became a huge sex symbol.[24] And not just to women. Both caused more than a few confusing erections in men.

Bowie soon moved on to poses new, leaving drag, androgyny and bisexuality behind,[25] but having already taken things to such extremes the pop mainstream moved over. Cross-dressing and dressing up became everyday in the British charts and glam rock was born. Acts like Roxy Music, Elton John and Gary Glitter divorced their dressing up from sexuality and used it as just another fancy dress outfit. Sweet and Mud, said at the time to look like 'brickies in drag', wore frocks – usually quite plain affairs, and they wouldn't wear make up or wigs – as a way of mocking the excesses of Bowie or Bolan.

Glam was pop as self-conscious camp. Not just because of the dressing up and the drag, but because it was about pop stars not taking themselves in the least bit seriously. At the back of all this was the reassurance that it was 'only a bit of fun'. Perhaps it could only have happened in Britain, where men in frocks are too redolent of childhood trips to the panto, or Les Dawson and Danny La Rue, to be truly shocking.

Certainly the groups glam helped inspire in the States were destined to remain on the margins. The New York Dolls first appeared as a four piece called Actress in 1971, and unveiled their new name and new look, more trash than camp, in May 1972. The New York Dolls took their sartorial cues from glam rock, the Warhol superstars, the Rolling Stones' early 1970s decadent look, and the gay bars where they would often seek refuge.[26] Commented photographer Bob Gruen: 'They were setting the pace. The thing that was funny was they said Uptown, "Oh, they're gay. They dress like girls." Well, no girls dressed like that. No girls walk around in cellophane tutus with army boots. They mixed the genders.'[27] They also had a teasing sexuality, lead singer David Johansen's most celebrated line was 'I'm trisexual ... I'll try anything!' But though they received much favourable coverage in Britain, the Dolls were unable to break out of their cult following in the States. They inspired a brace of frock rockers in New York: Cinderella Backstreet, Forty Second Street Harlots, the Miamis, Frankenstein and Teenage Lust. All were white trash, into confrontation, and none of them got anywhere. One American band managed to capitalise on their groundwork by downplaying the cross-dressing, polymorphous perversity and drag, and playing up the make-up and bubble gum punk sound. Kiss were clowns, and they became huge.

Wayne County was the scene's one true transvestite. Wayne had started out on the fringes of the Warhol set, and had acted in

Andy Warhol's play *Polk* in England in 1971, *Crawdaddy* magazine saw the singer's live act as taking the New York scene to its 'logical conclusion ... County's act is carried on in total drag; he wears a plastic cunt with straw hair, sucks off a large dildo, shoots 'come' at the audience with a plastic squirt gun, and for an encore eats dogfood out of a toilet bowl ... while these groups and their fans on this burgeoning scene profess to be parodying or 'camping on' various sexual styles (bisexuality, transvestism, sadomasochism), it is difficult to say where affectation ends and reality begins.'[28] County later relocated to England and became a part of the British punk scene with his new band the Electric Chairs. He used the same shock tactics on stage and wrote some great songs, most notably '(If you don't wanna fuck me) Fuck off' and 'Are you man enough to be a woman?' Punks demanded outrage, and County in his woolly hat, tatty nightie and 'plastic cunt', provided it.[29]

Arguably, glam's most enduring and successful by-product was the rock musical *The Rocky Horror Show*. This horror movie spoof transferred on to the big screen in 1975, with Tim Curry playing Dr Frank N Furter, the self-styled 'sweet transvestite from Transsexual, Transylvania' in black stockings, suspenders and bodice and plenty of tarty make-up. His drag was meant to suggest his deviant sexuality, but the movie itself is a celebration of sexual experimentation and nonconformity. All the leading characters, including the previously 'straight' young innocent couple, Brad and Janet, drag up like Frank N Furter for the grand finale, and sing the movie's great message song 'Don't dream it, be it.' *The Rocky Horror Picture Show* has had a formidable cult following at late night screenings in Britain and America ever since its release, with most of the audience dressing up, joining in with dialogue and providing their own special effects.[30]

As drag and effeminacy increasingly became seen by many heterosexuals as signifiers of homosexuality during the 1970s, some gay men reacted against such stereotyping by embracing a more masculinist look. The so called 'clones' were a kind of butch drag – a new form of dressing up by gay men and a way of fetishising their own bodies by turning themselves into one of Quentin Crisp's Great Dark Men.

The Village People took this butch drag into the charts, each member playing a character from the gallery of all-American males; cop, GI, construction worker, cowboy, native American and biker. But, like so many gay drag acts, their sense of camp humour and artifice served to disempower and deflate these symbols of hyper-masculinity. It was left to the black American singer Sylvester, to bring an image of the queen into the mainstream. Sylvester was happy to join the Little Richard tradition of the emasculated black male star – he had a beautiful falsetto voice and often performed in a flowing white robe – but unlike those that had preceded him, Sylvester was highly politicised, eloquent and unequivocally out.

Most of the other gay men involved in making disco music were working behind the scenes as songwriters and producers. And most of the records were sung by women – a continuation of the gay tradition of female worship that drag belonged to.[31] Disco produced no drag queen stars,[32] and yet the disco divas were drag at a distance. They were women, who sang songs about men, that were written by and aimed primarily at gay men. This became more explicit with Hi NRG during the early 1980s. Records like the Weather Girls' 'It's raining men', Sinitta's 'Cruising' and Miquel Brown's 'So many men, so little time' allowed songs that expressed sexually charged gay sentiments to still be covert enough to achieve a mainstream success that would have been nigh on impossible if they had been sung by men.

Before Hi NRG crossed over in Britain, something strange was happening in the charts. The 'new glam' of the New Romantics, pouting pretty boy pop stars with a touch of make-up and fussy clothes, gave way to the Gender Benders.

By the end of 1983 Culture Club's Boy George had established himself as the family's favourite pop star. Heavily but artfully made-up, with his hair in braids and a nice smock to top it all off, to many Boy George looked like a girl. Music journalist Simon Price remembers one playground conversation in 1982: 'Everyone: "Phwooar, did you see that girl out of Culture Club on *Top of the Pops* last night? Fancy her!" Me: "Actually chaps ..."'[33] *The Sun* took a rather different view of the same television appearance: 'Beautifully made up and wearing a tunic dress with trousers, it proceeded to prance about gracefully ... but it was impossible to tell from voice or prance whether the thing was male or female.'[34]

In November they ran 'a *Sun* exclusive on pop's newest sensation': 'Mister (*or is it Miss?*) Weirdo. He is number one in the charts and they call him the Gender Bender. He is the sensational singer who looks like a girl, sounds like a fella and behaves like something strangely in between.'[35]

Boy George came to be looked on and loved as the last of the great pantomime dames, rather than as a drag queen. Even America loved him – as another of those great English eccentrics. The most crucial part of his public image was his smile. He was *nice* and curiously asexual. Someone who famously claimed he'd 'rather have a cup of tea than sex.' Drag was a way of concealing any sexuality, rather than revealing homosexuality. But by the 1980s you could no longer get away with claiming frocks were only a bit of fun. George constantly had to justify his dressing up, and the main question being asked about Boy George soon ceased to be 'is it a he or a she?', and became 'is he or isn't he gay?'

He sang genderless love songs and his sexuality was chameleon like, depending on who was interviewing him.[36] In 1982, just as Culture Club were gathering attention, George reassured the *NME*: 'I'm not a transvestite. Everyone thinks I am, but I'm not. I wear y-fronts! I'm a man! I'm quite manly actually. I don't think I'm as poofy as I'm made out to be. I'm not gay or anything like that.'[37] He'd even make a Mr Fish like pitch for the manly tradition of men in frocks: 'I dress in a similar way to a priest or an archbishop. I wear robe's not dresses, and to be a transvestite you must wear womens' undergarments. I don't. I'm not fighting an oppressed need to be a woman. I'm proud to be a man. And if I wore a pot on my head I would not publicly assume the role of a kitchen. I would simply be being myself.'[38]

The last great pop star Britain has produced would assure the world that a man in a frock should be no big deal: 'I was quite shocked that the press could be so stupid. You just expect that after Danny La Rue and Quentin Crisp and God knows who else, someone would be able to accept someone with a bit of old make-up. England's like such a bunch of old drag queens anyway. If you pick up a history book . . . I'm quite tame compared to a lot of people.'[39] Though he showed typical perspicacity in understanding why he had caused such a fuss: 'I don't think it's being gay that's the problem. It's being effeminate. It's being not manly that's the problem. You see, when people accept Boy George they're accepting a million things about themselves. They're not accepting that I'm gay or straight; they're accepting that a man can act in a different way from how they're expected to act.'[40]

In George's wake came a ripple of cross-dressers that the press made out was a tidal wave of Gender Benders: his old friend and foe, Marilyn, a beautiful blonde with, hairy chest and dread-locks apart, more than a passing resemblance to Monroe, and the pervy midget Pete Burns of Dead or Alive. Even Divine finally broke through in 1984 with the rhetorical Hi NRG of 'You think you're a man'. After a butt slapping, lick lipping performance on *Top of the Pops* the BBC switchboard was deluged with a record number of complaints. Divine answered his critics with the bold assertion of his next single 'I'm so beautiful', and its follow up an ironic cover of the Four Seasons' 'Walk like a man'.

Divine was a character actor. A female impersonator who was lumped in with the Gender Benders for the sake of convenience. Divine was the stage name of Glenn Milstead, but 'Divine' became another character he created for highly lucrative personal appearances in clubs. Billing himself as 'the most beautiful woman in the world', he was a 375 lb man just about squeezed into a sequin dress and a shocking peroxide blonde wig. The joke being his sense of conviction of his own voluptuousness. He was brilliantly abusive and lewd on stage, but sweet as a pussy cat in interviews. Like many drag acts before him, Divine wanted to be recognised as an actor who specialised in playing female parts: 'I was on a big chat show in the States and he said, 'you're a transvestite,' and I said, 'I'm not, I'm an actor and entertainer,' and he said, 'So, if you're not a transvestite, why are you sitting here in a cocktail dress?' and I thought, well, he's got a very good point there.'[41]

Divine began playing a series of outrageous female lead characters during the 1970's in John Water's campy black comedies *Multiple Maniacs*, *Pink Flamingoes* and *Female Trouble*, as well as starring in Off-Broadway vehicles such as *Women Behind Bars*. In both the plays and the films he invariably was cast as a criminal, often murderous, outsider with few redeeming features. But in

Water's later, more mainstream, films, *Polyester* and *Hairspray*, he was equally believable playing the all-American doting mother.

Divine turned to recording in 1979 to embellish his night-club work. After making a couple of singles with New York's Hi NRG king Bobby O (which, like the early Water's films, were peerless but destined to remain cult classics), Divine was picked up in 1984 by Stock, Aitken and Waterman, the British production team who took Hi NRG out of the gay clubs and into the school discos. Mike Stock recalls this was a difficult decision, and reveals the hysteria that drag can cause in some people. 'Matt (Aitken) and I sat here agonising over the Divine song. We thought 'Are we leading impressionable young boys astray here? Are young boys going to turn gay because of Divine?'[42]

Divine's records were far more successful in Europe than in his home country. But the British Gender Benders helped spearhead what was dubbed 'the second British invasion of the American charts.' They were helped considerably by the rise of video and the arrival of MTV, which increased the value of an arresting visual style for pop acts. Commented the *Daily Mirror*, 'The Americans are getting very confused by the sex of the new British bands. First they thought Boy George was a girl and that Yazoo's Alf was really an Alfred. Now they are convinced that the Eurythmics' lovely Annie Lennox is actually a HE.'[43]

The androgyne female was a new development. Cross-dressing had previously been a male prerogative. Although in the 1950s the Beverley Sisters had caused a furore when they appeared on BBC television wearing trousers. Lennox went from a close cropped androgynous style to wearing Elvis drag at the Grammy Awards show and convincing man drag in the video for 'Who's that girl'. Grace Jones who'd been a butch disco diva since 1977, and had founded a career on, as she sang in one song 'feeling like a woman, looking like a man', was finally rewarded with her two biggest British singles in 1985.

As male artists had often found to their cost, many audiences were only interested in the surfaces. The bisexual and besuited female singer Ronny's career died a death, as did that of the butch lesbian folk singer Phranc. Just as gay men had been the standard bearers of male cross-dressing in pop, androgyny was used by lesbian singers, who were less worried about breaking gender codes, or appearing 'unfeminine'. But also to signify a sexuality they weren't yet fully prepared to announce. kd lang caused speculation through her masculine look, leading Madonna to quip, 'Elvis is alive and she's beautiful', and the Scottish singer Horse, much to her own consternation, was promoted in the States with the gruesome line, 'Is it a he or is it a she?' Few were that surprised when they both came out in the 1990s.

After glam had tested the waters in the 1970s, the American singer Jobriath marketed himself as the first out gay act, proclaiming, 'I think the world is ready for a true fairy'. The world wasn't quite ready, but ten years later the great Gender Bender boom did seem to ease the arrival of the first crop of out gay pop stars in Britain – Frankie Goes To Hollywood, Bronski Beat and Erasure.

However, after the AIDS crisis and its attendant moral backlash in the last half of the 1980s, drag withdrew from the pop arena and took refuge on the gay scene once more. Along with not talking to ugly people and passing round the poppers, drag was one of the few traditions of the gay scene – male strippers didn't appear until the mid 1980s. As ever there were the mime artists, and those that created a character. Some have taken these rather tired formulas a step further. Her Imperial Highness Regina Fong has developed a fanatical following on the London gay scene with an act more akin to sampling than miming – plundering an eclectic mix of sources from *Coronation Street*, to Helen Shapiro and a Marti Caine game show. His American equivalent Lypsinka, now an Off-Broadway star, splices together soundbites and songs from camp old movies into one continuous manic soliloquy. While the Italian Ennio Marchetto is a regular on the European festival circuit with his costumes and wigs made out of paper – a kind of origami karaoke.

By 1990 Lily Savage had established himself as the most popular drag act on the British gay scene. Paul O'Grady was a character actor, and Lily Savage a working-class Birkenhead single mother. Terry Sanderson has compared O'Grady with Alan Bennett – both have been 'mining a rich apparently inexhaustible seam of Northern childhood memories. Mainly memories of strong or eccentric women. Hasn't Bennett in fact been doing a drag act with his typewriter?'[44]

Lily is a comic heroine for many gay men. A gutsy, gritty and witty woman who is neither grotesque nor glamorous. Whilst satirising the brutal world from which gay men often have to flee, her experiences and entanglements with men resonate with our own. Lily is now more likely to be seen at the Edinburgh Festival and in small theatres, or doing television and radio guest spots, than on the gay scene where, one can't help feeling, she really belongs.

Though he had played a few shows in gay pubs, Julian Clary emerged out of London's alternative comedy circuit during the 1980s. Though this out gay comedian was given a platform by the politicised 'no sexist, no racist' scene, Clary was part of an older British comic tradition, more sauce than camp, that reached its apotheosis with the *Carry On* films. Originally operating under the name the Joan Collins Fan Club (until Ms Collins found out), Clary inhabited a world of innuendo and double entendres, talking about sex by talking around it. What was new was Clary's matter of factness about his own homosexuality.

Dressing up was a tactic, in full slap and glamorous outfits – often as breathtakingly ambitious as Dame Edna's – Clary presented a benign figure who could get away with mocking the naffness of the heterosexuals in his audience, and also with committing the cardinal sin of the late 1980s 'promoting homosexuality'.

After appearing in a disastrous Saturday evening game show, *Trick or Treat*, Clary's breakthrough came with the 1989 Channel 4 series, *Sticky Moments*, described by the eloquent Commissioning Editor of Channel 4 as 'Fucking brilliant! It's the *Generation Game* with frocks!'[45] Some have compared his act with such cosy camp comics of the 1970s as Larry Grayson and John Inman, but Clary was too much of an original ever to be a stereotype, and too out to ever allow his audience merely to 'laugh at the poof.'

Channel 4's 1992 sitcom, *Terry and Julian*, explored Clary's relationship with a straight male flatmate. As ever, Julian laughed in the face of dull suburbia. His sequins and glitter took on the shellsuit and won. A popular live act, Clary also acted in the revivalist film *Carry on Columbus*, and almost caused his own downfall with an uncharacteristically single entendre made about a former Chancellor of the Exchequer during the live broadcast of an awards show in 1994: 'I've just fisted Norman Lamont. Talk about a red box!'

Arguably, Julian Clary has made it easier for the first self revealed heterosexual transvestite celebrity, Eddie Izzard, to come out. This gifted and surreal British comic also has the benefit of a liberal 'alternative' audience. Initially Izzard broached the subject by talking in interviews about how he enjoyed wearing women's clothes around the house, and would continually have to point out that this kind of transvestism was something more common among heterosexual, rather than homosexual, men. Latterly Izzard has begun wearing make-up and the occasional frock at his live shows.

There was a resurgence of drag among gay clubbers from the late 1980s. To the generation of gay men who had grown up in the 1970s, drag had become 'ours'. As the Gender Benders had discovered, drag equalled queer: 'In a straight club the embodiment of everything queer is still a drag queen.'[46] Unlike the Skin 2 Balls, which divorced S&M gear from its roots and referents and turned them into fancy dress, drag was celebrated as something specifically gay. Yvette the Conqueror turned himself into the London gay scene's most successful hostess and all round mother figure, and Kinky Gerlinky grew into a hugely popular monthly residency at the Empire Ballroom. Gerlinde Kostiff began hosting Kinky Gerlinky in 1989. A continuum of the Porchester Hall's drag balls of the 1960s and a mass participatory version of Andrew Logan's Alternative Miss World pageants of the 1970s, at Kinky Gerlinky everybody was a star and dressed accordingly. 'It's all about entertainment – entertaining each other.' Kostiff told *Him* magazine, 'everyone is putting on show for everybody else.'[47] The Kinky Generation were a mixed crowd trying to have a good time during hard times. Ecstasy had helped to greatly relax both straight and gay clubbers gender and dress codes, and led to previously unthinkable integration between the two scenes. A post-clone look became popular with gay men, or 'boys', that married the erotic appeal of rough masculinity with feminine softness. This spirit was taken out of the clubs and onto the catwalks by gay designer Jean Paul Gaultier. Gaultier was asked to design the wardrobe for Madonna's live shows, and is still trying to get men to wear skirts. Though like Mr Fish, Gaultier would cite the manly kilt as his inspiration, 'It's a man's tradition that everybody knows, so there is no ambiguity about it. There is even some virility in it ... In the Madonna show the guys with the big cone bras – that wasn't me. That was Madonna. I don't put bras on guys, or if I did it would be a bra for the breast of a man – I don't do the changing roles. I make men as men.'[48]

Just as the word 'queer' had been reclaimed as a self-description, so was 'trannie'. The new stars of the club scene were its DJs, including the talented trannies Tashy Tim, Jon of Pleased Wimmin and Nick and Paul of Trannies With Attitude. TWA ran the mixed Leeds club night Vague in 1993, and began dragging up as they believed. 'Nightclubs have always been shows. It's theatre.'[49] But they didn't embrace the glamourous look so often seen at Kinky Gerlinky: 'British drag queens have a very down to earth persona. Especially the Northern ones. They're far more gutsy. They're far more ... Bet Lynch.'[50]

The British Kinky Generation had been preceded by America's Wigstock Generation, who had similarly mixed glamour with camp humour in their exaggerated costumes. The American keepers of the drag flame during the 1980s had previously been working-class black and Puerto Rican queens: 'They were the people who've been smeared by society, so they created their own place where they get their strokes and their adoration. They created a world down in the West Village where they are the stars.'[51] Jennie Livingston's 1992 documentary film *Paris Is Burning* captured the crowd of these house balls – centreing on a beauty pageant where points were awarded for 'real-ness' in the men's performance. A return to straightforward female impersonation, be it of a housewife or a supermodel. Madonna, a past master/mistress of genderfuck, appropriated Vogue-ing, the dance style that evolved from this scene (which involved 'striking a pose' as if being shot for a fashion magazine spread), and took it mainstream. Though Madonna neglected to mention the dance's roots on the gay drag scene in interviews.

Drag was embraced back to the bosom of gay activism in the 1990s. Queer politics celebrated difference and the breaking of gender rules. Like the GLF before them OutRage!'s Work It Girl subgroup took their frocks out onto the streets, the tube trains and the department stores: 'Drag has always been the most visual way of expressing your queerness,' explained WIG's Patrick McCann, 'It says you're not interested in being tolerated or accepted if the price is to succumb to some dreary conformity.'[52] London also got its own chapter of the Sisters of Perpetual Indulgence, 'gay nuns', that had first appeared in San Francisco in the 1970s as a satirical dig at the institutionalised homophobia of the Catholic Church. The nuns were prominent on demos, and went round the gay scene collecting for AIDS charities and forgiving customers their 'sins'. They also undertook some well-publicised canonisations of 'queer saints' such as Derek Jarman.

Drag even became a tool for political comedy. The impressionist Mike Yarwood's career went into permanent decline during the Thatcher years, just as Steve Nallon's faultless take on Mrs Thatcher became as permanent a fixture on television as it was on Gay Pride marches. Nallon was much more convincing (and popular) than female impressionists such as Faith Brown and June Brown had been. He even provided the voice for the suit wearing, cigar smoking Thatcher puppet on television's *Spitting Image*. Perhaps this was because Thatcher was a drag queen of sorts herself – famously described as 'the only real man in the cabinet', only she could have led to the innocuous sounding phrase 'handbagging' being used as a euphemism for political annihilation.

Like Barry Humphries, the chief creation of the South African impressionist Pieter-Dirk Uys, was a suburban housewife with ideas above her station. But whereas Dame Edna's delusions of grandeur were benign, those of Mrs Evita Bezuiderhout's were malign and provided a brilliant deflation of the arrogance that shored up the apartheid system. More latterly Uys has incorporated an equally chilling impression of Winnie Mandela into his act.

Drag finally became a regular part of the landscape of American rock in the 1990s, where it had remained a taboo subject.[53] When all four members of Queen paid homage to *Coronation Street* by dragging up for the video for their 1984 single 'I want to break free', they felt it dealt a severe blow to their career Stateside. Guitarist Brian May commented that, 'In Britain everyone thought the idea was just a laugh but in America they hated it and thought it was an insult.'[54] Some American rock bands embraced drag for this very reason. Nirvana's Kurt Cobain was the first to bring sexual politics into this arena. All the band wore drag in their 'In bloom' video, Kurt wore a lovely floral print dress on the cover of *The Face* and would regularly wear a comfortable smock on stage, telling interviewers that he also preferred to wear one around the house. Kurt was a rock star who didn't want the adoration of many of his fans. He was passionately pro-gay and drag seemed a way of deliberately confronting and provoking his audience, even of wilfully alienating the more reactionary elements.[55]

Cobain inspired a mini outbreak of dress wearing by the cream of the American alternative rock establishment, including Evan Dando of the Lemonheads, Greg Dulli of Afghan Wigs and Billy Corgan of Smashing Pumpkins. America even got its first glam rock band, androgyny and all, twenty years too late, with Nancy Boy, who were led by the son of 1960s star Donovan. Faith No More brought in a gaggle of drag queens for their video for 'Easy'. Manchester's James dragged up in Laura Ashley for the cover of their 1993 album *Laid*, and Ireland's U2 dragged up for the video for 'One', but decided to shoot another version as they felt the frocks detracted from the seriousness of the song's message about Aids. It looked like just another fad, but most of these bands were sincere. Wearing frocks wasn't meant to be merely amusing but was done as an act of solidarity.[56]

For even in Britain drag was still far from unproblematic. Frocks were faggoty and had to be avoided lest people got the 'wrong' idea. East London's purveyor of 'TV filth rock', Sexton Ming, says that he took to wearing drag on stage as it was the simplest way of announcing his homosexuality. Dave Rimmer recalls how Jimmy Somerville's father 'hadn't dared tell any of his friends when his son first appeared on television. He was worried Jimmy would be decked out in ribbons and frocks, "just like Boy George"'.[57] Erasure's gay singer Andy Bell had been warned off by his record company, after he and Vince Clarke dragged up for their first video. 'Who needs love (like that)?' They only returned to frocks long after they had consolidated their success in 1992, when Vince and Andy posed as Abba's Agnetha and Anni-Frid in 'Take a chance on me', whilst simultaneously flirting with their real selves. Thus it was courageous of teenybop group Take That's Jason

Orange to make brief appearances on stage in 1993 dancing with Howard Donald whilst wearing a rather fetching polka dot dress and blonde wig. But Take That have always remained laudably unflustered by rumours about their sexuality.

Drag reached its pop zenith with RuPaul. A six foot black man in a blonde wig, looking every inch the supermodel, he describes his look as 'total glamour, total excess, total Vegas, total total.' Ironically his single 'Supermodel' was only kept off the number one spot on America's Billboard dance charts in 1993 by Whitney Houston's 'I'm every woman'. RuPaul first got into genderfuck 'boppers' drag' in Atlanta during the 1980s, where he performed under the name Star Booty, but got into glamour drag when he moved to Wigstock-era New York.

Monica Lynch, who signed RuPaul to Tommy Boy records, has likened him to *Sesame Street*'s Big Bird, echoing Little Richard's self description, 'RuPaul's so unthreatening, he's harmless.' It's a mistake a lot of people make, RuPaul's beauty is that he just seems harmless. But Ru is defiantly out, proudly black, a chat show host's dream and a highly effective spokesperson for personal freedom and gay liberation: 'My act is all about loving yourself and learning how to love yourself, cause if you don't love yourself how you gonna love somebody else?'[58]

RuPaul is a spectacular act of self-reinvention and of drag reclamation. He's created a character – sassy, strong, beautiful and black – but disputes that his act is female impersonation, claiming he doesn't look like a woman, he looks like a drag queen: 'I don't think I could ever look like a woman. They don't dress this way. Only drag queens dress this way.'[59]

Drag has always been a powerful weapon. But it is rarely loaded and pointed in the right direction. RuPaul uses drag to assert his own homosexuality, to celebrate femininity, and to escape the constraints of masculinity. Rousseau knew that 'man was born free, but everywhere he is in chains'. RuPaul knows what those chains can be made of: 'I always say "we're born naked and the rest is drag." Any performer who puts on an outfit to project an image is in drag. Everything you put on is to fit a preconceived notion of how you wanna be seen. It's all drag. Mine is just more glamorous.'[60]   RS

Notes

1. Ned Ward, *The History of the London Clubs*, quoted in Roger Baker, *Drag: A History of Female Impersonation on the Stage* (London: Triton Books, 1968), p 26.
2. I use the word 'queen' to describe a gay acting, gay looking gay man (as opposed to a straight acting, straight looking gay man).
3. For an interesting fictionalised account of one travelling drag troupe, the Merrie Belles, see Paul Buckland, *A Chorus of Witches* (London: WH Allen, 1959).
4. Christopher Isherwood, *The World in the Evening*, (London: Four Square, 1960), p 94.
5. Quoted in Mario Mieli, *Homosexuality and Liberation*, (London: GMP, 1980), p 193.
6. Quoted in Kris Kirk and Ed Heath, *Men in Frocks*, (London: GMP, 1984), p 104.
7. *Come Together*, January 1972.
8. Ibid.
9. Quoted in Kirk and Heath, p 106.
10. *Come Together*, January 1972.
11. Ibid.
12. Quoted in Kirk and Heath, p 102.
13. 'Got your mother in a whirl, she's not sure if you're a boy or a girl,' David Bowie, 'Rebel rebel'. The American garage band the Barbarians superb 1965 single, 'Are you a boy or are you a girl?' turned the parental cliché of its title into a statement of approval and, because of the band's own hair length, defiance.
14. Quoted in Charles White, *The Life and Times of Little Richard* (London: Pan, 1985), p 71.
15. Quoted in Christopher Sandford, *Mick Jagger: Primitive Cool* (London: Victor Gollancz, 1994), p 129.
16. For a profile of Mr Fish (and other key figures in British fashion) see 'Today there are no gentlemen', in Nik Cohn, *Ball The Wall* (London: Picador, 1989).
17. In the 1950s Little Richard had written 'Lucille' about a drag queen acquaintance, but the lyrics were rewritten before they were thought suitable for release.
18. The 'man picks up woman only to find out it's a bloke' comic *denouément*/drag cliché would later pop up in the 1990's hit singles, 'Dude (looks like a lady)' by Aerosmith and 'Funky cold medina' by Tone Loc. It has long been popular with otherwise strait-laced television situation comedies and sketch shows, and was used in the teen movies *Bachelor Party* and *Risky Business* (Flip Wilson played the 'hooker' in the latter). One episode of

Blackadder gave it a fine *Sylvia Scarlett* twist by having its Elizabethan hero questioning his own heterosexuality after falling for a
young lad called Bob – before Bob revealed her true gender.

19.   Quoted on the video history *Rolling Stone: Twenty Years of Rock*.
20.   Quoted in *The Bowie Companion*, ed. Elizabeth Thomson and
        David Gutman (London: Macmillan, 1993), p 12.
21.   See Richard Smith, 'Ambisexuality', *Melody Maker*, 12 December
        1992.
22.   Michael Watts, 'Oh you pretty thing', *Melody Maker*, 22 January
        1972.
23.   Of course all pop stars are to some extent playing a role. Bowie was
        just the first to admit it.
24.   Sheryl Garratt has argued that young female fans have always
        found the androgynous erotic in teenybop stars; 'The people most
        attracted to the ideal of the hard, hairy, virile hunk of male, are, in
        fact, other men, who form the majority of the audience at any
        heavy metal gig. Women seem far more excited by slim, unthrea-
        tening baby-faced types who act vulnerable and resemble them.
        Androgyny is what they want: men they can dress like and identify
        with as well as drool over.' 'All of us love all of you', in Sue
        Steward and Sheryl Garratt, *Signed, Sealed and Delivered: True
        Life Stories of Women in Pop* (London: Pluto, 1984), p 144.
25.   Save for one last glorious appearance in drag triplicate in the video
        for the 1978 single 'Boys keep swinging'. Bowie's assessment of
        what his sexuality 'really' was in the early 1970s would change
        every few years. For his most recent position, ('Now even I have a
        problem relating to my life and my sexuality in the early Seven-
        ties'), see the interview with Tony Parsons in *Arena*, May/June
        1993.
26.   'Since the (transvestite) Club 82 had this outcast image for so long,
        the punks and the early glitter kids were treated very openly by the
        management. They didn't think they were weird and didn't try to
        cash in on 'em – they'd been dealing with weirdos for forty years!'
        Bob Gruen, quoted in Clinton Heylin, *From the Velvets to the
        Voidoids* (London: Penguin, 1993), p 188.
27.   Quoted in Heylin, p 79.
28.   Quoted in Heylin, p 78.
29.   Wayne County had a sex-change operation in 1981 and re-emerged
        as Jayne County. The actress and singer Lana Pellay and magician
        Fay Presto have also had the operation. Amanda Lear, the cover star
        of Roxy Music's *For Your Pleasure*, one time girlfriend of Bryan
        Ferry and disco star on the continent during the late 1970s, now
        manages to fool many journalists she has always been a woman and
        that she only pretended otherwise for publicity purposes. For an

account of Lear's early life see Duncan Fallowell and April Ashley, *April Ashley's Odyssey* (London: Jonathan Cape, 1982).

30. British fans can be rather boorish, but many American gay teenagers have come out through the 'freaks' they met at local screenings. See, for example, Aaron Fricke, *Reflections of a Rock Lobster* (Boston: Alyson, 1981).

31. Folk singers used to consider it an insult to the song to change the gender of its lyrics to suit a new singer – listen to Bob Dylan's rendition of 'House of the rising sun' on his debut album. This wasn't passed into pop. The Animals' Eric Burdon sang the same song as a ruined boy, not a girl. But hear Marc Almond's 1986 single 'A woman's story' (and his cover of Charles Aznavour's 'What makes a man?' – a drag queen's story). Patti Smith's cover of Van Morrison's 'Gloria', like Sarah Jane Morris and Sandra Bernhard's respective versions of 'Me and Mrs Jones', is not heard as a male impersonation, but as lesbian appropriation.

32. New York's Noel, under the tutelage of Sparks, had tried and failed in 1979. Noel was more successful when he reappeared much later out of drag. His 1988 single 'Silent morning' is one of the best songs to have come out of the Aids crisis.

33. *Melody Maker*, 15 January 1994.

34. Quoted in *When Cameras Go Crazy: Culture Club*, Kasper de Graaf and Malcolm Garrett (London: Virgin, 1983), p 8.

35. Ibid. p 88.

36. George came out fully in 1985, just as Culture Club were falling apart. He's continued dressing up throughout his solo career, and once kept me waiting for fifteen minutes before an interview while he put his make-up on.

37. *NME*, 1 May 1982.

38. Quoted in Kirk and Heath, p 112.

39. Quoted in Dave Rimmer, *Like Punk Never Happened: Culture Club and the New Pop* (London: Faber and Faber, 1985), p 94.

40. Ibid, p 98.

41. Quoted in Bernard Jay, *Not Simply Divine* (London: Virgin, 1993), p 126.

42. *NME*, 19 December 1987.

43. Quoted in Jon Savage, 'Androgyny', *The Face*, June 1983. One of the few contemporary accounts of Gender Bending worth reading.

44. Terry Sanderson, 'The Two Faces of Lily Savage', *Gay Times*, June 1993. Similar comments have often been levelled at Tennessee Williams' female characters.

45. *The Guardian*, 24 December, 1990.

46. Paul Fryer, quoted in Richard Smith, 'Dragged into the Future', *Gay Times*, November 1993.

47.   Andy Saxton, 'Kinky Girls and Boys', *Him*, February 1992.
48.   Richard Smith, 'Half a Rebel', *Gay Times*, January 1994.
49.   Smith, *Gay Times*, November 1993.
50.   Ibid.
51.   RuPaul, unpublished interview with the author, August 1993.
52.   Neil Wallace, 'From Drag To Bitches', *Him*, February 1992.
53.   Many heavy metal bands use the trappings of drag: poodle perms, spandex and glitter, that, in their minds, refer back no further than to Aerosmith or the Rolling Stones. Dee Snyder of Twisted Sister took the look to such an extreme that he was often labelled a Gender Bender. Boy George has noticed a possible inspiration for the metal style: 'If you go to middle America all the housewives dress exactly like that.' (Unpublished interview with the author, December 1992.) The rampant homophobia of the same scene was neatly satirised by the 'polysexual rockers' RPLA's 1993 single and video 'Last night a drag queen saved your life'.
54.   Quoted in Rick Sky, *The Show Must Go On: The Life of Freddie Mercury* (London: Fontana, 1992), p 108.
55.   See the interview with Cobain, 'All Dressed Up', *Melody Maker*, 12 December 1992. Cobain wrote on the sleeve of Nirvana's *Incesticide*, 'If any of you in any way hate homosexuals ... please do this one favour for us – leave us the fuck alone!'
56.   In 1993 the Lemonheads recorded the pro-gay song 'Big gay heart' and Roddy Bottum of Faith No More came out. Both actions are as rare in American rock as they are brave.
57.   Rimmer, p 97.
58.   Richard Smith, 'The Queen of New York', *Gay Times*, July 1993.
59.   Unpublished interview with the author, August 1993.
60.   Smith, *Gay Times*, July 1993.

Select Bibliography

Ackroyd, Peter. *Dressing Up: Transvestism and Drag, The History of an Obsession*, New York: Simon & Schuster, 1979.

Arundell, Dennis. *The Critic at the Opera*. London: Ernest Benn, 1957.

Bartlett, Neil. *Who Was That Man? A Present for Mr Oscar Wilde*, London: Serpent's Tail, 1988.

Bayard (editor). *Sunday Chronicle Pantomime Annual*, London: Sunday Chronicle, 1908–1909.

Bloch, Ivan. *Sexual Life in England*, London: Corgi, 1965.

Boas, Guy. *Shakespeare & the Young Actor*, London, Rockliffe, 1955.

Bradbrook, M C. *The Rise of the Common Player*, London: Chatto & Windus, 1962.

Braybrooke, Lord (editor). *Diary and Correspondence of Samuel Pepys, FRS*, Volumes I–IV, London: George Allen & Unwin, 1890.

Bridges-Adams, W. *The Irresistable Theatre*, London: Secker & Warburg, 1957.

Brown, Ivor. *Shakespeare*, London: Collins, 1949.

Brown, Ivor. *How Shakespeare Spent the Day*, London: The Bodley Head, 1963.

Buckland, Paul. *Chorus of Witches*, London: W H Allen, 1959.

Bulliot, J C. *Venus Castina*, New York: Bonanza Books, 1928.

Burnett, Al. *Knave of Clubs*, London: Arthur Barker, 1963.

Byng, Douglas. *Byng Ballads*, London: John Lane, The Bodley Head, nd.

Byng, Douglas. *More Byng Ballads*, London: John Lane, The Bodley Head, 1935.

Byng, Douglas. *As You Were: Reminiscences*, London: Duckworth, 1970.

Carey, Gary. *Katherine Hepburn: A Biography*, London: Robson Books, 1983.

Cauldwell, David O (editor). *Transvestism*, New York: Sexology Corporation, 1956.

Costa, Mario A. *Reverse Sex*, London (?): Challenge Publications, 1962.

Coward, Noel. *Collected Sketches and Lyrics*, London: Hutchinson, nd.

Curtis, Tony & Paris, Barry. *Tony Curtis: The Autobiography*, London: Wm Heinemann, 1994.

Damase, Jacques. *Les Folies du Music-Hall*, London: Anthony Blond, 1965.

Darlington, W A. *The World of Gilbert & Sullivan*, London: Peter Nevill, 1951.

De Choisy, Abbe (translated and with an introduction by R H F Scott). *The Transvestite Memoirs*, enlarged edition, London: Peter Owen, 1994.

Dent, Edward J. *Mozart's Operas*, Oxford: Oxford University Press, 1947.

Dick, Kay. *Pierrot*, London: Hutchinson, 1960.

Dickens, Homer. *What a Drag*, London & Sydney: Angus & Robertson, 1982.

Edwards, Anne. *Katherine Hepburn: A Biography*, London: Hodder & Stoughton, 1985.

Findlater, Richard. *Grimaldi: King of Clowns*, London: MacGibbon & Kee, 1955.

Gaillardet, F. (translated by Antonia White, with an introduction and notes by Robert Baldick). *Memoris of the Chevalier d'Éon*, London: Anthony Blond, 1970.

Ford, Boris (editor). *The Age of Shakespeare*, Harmondsworth: Penguin Books, 1955.

Garber, Marjorie. *Vested Interests: Cross-dressing & Cultural Anxiety*, New York & London: Routledge, 1992.

Gore-Brown, Robert. *Gay Was the Pit*, London: Reinhardt, 1957.

Granville Barker, Frank & Handley-Taylor, Geoffrey. *John Gay and the Ballad Opera*, Hinrichsen Editions, 1956.

Gray, Simon. *Wise Child*, London: Faber & Faber, 1968.

Grimaldi, Joseph (edited by 'Boz' – Charles Dickens). *Memoirs of Joseph Grimaldi*, London: George Routledge & Sons, 1903.

Guinness, Alec. *Blessings in Disguise*, London: Hamish Hamilton, 1985.

Halliwell, Leslie. *Halliwell's Film Guide*, 3rd edition, London: Paladin, 1979.

Harding, James. *George Robey & the Music-Hall*, London: Hodder & Stoughton, 1990.

Harrison, G B. *Introducing Shakespeare*, Harmondsworth: Pelican Books, 1939.

Hauser, Richard. *The Homosexual Society*, London: The Bodley Head, 1962.

Heriot, Angus. *The Castrati in Opera*, London: Secker & Warburg, 1956.

Howes, Keith. *Broadcasting It*, London: Cassell, 1993.

Hughes, Glyn. *The Antique Collector*, London: Simon & Schuster, 1990.

Humphries, Barry. *A Nice Night's Entertainment: Sketches and Monologues 1956–1981*, London: Granada, 1981.

Humphries, Barry. *My Gorgeous Life: An Adventure by Dame Edna Everage, housewife and megastar*, London: Macmillan, 1989.

Humphries, Barry. *The Life and Death of Sandy Stone*, Harmondsworth, 1991.

Humphries, Barry. *More Please*, London: Viking, 1992.

Incognito Guide, 1972, Paris: ASL, 1972.

Jay, Bernard. *Not Simply Divine*, London: Virgin, 1993.

Jay, Monica. *Geraldine: The Story of a Transvestite*, revised edition, London: Mandarin, 1992.

Kendall, Henry. *I Remember Romanos*, London: Macdonald, 1960.

Kirk, Kris & Heath, Ed. *Men in Frocks*, London: GMP, 1984.

Kott, Jan. *Shakespeare Our Contemporary*, London: Methuen, 1964.

Lahr, John. *Dame Edna Everage and the Rise of Western Civilisation: Backstage with Barry Humphries*, London: Bloomsbury, 1991.

La Rue, Danny (with Howard Elson). *From Drags to Riches: My Autobiography*, London: Viking, 1987.

Laver, James (editor). *Fashion*, London: Paul Hamlyn, 1965.

Leno, Dan. *Hys Booke*, London (?): Greening, 1903.

Lucas, Ian. *Impertinent Decorum: Gay Theatrical Manoeuvres*, London: Cassell, 1994.

McLaren, Jay. *Out Loud! The Encyclopedia of Gay and Lesbian Recordings*, Amsterdam: Out Loud Press, 1994.

McRobbie, A (editor). *Zoot Suits and Second Hand Dresses: An Anthology of Fashion and Music*, London: Macmillan, 1989.

Magee, Bryan. *One in Twenty*, London: Secker & Warburg, 1966.

Mander, Raymond & Mitchenson, Joe. *British Music Hall*, London: Studio Vista, 1965.

Mann, William. *Richard Strauss*, London: Cassell, 1964.

Marlowe, Kenneth. *Mr Madam*, London: Mayflower-Dell, 1967.

Masters, Brian. *The Swinging Sixties*, London: Constable, 1985.

Masters, John. *Casanova*, London: Michael Joseph, 1969.

Milton, Billy. *Milton's Paradise Mislaid*, London: Jupiter Books, 1976.

Morley, Sheridan. *Spread a Little Happiness: The First Hundred Years of the British Musical*, London: Thames & Hudson, 1987.

Nagler, A M. *Shakespeare's Stage*, New Haven: Yale University Press, 1958.

Nichols, Peter. *Feeling You're Behind*, London: Weidenfeld & Nicolson, 1984.

Nichols, Peter. *Plays: One* (including *Privates on Parade*), London: Methuen, 1987.

Nixon, Edna. *Royal Spy*, London: Wm Heinemann, 1966.

Norton, Rictor. *Mother Clap's Molly House: The Gay Subculture in England 1700–1830*, London: GMP, 1992.

Oakley, Gilbert. *Man Into Woman*, London: Walton Press, 1964.

Paglia, Camille. *Sexual Personae: Art and Decadence from Nefertiti to Emily Dickinson*, London & New Haven: Yale University Press, 1990.

Paglia, Camille. *Sex, Art and American Culture*, London: Viking, 1993.

Pronko, Leonard C. *Theatre East and West*, University of California Press, 1967.

Rimmer, Dave. *Like Punk Never Happened: Culture Club and the New Pop*, London: Faber & Faber, 1985.

Roberts, Peter. *The Best of Plays and Players 1953–1968*, London: Methuen, 1988.

Roberts, Peter. *The Best of Plays and Players 1969–1983*, London: Methuen, 1989.

Roscoe, Will. *The Zuni Man-Woman*, Albuquerque: University of New Mexico Press, 1991.

Rowell, George. *The Victorian Theatre*, Oxford: Oxford University Press, 1956.

Rowse, A L. *Shakespeare's Southampton*, London: Macmillan, 1965.

Russo, Vito. *The Celluloid Closet: Homosexuality in the Movies*, revised edition, New York: Harper & Row, 1987.

Savitsch, Eugene de. *Homosexuality, Transvestism and Change of Sex*, London: Wm Heinemann Medical Books, 1958.

Scott A C. *The Classical Theatre of China*, London: George Allen & Unwin, 1957.

Scott A C. *The Kabuki Theatre of Japan*, London: George Allen & Unwin, nd.

Scott, Clement. *The Drama of Yesterday and Today*, London: Macmillan, 1899.

Short, Ernest. *Fifty Years of British Vaudeville*, London: Eyre & Spottiswoode, 1946.

Sinfield, Alan. *The Wilde Century*, London: Cassell, 1994.

Steegmuller, Francis. *La Grande Madamoiselle*, London: Hamish Hamilton, 1955.

Thompson, C J S. *Mysteries of Sex*, London: Hutchinson, 1938.

Thomson E & Gutman D (editors). *The Bowie Companion*, London: Macmillan, 1993.

Thornton, Michael. *Jessie Matthews: A Biography*, London: Hart-Davis, MacGibbon, 1974.

Trewin, J C. *The Turbulent Thirties*, London: Macdonald, 1960.

Underwood, Peter. *Danny La Rue: Life's a Drag*, London: Leslie Frewin, 1974.

Wadler, Joyce. *Liaison*, Harmondsworth: Penguin Books, 1993.

Waters, John. *Shock Value*, London: Fourth Estate, 1991.

The Kenneth Williams Diaries, edited by Russell Davies, London: HarperCollins, 1993.

Wilson, Lanford. *Home Free!: The Madness of Lady Bright*, London: Methuen & Co, 1968.

Zadan, Craig. *Sondheim & Co*, revised and updated edition, London: Pavilion, 1987.

Zadan, Craig. *Sondheim & Co*, revised and updated edition, London: Nick Hern Books, 1990.

Also particularly helpful were back issues of the international gay press, notably *Gay News* and *Gay Times*.

Index